Everett McCourt

About the Author

Alan Huffman is a freelance journalist and the author of the highly acclaimed *Mississippi in Africa*. He has appeared on numerous National Public Radio shows and has contributed to many publications, including *Smithsonian* magazine, the *Los Angeles Times*, the *New York Times*, and the *Washington Post Magazine*. He divides his time between Bolton, Mississippi, and Brooklyn, New York.

⊛ Smithsonian Books

HARPER

NEW YORK · LONDON · TORONTO · SYDNEY

SULTANA

*Surviving Civil War, Prison, and
the Worst Maritime Disaster
in American History*

...

ALAN
HUFFMAN

HARPER

A hardcover edition of this book was published in 2009 by Collins.

SULTANA. Copyright © 2009 by Alan Huffman. All rights reserved. Printed in the United States of America. No part of this book may be used or reproduced in any manner whatsoever without written permission except in the case of brief quotations embodied in critical articles and reviews. For information address HarperCollins Publishers, 10 East 53rd Street, New York, NY 10022.

HarperCollins books may be purchased for educational, business, or sales promotional use. For information please write: Special Markets Department, HarperCollins Publishers, 10 East 53rd Street, New York, NY 10022.

FIRST HARPER PAPERBACK PUBLISHED 2010.

Designed by Lovedog Studio

Library of Congress Cataloging-in-Publication Data is available upon request.

ISBN 978-0-06-147056-1 (pbk.)

10 11 12 13 14   OV/RRD   10 9 8 7 6 5 4 3 2 1

For A. D. Huffman
August 6, 1916–August 19, 2008

CONTENTS

FOREWORD

THERE WERE SIX OF THEM, FIVE YOUNG MEN AND ONE woman, dressed in brand-new desert camo and pristine combat boots, posing for a cell-phone photo at the terminal gate. They were the sort of soldiers you see everywhere in American airports these days: Guys with Oakley shades perched atop freshly shaved heads, women with hair tucked inside their caps, moving purposefully and a little furtively, separate from everyone else.

Their expressions seemed both confident and a little edgy. No one knows what the future holds, but it is seldom as obvious or meaningful as when a person sets off for armed conflict. From that moment on, anything can happen. The soldiers were documenting a true departure, the beginning of a very personal and potentially fatal group experiment: *This is us leaving Atlanta, leaving the known world behind.*

The scene has been repeated, in various incarnations, for as long as people have been going off to war. It would have been much the same for Romulus Tolbert, a soldier I was trailing, nearly a century and a half after the fact. In the fall of 1863, Tolbert was waiting with his fellow soldiers in the Indianapolis train station, in his own crisp uniform and unsullied boots, preparing to ship off to the American Civil War. He was about to step across a similar threshold, and he faced the same basic question: Will I make it back? He had no way of knowing how bad things would get, which was probably just as well.

I came across Tolbert's story while researching a comparatively obscure historical episode that had made the local news two decades before, when a farmer and a Memphis lawyer reported finding what they believed to be the remains of a steamboat known as the *Sultana* buried beneath an Arkansas soybean field. The *Sultana* saga was by then largely forgotten, despite its epic proportions and the fact that it branched off into a network of intriguing subplots, one of which concerned Tolbert. The interwoven stories of the *Sultana* disaster have a lot to say about human survival, and they are particularly attractive to those of us eating frozen yogurt in Concourse E. They show us what a full onslaught is like, with everything the Fates can throw at you.

The *Sultana* disaster was remarkable primarily for its magnitude. More than seventeen hundred people died after the grossly overloaded boat exploded, burned, and sank in the flooded Mississippi River at the end of the Civil War, making it the worst maritime disaster in American history. It also represented the climax of a series of momentous trials for most of those aboard, including Tolbert, his friend John Maddox, and, among the more than two thousand recently released Union prisoners of war, two others from the same region of Indiana, J. Walter Elliott and Perry Summerville. Aside from Tolbert and Maddox, these four men had not crossed paths before the war.

Looking back now, when their lives can be considered of a piece, it is clear that they and most of the other *Sultana* survivors were capable of enduring almost anything, and for an extended period of time. The bar was continually being raised. At each level they watched stronger, smarter, and seemingly luckier people disappear from the frame. It would have been nice if they could have known that the bullets piercing the air at Chickamauga would not find them, that the diseases they suffered in prison would eventually abate, and that they could wake up on a burning boat on a flooded river and somehow make it to shore, but they could not know what the future held, nor how much they could survive. Only in looking back can the results of their experiment be known.

Survival is not an achievement. It is a process, and it is impossible to know, at any given moment, where you are in that process. The soldiers in the Atlanta airport could (or might) have been embarking on an uneventful tour, a dramatic sidebar of the war in Iraq or Afghanistan, set to an iPod soundtrack of Drowning Pool and Ludacris songs, or they might have been on their way to getting their throats slit, live on a streaming Internet video, and it would have been much the same for the soldiers aboard the *Sultana*. Even before they boarded the boat, Tolbert and most of the other recently paroled prisoners had burned through their reserves of physical, mental, and emotional calories in what was essentially a phased experiment in human survival, the results of which would not be revealed for decades, until the last of them lay on their deathbeds as old men. By the time the *Sultana* went down, they had endured pretty much everything the world can throw at you: Violence, deprivation, sickness, humiliation, loss of friends and brothers, betrayal by their own country and in some cases their own countrymen. All that was left was the specter of a sudden and complete disaster, and soon that came, too. At no point did they know the logarithm of their survival. The dangers were diffuse. Even after the disaster, they knew only that a crowning blow had been delivered at the precise moment when they had every reason to believe they had left their troubles behind. Under the circumstances, their survival must have come as something of a surprise, and even after they made it to shore, it would have been hard to breathe a sigh of relief.

A body and brain under extreme duress go through all sorts of chemical transformations, which influence how a person responds and, to varying degrees, what happens next. Faced with a mortal threat, an otherwise normal life can become so magnified, so pixilated that it may be hard to remember what it was like before or to imagine how it will be afterward, to even clearly recall that day in the Atlanta airport or in the Indianapolis train station when your boots were untainted by mud and blood, and when survival was just an idea for the very last time.

SULTANA

Chapter One

MIDSTREAM,
APRIL 27, 1865

J. WALTER ELLIOTT TOOK THREE DOSES OF QUININE the Sisters of Charity had given him on the boat, all at once. It was a futile gesture, but it was all he had at the time. Elliott, an army captain from southern Indiana, lay shivering on a cypress log, snagged in drift on the Arkansas side of the river. He was so exhausted that for a while he could not sit up. He was tormented by mosquitoes. In the darkness nearby, he heard a young man gurgling and moaning. The young man seemed to be losing his hold on a flooded tree.

Elliott listened to the gurgling and moaning for hours, and not long after the source was revealed by the faint light of dawn, the young man died. By then, rescue boats were slowly pirouetting on whirlpools in the open channel, and he noticed another man a little farther away, fully out of the water, clinging to another flooded sapling, his grasp weakening, too. The man inched lower and lower until his head slipped beneath the muddy water, then unexpectedly broke the surface again, clawing at the trunk and pulling himself up, though not quite as high as before. The scene kept repeating, stuck in frustrating denouement. The man went under; the man came up; the man went under again. Elliott could not get to him because he could not swim.

When he was finally able to stand, Elliott focused his attention on a nearly naked man who lay at his feet on a thin, sodden mattress. The man was shivering uncontrollably, as everyone was. The shakes could represent the insistent quivering of life or the final shuddering of death. All of them had engaged in mortal parlay many times before, had felt their hearts in their throats at Perryville and Stones River and Chickamauga, had lain sleepless at night in the purgatory of the prisons, watching their breath fade out before them in the cold. They had been sick, wounded, or both. They had been close to giving up and could have done so in a single breath. Each time, when they thought they had endured the worst, it had reappeared ahead of them, but each time, when they thought they had reached the end, it had been delayed.

Elliott had feared death both on the burning boat and in the river, but he was still there, rhythmically striking the nearly naked man with a switch. He was intent on keeping the man alive, and pain was the only tool at his disposal. The man, whom he did not know, feebly begged him to stop. There were others nearby, and soon the bodies of two men and of a young woman lay at Elliott's feet, evidence of his failures. Up and down the river he saw men clinging to flooded trees, which bowed under their weight and in the tug of the currents. Some clung with death grips; others hung limply like snagged debris. For miles down the river, he could see people floating away lifelessly or barely alive, on driftwood and pieces of the boat. Somewhere among them was Romulus Tolbert, a private, also from southern Indiana, who grasped a board or a piece of driftwood (the detail would be lost in the telling). Tolbert had lost sight of his boyhood friend John Maddox, a fellow private, who until then had been with him nearly every step of the way. Tolbert and Maddox had served together in the local militia back in Indiana, had endured enemy fire and wearying marches through Georgia, and had survived the squalid Confederate prison in Alabama before boarding the *Sultana* on their way home.

Private Perry Summerville, who grew up not far from Elliott, Tolbert, and Maddox in rural Indiana, and had also been in the Alabama pen, was now miles downstream, carried helplessly on the unyielding currents, floating toward Memphis between two wooden boards, one clutched between his shriveled, aching hands, the other hooked under his feet. Another refugee from the Alabama pen, George Robinson, a private from Michigan, was already beyond the city, floating senselessly on a dead mule amid bobbing barrels, discarded clothes, deathly quiet bodies, and smoldering splinters of the boat.

From his perch on the log, Elliott watched men hanging over the sides of the distant boats, dragging survivors and bodies aboard. He heard voices echoing across the river, and here and there someone crying out deliriously or moaning so pitifully and interminably that it was a relief when the voices finally quieted and faded away. Men mimicked the calls of birds and the croaking of frogs, or sang favorite songs from childhood or the war: *Come on, come on, come on, old man, and don't be made a fool, by everyone you meet in camp, with "Mister, here's your mule!"* Beyond the man hanging on the tree Elliott saw a pirogue piloted by a misplaced Rebel soldier, nosing in and out among the trees. It was a curious sight. Elliott called out to him and pointed to the young man clinging to the tree, and the Rebel took his cue and saved him. In the distance, in a flooded field, he saw a group of men crouched together on the roof of a barn, hugging themselves against the chill, occasionally swatting stiffly at mosquitoes. It might have seemed strange, mosquitoes in the cold, raising welts amid the goose bumps, but there was no logic to anything now. The world and the mind played tricks.

He tried to commit every detail to memory. Years from now he would struggle to make sense of it all, to put it into words, to impose order, to impress anyone who was willing to listen. Nothing would be too preposterous to believe: The hapless man rolling over on a twirling barrel, like some macabre sideshow; the man who had tied a tourniquet around the ruptured, pulsing veins of his broken legs to keep from bleeding to death, who asked to be thrown overboard to drown rather than face being burned alive; the six or seven men clinging to the back of a terrified horse as it swam down the fire-lit channel; the sister who stood on the bow of the *Sultana*, attempting to calm the drowning masses until the moment the flames consumed her; the woman who drifted serenely through the mayhem, buoyant as a water lily in her hoopskirt, as if in a dream—which she may well have been. They would be characters in Elliott's stock scenes. He would use them to populate his mythopoeic tale.

Other survivors would keep their memories to themselves. But even now, in the aftermath, all of them faced the same questions that had raced through Perry Summerville's mind when he awoke, flying through the air above the darkened river: *How did I get here, and what do I do now?*

Chapter Two

GETTING THERE

O N A SUMMER MORNING IN 2007, A DIESEL TOWBOAT churned the placid Ohio River as the day's first tourists strolled the waterfront promenade of Madison, Indiana, squinting at their guidebooks, alert to any meticulously restored cottage or mercantile-store-turned-candle-shop. Madison is an old port town that looks as if it sprang full-blown from the collective mind of a well-heeled preservationist society, which is what most tourists come to see.

A few blocks up the hill from the river, a beer truck discharged kegs at the historic Broadway Tavern and Inn, where the night before a crew from the Discovery Channel had filmed a TV segment on ghosts. The Broadway has been in continuous operation since 1834 and has never been remodeled, aside from the addition of electric heat and in-room baths, and its atmosphere of studied inertia is said to provide an attractive venue for ghosts. The steep stairs creak creepily underfoot, and the décor, despite an overlay of care-worn 1980s upholstery, is appropriately antiquated. The downstairs tavern, with its massive oak bar and nicotine-stained walls, feels both historic and rowdy. It is easy to imagine newly enlisted Union soldiers and workers from the nearby International Paper Company plant feeling equally at home there.

As the Discovery crew filmed in the inn's dining room two local guys sat at the bar sporting barbed-wire tattoos and fashionably ripped jeans. When the director came into the bar, one of them stretched elaborately, trying unsuccessfully to catch his attention. Everyone wants something big to happen, and the guy might have gotten his break playing the role of Romulus Tolbert or John Maddox, had anyone known their stories. But the focus of the show was on the sort of apparitions who slam hotel doors. No one knew Tolbert's and Maddox's stories, and no one recognized the young guy's willingness to play.

There was a time when Tolbert and Maddox were trawling for their own recognition, and Madison was their venue, too. Tolbert was a young farmer from nearby Saluda, a quiet guy with a handsome, slightly pensive face. Maddox, whose blue eyes glimmered against an otherwise dark visage, was a friend of Tolbert's from down the road. They had served together for three months in the local militia in 1862 but did not enter the actual Civil War—the launching pad for their series of mounting trials—until the following September. When they set out, Tolbert was twenty. Maddox was seventeen and had lied about his age to get in. It was their first trip far from home.

Madison, Indiana, is known for its history, but few locals knew or cared about Tolbert and Maddox other than Robert Gray, a veteran of World War II who spends his free time purposefully roaming the back roads of Jefferson County in his aging Plymouth, or in whatever car his grandson, a used-car dealer, lends him to drive.

Gray never tires of scouring abandoned graveyards and other places of historical interest, many of which are forgotten. His grandson, Beau, who sat at the bar the night the Discovery crew filmed, said he was proud of the old man's love of history and his fidelity to the momentous details of forgotten lives, but like most people—no doubt including Tolbert and Maddox in 1863—he was more concerned about where his own life was leading him.

Gray stumbled upon Tolbert's Civil War record in the National Archives a few years back while researching a group of local soldiers, and he wanted to know more. He began asking around but found no one, including among Tolbert's local descendants, who had much information to share. Here was a young man—for in Gray's mind Tolbert would always be a young man, though he died at nearly eighty, as many years ago—who went through an astonishing series of survival trials, yet afterward retired to the quiet life of a farmer and rarely spoke of any of his ordeals again. Tolbert had mailed home a postcard during the war, but it had been somehow lost. A trunk containing his small cache of memorabilia was likewise abandoned when his descendants moved out of his old clapboard farmhouse, which was eventually torn down. The imposing brick farmhouse where he grew up still stands, but the people who live there know nothing about him. Maddox's family home is gone. The elderly woman who last lived in it recalled the night it burned and said she and her late husband were lucky to get out alive. The overgrown Maddox family cemetery is tucked away in a hollow along the abandoned Saluda pike. Tolbert's dates are chiseled in stone in the well-tended graveyard of the New Bethel Church a few miles away. On the surface, that seemed to be all there was. None of the numerous local historical markers mentions Tolbert or Maddox, and a search of their names in the local historical society's database produced no hits. Their stories remain deeply submerged, which in Tolbert's case seems to have been by design.

Tolbert's great-granddaughter, Anne Woodbury, who never actually knew him but has heard, said he was reticent by nature. He scribbled a sketchy summary of his war experiences when he applied for a military pension, and he offered a few terse replies to one of his son's persistent questions. Otherwise, he remained mum about what he went through between September 1863, when he and Maddox joined the U.S. Army, and May 1865, when he finally made it home. A casual observer would not have suspected anything remarkable about him afterward, though he had endured enough pathos and drama by the time he was twenty-one to blanche the apparitions trotted out for the Discovery Channel crew. Among his extraordinary feats of survival was one that seemed to ensure he would be forgotten, but which intrigued Robert Gray: Managing to become outwardly ordinary again. From all appearances, Saluda was the only place Tolbert ever wanted to be, and he spent two long years in an epic struggle to get back, and the rest of his life getting over what had stood in his way.

The Tolberts farmed on a high, rolling plateau along the Ohio River, where the rock ramparts of Kentucky tower over broad fields of corn, tobacco, and wheat. Saluda was then, and remains today, a pleasant outcropping of rural Americana, of neat farmhouses and calendar-worthy barns, with open land serrated by hollows shrouded in sycamore, poplar, locust, and hickory trees, where ferny creeks plunge in minor cataracts to the floodplain of the river. At the center of the farm stood the Tolberts' two-story red-brick house, large but unpretentious, with a few curlicues embellishing an otherwise restrained façade. From the front porch the family could see the quaint Tryus Church, where they attended services and whose very name seemed to entreat new supplicants. Through the wavy glass of the dining room windows the landscape tilted down to the family cemetery, where, by the time the war broke out, Tolbert's father lay. As late as the spring of 1862, Tolbert was still helping to cultivate the crops and tend the livestock, eating his fill at his mother's table and sleeping each night in his own bed. Jefferson County remained—on the surface at least—comparatively serene, though it existed in a border zone between the solidly pro-Union western states (as the Midwest was then known) and the sprawling slave plantations of the South. The county was home to both rabid abolitionists, some of whom were involved in the Underground Railroad, and Copperheads, who supported the Confederacy. Today Jefferson County has its share of shrines to the Union cause, but it is not unusual to see pickup trucks traveling the back roads sporting Rebel flag decals. On the outskirts of Hanover, on Route 56, stands the Johnny Reb Lounge.

During the Civil War, there was talk of Indiana seceding from the Union to form a separatist government with other western states. A local soldier named Andrew Bush wrote home to his wife in January 1863 to express his dismay over the news, saying, "I trust that it aint so for if it is so us pore soldiers will have to Suffer." Bush did not share the enthusiasm of certain soldiers who believed that secession would provide a ticket home. He had sworn allegiance to the United States, though he disagreed with "old Abe's proclamation" and wrote that he would not have enlisted had he believed the war was about freeing the slaves, whom he did not consider human. Such a paradox—men who fought a war to prevent secession, harboring a desire to secede—was not unusual in Jefferson County. The county's bucolic air belied inner turmoil.

From the outset of the fighting, Jefferson County stockpiled war matériel—kegs of gunpowder, rifles, muskets, revolvers, bullet molds, cannonballs, bridles, and spurs—to outfit and train what was known as the Home Guard. In the summer of 1862, Tolbert and Maddox served their three-month stint in a militia known as Captain Monroe's Independent Company, an initiation that proved uneventful and took them only as far as Indianapolis, where they were assigned to guard Confederate prisoners of war. By then, four of Tolbert's five brothers were in the active Union Army.

Then, in July 1863, a few days after the Union victories at Vicksburg and Gettysburg, a Confederate cavalry division known as Morgan's raiders swept through southern Indiana and Ohio, looting farms, stealing horses and generally terrorizing the citizenry. Afterward, everything changed. A local woman who wrote an account of the raids seventy years later noted that people were already discouraged about the war and fearful of a possible Rebel invasion. The woman, who was a child at the time, recalled that Morgan's raiders stole all the horses and guns and forced her and her sisters to bake them bread. As the girls baked, the men sat in the kitchen and read the local newspaper. After the raiders left, as darkness fell, a group of relatives and friends arrived to hold vigil during the night. The next day, a group of Union soldiers passed through on their way to southern Ohio, where they joined other troops who captured or killed more than eight hundred of the raiders near Athens. Morgan himself was captured a week later.

As invasions go, it was not exactly the Mongol hordes, and in fact the raid was as remarkable for its relative tameness and civility as for its unexpectedness and could not compare with Union assaults against Southern civilians. But Morgan's raid brought the conflict home to a large, previously remote population and prompted a general call to arms. Tolbert, who was of draft age, and Maddox, who was approaching it, were among those who responded two months later. They departed Saluda on the familiar winding road to Madison, the county seat; filled out the necessary paperwork; enlisted for three years in the 39th Indiana Volunteer Infantry; collected their respective $25 bounties; and caught the train to Indianapolis to muster in. Neither apparently took the opportunity to document the occasion in a photograph, though many new recruits did.

Vincent Anderson, a fellow Indiana soldier, recalled that he set off in search of a photographer "as soon as I donned my soldier suit." The photographer he found kept a few guns and swords as props to place in the hands of soldiers, and "When I went to get my picture taken, and he saw I was a private he took a musket with the bayonet fixed and knelt down and showed me how to form a hollow square out of myself and resist a cavalry charge, I at once took to his idea and down on one knee I went, and with the gun and bayonet, as directed, my picture was taken."

Most recruits had little or no actual military experience. Ideally they would be given months of drills and training, but that was not always possible. Sometimes they were pulled directly from the farm, or from their jobs, and thrust into the violence of war with a few choice words and the guidance of a two-bit photographer.

Tolbert and Maddox remained in Indianapolis for only a week or so, then headed south to Nashville. A Jefferson County soldier who made the same journey noted that none of the recruits in his group even knew how to pitch a tent and were therefore put up in a hotel upon their arrival in the city. Few had ever ventured far from home, which was a quieter and more self-contained place than most Americans can imagine today. In Saluda, Indiana, in 1863, noise was invariably associated with a meaningful event: The passage of a steam locomotive, the report of a hunter's gun, the bawling of a cow stuck in a swamp, the thunder of an approaching storm. Tolbert and

Maddox had never experienced anything like the unending, insidious, ear-shattering din of battle, and they had no idea whether they were remotely prepared. All they knew was that something big was about to happen.

At the time of their enlistment, the recruits were required to fill out a questionnaire about their physical and mental health. One question was whether they had ever experienced "the horrors," which is something akin to panic attacks. Tolbert and Maddox both answered no, but in hindsight a more accurate answer might have been *not yet*.

THE TRAIN THAT CARRIED THEM to war traveled south from the Ohio River into the Kentucky bluegrass. Most of those aboard were novice soldiers on their way to "see the elephant," as the saying went—to lay their eyes upon the much-ballyhooed beast of war. The recruits wore crisp blue uniforms and carried the essentials in their knapsacks: Fresh underwear and socks, soap, a knife and fork, a toothbrush, a supply of paper and envelopes, pen and ink, perhaps a few photographs, some twine, a needle and thread, a mirror, and a comb or brush (certainly for Tolbert, who tended to fuss over his hair, judging from photos of him). The knapsacks were both their overnight bags and survival kits. Most also carried smaller haversacks of leather or painted cloth, along with their canteens, guns, and up to forty rounds of ammunition. Soon, when they became cavalrymen, Tolbert and Maddox would carry sabers—elegant and deadly props.

The recruits would hold on to their personal possessions while circumstances allowed, but that was not usually for very long. Their accoutrement and baggage would become a burden. The knapsacks alone weighed as much as twenty pounds, and soldiers inevitably discarded their treasured possessions one by one during long marches, or stowed them on the eve of engagements and never saw them again. In the end, most would retain only those items they carried in their pockets, and often those would be lost, too. They would start out sleeping in shared tents, but those would later be left behind, and they would lie on the ground beneath the stars or under a rubber blanket in the pouring rain. Eventually, even the blankets would go.

As the train rocked into Tennessee the physical evidence of the war began to drift past the windows: Burned buildings, abandoned towns, clumps of bedraggled refugees. It was obvious they were getting close. For two years Tolbert and Maddox had heard the news from afar, from soldiers on furlough, in letters, in the local newspaper. The headlines had grown increasingly shrill as the fighting intensified and moved closer to home. In the fall of 1862, beside an ad for Dr. Roback's Blood Purifier and Blood Pills, the Madison *Courier* had exclaimed:

BRAGG ADVANCING IN KENTUCKY!
GREAT EXCITEMENT!
A FARMER HAS JUST COME OVER FROM MILTON TO
GET HIS GUN FIXED!
STILL LATER!
A Small Boy Passed up Main Cross Street Displaying
A SECESH FLAG.
The People Greatly Excited

The sudden militancy of a local farmer and public outrage over a boy bearing a secessionist flag were evidence of the increasing threat posed by the army of Confederate General Braxton Bragg, who was stirring up trouble in Kentucky, just across the Ohio River. The *Courier* reported from Perryville, Kentucky, on October 9, 1862: "A portion of Bragg's army attacked a portion of McCook's corps d'armee at this place on Tuesday. The fighting was desperate." Three days, later the newspaper reported that sixteen thousand Union soldiers had engaged an unknown number of Confederates at Perryville and that perhaps six hundred of them, as well as thirteen hundred Rebels, had been killed. Later accounts put the number of troops engaged as thirteen thousand Yankees and nearly seventeen thousand Rebels. The article noted: "Doctor Heard, medical director, has been required to prepare for the reception of three thousand of the Perryville wounded."

On October 22, the *New Albany Ledger* reported that the troops had fought hand to hand with the Rebels and that the 22nd Indiana, in which Tolbert's brothers Tyrus, Silas, and Daniel served, "went in like tigers. They were in the front of the battle throughout the day, and suffered terribly—being cut to pieces. We have heard their loss at over 175 killed, and 350 wounded. They repulsed seven charges of the rebel cavalry."

This was news that everyone devoured, particularly in the Tolbert household. Among those killed was one of Tolbert's brothers, identified by the *Courier* as Second Lieutenant Tyrus Talbert, who was shot through the heart at twenty-nine and left behind a wife and a three-year-old son. For Romulus Tolbert, who was old enough to fight, the news must have been both grievous and provocative. With three brothers now in the army, he was left waiting in the wings alongside his younger brother Samuel, who was just a boy.

Amid the war news was this advertisement: "MANHOOD; How Lost! How Restored!" which offered, for six cents, a lecture by one Dr. Robert J. Caldwell, delivered in a sealed envelope, on the nature, treatment, and cure of "Spermatorrhoea, or Seminal Weakness, Involuntary Emission, Sexual Debility and Impediments to Marriage generally," along with related problems of nervousness and mental and physical incapacity resulting from self-abuse. Also: "Ohio River Farm for Sale!"

Chapter Three

WAR

DURING THE BRIEF PERIOD THAT THE 39TH INDIANA recruits were pacing around Indianapolis in September 1863, marching in regimental drills and preparing to ship out, Tolbert's brother Mathew was shot and captured at the battle of Chickamauga. The 22nd Indiana Infantry, in which his brothers Silas and Daniel fought, arrived on the battlefield a few hours before the end, after Mathew was gone. Tolbert now had two very personal disastrous models in which he could imagine himself, both of which involved people he knew well and identified with who had been targeted in different ways.

By the time he and Maddox caught up with the 39th Indiana in October, Chickamauga was already legendary, and once again, though they were soldiers, they had to settle for hearing about it after the fact. They would have little to add when the other soldiers sat around the campfire commiserating about the momentous charge across the Widow Glenn's farm. The most Tolbert could have contributed was, *My brother Mathew got captured there.* Perhaps it seemed they had missed the big scene.

Soldiers on the cusp of combat naturally try to imagine what it will be like, though no one knows how they will react to a full-blown mortal assault until it unfolds. A new recruit's self-image relies a lot on conjecture—on stories he has heard from other soldiers and on his own behavior in stressful situations in the past. Tolbert left no record of how he imagined war to be, or how he felt he had measured up, and as a result a great many of the contours of his life have been lost. But the path he followed is well documented, whether in his own record or in the accounts of others, and for the cast of thousands with whom he shared a succession of dramatic scenes, Chickamauga was pivotal. There were lessons to be learned.

In addition to Tolbert's brothers, most of the soldiers whose sagas overlapped with his fought at Chickamauga: Lieutenant Colonel Thomas Harrison, who would earn accolades for his command of the 39th Indiana (soon to be reorganized as the 8th Indiana Cavalry); the fearless Lieutenant Colonel Fielder Jones, who would later lead the 8th under Harrison; Perry Summerville, also a cavalryman from Indiana, and George Robinson, a cavalryman from Michigan, both of whom would end up in the same Confederate prison and aboard the same doomed boat; and J. Walter Elliott, whose hapless tale would intersect with his near the end. For those who were there, Chickamauga would have been enough of a war story for a lifetime. Yet, for many of them, it was only the prelude.

Chickamauga, fought just south of Chattanooga, Tennessee, was not the kind of warfare most of the soldiers envisioned. The battle, which swept back and forth across a patchwork of cornfields and woods near West Chickamauga Creek on September 19 and 20, 1863, was more a series of brutal, chaotic charges and countercharges than a conventional engagement. At times it devolved into what amounted to armed mob violence, with troops appearing out of the blue and disappearing almost as suddenly into a dense pall of smoke. Soldiers are often thought to put their emotions aside, but combat is about surrendering to one of the most powerful emotions there is—instinctive aggression. Because of the terrain at Chickamauga, the number of troops involved, and the range of weapons, that aggression was channeled in a thousand different directions at once. The 39th would never see anything on its scale again. Over the two-day period, about 125,000 soldiers were involved. But the battle's irregularity foreshadowed the skirmishes and guerilla attacks that they—including Tolbert and Maddox—would come to know well as the Union Army pushed deeper into Georgia.

No one had it easy at Chickamauga, even those who received what might have seemed comparatively safe assignments, such as George Robinson, the Michigan soldier who was detailed to guard a cavalry supply train. There was no safe place at Chickamauga—no backstage. The fighting was all over the map, and everywhere intense. Colonel John Wilder, who commanded a brigade of mounted Union troops alongside the 39th Indiana on the Widow Glenn's farm, recalled that when he came upon a group of Confederate soldiers trapped under his men's fire in a ravine just east of the widow's house, "It seemed a pity to kill men so. They fell in heaps, and I had it in my heart to order the firing to cease, to end the awful sight." Noting the defining anarchy of the battle, Wilder later wrote, "All this talk about generalship displayed on either side is sheer nonsense. There was no generalship in it. It was a soldier's fight purely, wherein the only question involved was the question of endurance. The two armies came together like two wild beasts, and each fought as long as it could stand up in a knock-down and drag-out encounter. If there had been any high order of generalship displayed, the disasters of both armies might have been less."

For someone like Tolbert or Maddox, hearing of the battle from afar, it would have been hard to know how to prepare for what was to come. Almost as soon as the fighting began, droves of men went tumbling to the ground across the uneven terrain, killed instantly or twisting in agony amid the wildly stamping hooves and boots. A soldier such as Mathew Tolbert, who was wounded on the battlefield, was horribly exposed. Every bullet that pocked the ground nearby or screamed past overhead presented a new terror, and if a downed man managed to avoid being run over by a horse, he was likely to be shot again or, as happened in Mathew's case, captured. Everywhere blood flowered on dusty clothes. Bullets and canister shot penetrated arms, legs, trunks, mouths, eyes, and groins, spewing tiny geysers. Men disintegrated before the relentless cannon fire. Death was everywhere; if a man was lucky it only tapped him on the shoulder to say *Hey*, but everyone got noticed sooner or later. Not that the killing was easy. A soldier who kills, at close range, another man bent on killing him initially feels euphoria, then guilt. Sometimes he vomits.

Across the interconnected battlefields, the fighting grew so fierce that at times the soldiers found their guns too hot to hold, and they had to cast them aside and grab one that had been discarded on the ground or from the arms of a dead man, and begin shooting again. But as long as a man continued to breathe and move and shoot, he had hope that he would survive. That was the nature of war.

For the 39th Indiana, it was all about the Widow Glenn's farm, which was to be their ultimate proving ground during the war. Eliza Glenn earned her sobriquet after her husband, a Rebel soldier, was killed, leaving her alone with two young children, and unexpectedly found herself in the middle of the first day of conflict inside her crude log cabin. Union General William Rosecrans chose the cabin for his field headquarters, had a temporary telegraph line run to it, and spread out his maps on her parlor table. The maps turned out to be unreliable, and Rosecrans had difficulty ascertaining the patterns of the distant fighting. The terrain along west Chickamauga Creek was broken into hills and bottoms—some open, some wooded—and the noise seemed to be coming from every direction. The Widow Glenn, trapped in her house with an enemy general, decided to help him monitor the fighting by ear. Perhaps she, too, wanted only to keep the assault at bay. As Shelby Foote noted in his seminal trilogy *The Civil War*, "She would make a guess, when a gun was heard, that it was 'nigh out about Reed's Bridge,' or 'about a mile fornenst John Kelly's house,' and he would try to match this information with the place names on his map." Soon the roaring extended across the entire front, and, Foote wrote, "A reporter thought he had never witnessed 'anything so ridiculous as this scene' between Old Rosy and the widow." After the Rebels broke through the Union lines, the widow was removed to a safer location.

At one point during the first day of fighting, Mathew Tolbert's 38th Indiana was cut off from the main army, along with the 2nd Indiana Cavalry, in which Perry Summerville fought, and was not reunited with the main army until sunset, at Crawfish Springs, where the 38th continued to fight well into the night. The flashing volleys of guns and cannons created what one soldier described as "a display of fireworks that one does not like to see more than once in a lifetime." By then the fields and forests were a wreckage of splintered farm buildings and trees, as if a tornado had passed through, and littered with wounded and dying men.

The temperature fell rapidly after dark, and few of the soldiers had blankets or water. Lieutenant Colonel Thomas Harrison, commanding the 39th, instructed his troops to gather all the canteens they could find, which turned out to be about a thousand, and deliver water to the men languishing on the field. Soldiers from both sides, as well as local civilians, roamed the dismal scene by the light of lanterns, trying to tend to the injured and the dead. A group including Confederate soldier Sam Watkins encountered a party of women probing the darkness for their men, the hems of their dresses no doubt stained with dirt and blood. When one of the women located her husband cold on the ground, Watkins watched her fall to her knees, cradle his face in her hands, and cry out. He helped her carry the body away, staggering past bodies with grotesquely cocked arms and legs, and men who moaned and begged for water.

Through the night the men of the 39th busied themselves building breastworks for the fight they knew would resume the next day, a Sunday, or if not then, the day after. There was talk that the generals might avoid fighting on the Sabbath, but it was impossible to tell, and they had to be ready. It was too cold, and most of the men were too jumpy to sleep anyway, so they labored on their trenches and breastworks, bolstering them with whatever materials they could find—logs, sections of rail fences, rocks. There was only so much anyone could do to prepare, but if you were smart you did what you could, made sure your weapons were in order and, as the actual moment of the battle approached, tended to last-minute details, such as relieving yourself, because no one wanted to need to pee during a fight. In the final moments before a battle, men prayed or sang favorite songs. Sometimes they recalled the death of a friend, to stoke the desire for revenge. Maybe they tried to purge their minds of disturbing images, like the sunburned face of a Rebel who had pointed his gun at them the day before but for some reason did not fire, whose upper lip curled back menacingly and whose knife-edged features and angular jaw brought to mind the head of a poisonous snake. It was crucial to find the right place to be when the moment came, to ignore the tightness in your chest, your racing heart and quivering knees, the lump in your throat, the dry mouth, the nervous belching. Most of all, you had to forget the worrisome thoughts the veterans were always planting in the less experienced soldiers' minds. No one ever forgot the first time they watched someone die, they said, though the shock was muted somewhat by repetition, which was a good thing because otherwise no one would continue to fight.

Even the experienced soldiers were out of their element during a battle on the scale of Chickamauga. Over time a soldier might learn to decipher patterns, to speculate on the basis of past experience about how the fight would unfold, and to consider whom he could count on. But there was no way to fully understand or to plan for barely controlled chaos. The soldiers' clear narrative arcs, their judgments of others, their understanding of all the variables that came into play, would be created afterward. At the time there were only the simultaneous battles within and without: The physical conflict with the enemy and the interplay of emotions and reason that governed survival on the fly. Inevitably, some details could never be reconciled. Maybe a soldier fired at a Rebel kid in a floppy hat with holes in his pants, and the bullet hit him and he fell over in the weeds and no one saw him, and he lay kicking but not dying, so that whenever the soldier stole a glance the kid was always still there, writhing, unnoticed, and for the long half-second he glanced, he could already imagine the impact of the bullet he left himself open to—exploding his head like a gourd that someone had balanced on a fence rail. Maybe a soldier accidentally shot one of his own men and no one else knew, and he never told. Some episodes would never fit into a veteran's life afterward, but a soldier did what he had to do to survive. Whether he succeeded, and whether he crossed an unacceptable line, he had to move on. The challenge was far from over.

In the heat of battle there was often too much happening for soldiers to feel rationale fear, but they almost always felt it beforehand. One soldier wrote that "it is the belief of nine out of ten who go into battle that that is their last. I have never gone into battle that I did not expect to be killed." A soldier might convince himself and everyone else that he was brave, then run like a hen caught in the open by a pack of dogs, then become brave again as he crouched alone in the thundering trees. Each variable contained infinite sub-variables. None of it made sense except in hindsight.

At first light on the second day of Chickamauga, fog settled over the bottomlands, and there was talk that if the generals were willing to fight on a Sunday, they would not do so when no one could see. But the fog burned off, and the Sabbath was more or less forgotten. The first shot pierced the air on the Widow Glenn's farm at about 11 a.m., and soon hundreds of screaming Rebels poured from the brambles at the foot of the long sloping field, heads down so that the tops of their hats showed, unleashing a fusillade of gunfire that, along with the Yankees' replies, shrouded the scene with smoke. The Widow Glenn's house was hit by an exploding shell and burst into flames.

From his position near the burning house, Colonel Harrison watched the renewed contest unfold. Men swept through the shadowy forests into the open sun, guns and sabers glinting, shouting and raising clouds of dust, while canister shot and cannonballs and bullets tore through the air with whistles and screams. Harrison believed his position was strong. He commanded the field of fire. He

could cover a retreat if necessary. His men seemed to be performing well, though it soon became evident that they were engaged
in a terrible sideshow to an even worse fight taking place to the
north, near the Snodgrass cabin. Harrison did not know precisely
what was happening there, but for that matter it was unclear from
moment to moment what was going down on the Widow Glenn's
farm. There was just the blinding smoke and deafening noise, men
shouting wordlessly, faces streaming with muddy sweat and blood.
The fight whirled first one way and then the other, growing in size,
contracting and then spreading out again. Through his field glasses
Harrison watched for outcroppings of strength and weakness, and
for feints, trying to read ahead. It was like a fast and violent game
of chess. Men ran headlong into the check, dropped back, and then
delivered crowning blows. Here and there the injured could be seen
crawling away. They seemed to be generally attracted to a distant
stock pond, where they crowded the water's edge, vying for space
with lost and riddled horses.

It seemed impossible that men could charge through the melee
and not get hit by something; yet, most of the bullets spent themselves ineffectively. By some estimates, nine out of ten bullets fired
during an average Civil War battle failed to find their mark, and
many more were dropped in the excitement of loading on the run.
Some men never fired their guns at all but only ran with them,
more or less as menacing props. But there were more than enough
bullets to go around, and each one that was dropped held the potential to get the fumbling shooter killed, leaving open the window
just long enough for someone else's bullet to reach him. It was no
easy matter to load a gun under such conditions, often while running, with shaking hands, as thousands of men fired at you. It was
a maddeningly painstaking process: Tear open the cartridge with

your teeth, empty the gunpowder into the barrel, tamp the minié ball into the barrel with your thumb, pull out the ramrod to push the bullet home, cock the hammer, insert a percussion cap over the nipple, and finally pull the trigger. Eventually the loading became second nature, even mindless, but it was still slow, and it was done with the knowledge that at that moment someone might be taking careful aim at you. The men of the 39th were fortunate to have repeating Spencer rifles, which could fire up to seven bullets in a row before the magazine needed reloading, and turned out to be a stunning advantage. The guns were an excellent investment that some soldiers had made with their own money before they were standard issue in the Union Army. But even the Spencers had to be loaded again and again, and there was little consolation in knowing that the Rebels had to reload, too. When a bullet hit a man, every soldier within earshot recognized the awful thud.

To Colonel Harrison, watching from his hill, it appeared that the Rebels were losing ground. The noise of the battle seemed to be inching incrementally back toward the line of trees. Then he watched in dismay as the blue-coated troops on his left began to waver, and the shape of the battle again changed. Suddenly the Union line was breached. His men could not see what was happening; they were aware only of the ebb and flow, of the sharp rattle of musketry, rifle and cannon fire fading away or growing more distinct, increasing in volume. A distant cheer might be the only indication of victory or loss. But Harrison could see that his troops, together with Wilder's horsemen on his right, were about to be cut off from the main army again. In a matter of moments they ceased to be part of an organized force. Using the buglers, flag signals, and shouts carried through the noise, he directed his troops to begin pulling back, and soon a courier arrived with orders for a retreat toward the long escarpment of Lookout Mountain, and from there back to Chattanooga. The fighting began to fragment. The firing grew sporadic and scattered. The 39th withdrew past the burning embers of the Widow Glenn's house, fighting backward, into the trees.

By then the situation was similarly dire near the Snodgrass cabin. Rosecrans, whose reputation would never fully recover, reportedly turned to his staff and said in a surprisingly calm voice, "If you care to live any longer, get away from here." Union General Charles Anderson Dana, a former journalist who would later be assistant secretary of war, said he knew his line was in trouble when he saw Rosecrans crossing himself.

As the Union troops retreated a Confederate general noted the grandeur of the scene, with flags waving and weaponry flickering in the sun, but Watkins, the Rebel soldier, found the aftermath bleak. "Men were lying where they fell, shot in every conceivable part of the body," he later wrote. "Some with their entrails torn out and still hanging to them and piled up on the ground beside them, and they still alive. Some with their under jaw torn off, and hanging by a fragment of skin to their cheeks, with their tongues lolling from their mouths, and they trying to talk . . . And then to see all those dead, wounded and dying horses, their heads and tails drooping, and they seemed to be so intelligent as if they comprehended everything."

At the end of the two-day fight, more than three thousand Union and Confederate troops were dead and more than thirty thousand had been wounded or captured, including Mathew Tolbert, whose whereabouts was now unknown.

It would be said that the 39th had kept the Rebels engaged long enough to enable the rest of the Union Army to form a new line of defense and eventually to make an orderly retreat. The Confederate Army, meanwhile, missed a chance to fully rout its retreating enemy, meaning its strategic victory was nil. Still, everyone on the Union side knew the day had been lost.

The 39th was among the last to leave the field. They were at the end of a long retreating column, along a road crowded with stragglers, weary disoriented troops, and horses and mules pulling gun caissons, wagons, and ambulances. Perry Summerville's 2nd Indiana Cavalry, which was not far ahead, had been worn down before the fighting at Chickamauga even began, after reconnoitering through northern Alabama and Georgia for two weeks, destroying Confederate salt works, capturing stragglers and Rebel pickets, and driving away or running from enemy cavalry.

The Rebel cavalry sporadically assailed the retreating column most of the way, but by nightfall the Union Army arrived at its stronghold in Chattanooga. From there, Summerville and the rest of the 2nd continued north toward Bridgeport, Tennessee, where they would spend the next few weeks chasing Confederate guerillas and ferrying supplies across the river. By then, the battle was on its way into history, and when Tolbert and Maddox finally arrived in Nashville, the only record of Mathew's whereabouts was a dispatch noting that he had been wounded and was in the hands of the enemy. Prison camps were squalid, dangerous, disease-ridden places, particularly in the South, and Andersonville, the nearest in Georgia, was by far the worst. But Tolbert likely had more than just his brother's capture to worry about. He had a lot to learn, and he had to learn it on the run. More than sixty different bugle calls directed the choreography of military life, and a mistake in understanding could be fatal. Added to that, the 39th was about to be reconfigured as the 8th Indiana Cavalry, and Tolbert, who had experience plowing behind a horse, would have to learn quickly how to shoot, and avoid being shot, from the back of one.

THERE IS A REASON WHY recollections of dangerous episodes tend to be more vivid. The same part of the brain that prompts sudden emotional reactions initiates the storage of memory, so memories that illustrate the greatest threat naturally tend to receive highest priority. But because the nervous system becomes extremely selective under emotional stress, and the brain later analyzes and even updates memories with new information, how an event is recalled can be as unpredictable as the event itself. That is why the men of the 2nd Indiana could be frequently cited for gallantry on the battlefield but at other times be said to be ill disciplined, thieving, rude to other soldiers and civilians, and gutless during a fight. The truth may be immediate and undeniable, but the record evolves over time.

All the conflicting forces that war brought to bear—the weather, the individual soldiers' moods, the acumen of the generals, and the lay of the land—were subject to continual change. In camp, on the battlefield, and on the march, everyone triangulated to determine the character of those they fought alongside, and a significant failure of courage or strength would likely follow a man all the way through. The ability to gauge the impact of such behavior might be difficult when the threat was actually unfolding, but everyone wanted to be remembered as the guy others could count on, like the sergeant in the 2nd Indiana who braved enemy fire to retrieve a dying comrade deserted by the retreating infantry. No one wanted to be remembered as the guy who got someone killed.

There was always posturing in the aftermath of a crucial encounter, and J. Walter Elliott seemed particularly concerned with framing his experiences, sometimes even as they unfolded. He suffered three almost embarrassingly minor war wounds, none of which qualified as a red badge of courage. He missed the battle of Perryville because of a spider bite, got shot in the tip of his ring finger the day before Chickamauga, and was lightly grazed in the shoulder by a bullet during the actual battle. Yet, he incorporated those awkward episodes into a plausibly valiant identity by playing up both the best and the worst. There is no evidence that he actually lied, but he made the truth work for him.

To some extent everyone was intent on composing what Stephen Crane, in his Civil War novel *The Red Badge of Courage,* described as the song of their life. The stories the soldiers had been told by others and would later tell themselves were part of an evolving survival equation, illustrating what worked and what did not, who could be counted on in times of danger, and how their actions might be viewed in hindsight.

After Chickamauga, the slightly wounded Elliott was directed to a military hospital in Nashville, but he chose instead to remain at large in the city until it was besieged. This would be an important detail in his accounts. A new front was taking shape along Missionary Ridge, just east of town, and he wanted to be there. The battle would restore the Union Army's position in the region, and it would give those involved stories that they could be proud to tell. With the help of reinforcements, the Yankees routed the Rebels at Missionary Ridge, opening the way for a drive into Georgia, and after a year of relentless cavalry raids, foraging expeditions, and ambushes, General Sherman would embark upon his infamous March to the Sea. For Elliott, Tolbert, Maddox, and Summerville, it would also usher in a series of personally fateful events.

From all appearances, Elliott tried to do what was right as a soldier, even considering his doctor's excuse at Perryville, which might have been justified. But after undergoing a mortal threat, a person has a tendency to accommodate, rationalize, and lay or deflect blame. A soldier who misses a fight because of a spider bite can be seen as a dangerous variable, and Elliott was intent on creating a narrative in which his perception of honor and presence of mind were on full display.

Elliott was physically a dark presence, with black hair, beard, and eyes and a dusky complexion. He had grown up in Hanover, Indiana, not far from where the Tolberts and the Maddoxes farmed, in a locally prominent family who had donated land for both a school and the Lancaster Church, New Style, which they had helped found. An uncle was involved in the Underground Railroad. Before the war, Elliott worked as a school teacher in Lafayette, Indiana, where he married and fathered a child. His wife died a year later, and he left their daughter in the care of his own mother when he enlisted in the 10th Indiana in 1861. No doubt his abandonment of the child—he never actually retrieved her—was the subject of some careful spin-doctoring, too, but whatever license Elliott took with the facts, his penchant for calm calculation undoubtedly helped him survive.

As Laurence Gonzales wrote in *Deep Survival: Who Lives, Who Dies, and Why*, "Only 10 to 20 percent of people can stay calm and think in the midst of a survival emergency. They are the ones who can perceive their situation clearly; they can plan and take correct action, all of which are key elements of survival. Confronted with a changing environment, they rapidly adapt." Survival involves more than being smart or brave. Body and brain chemistry play a major role and can transform a previously brave man into a liability or a weak one into a hero. Disaster can befall anyone, and sometimes how a person reacts is inconsequential, because forces are utterly beyond their control. But at other times those reactions influence what happens next, and who survives. It is important to respond decisively and sensibly to actual circumstances rather than cling to an imagined model of what those circumstances should be—or worse, to panic. Elliott, Tolbert, Maddox, and Summerville proved lucky (though they might have disagreed with that assessment at certain junctures) and never made decisions or reacted in such a way that got them killed. That was the unifying theme of both their most dramatic experiences and their lives afterward.

Survival decisions are made, more or less, in two parts of the brain: The amygdala and the neocortex. The amygdala is a comparatively primitive part of the brain and acts as the watchdog. The neocortex is responsible for conscious decisions and analytical thought. As Gonzales wrote, perceptions about the environment first reach the amygdala, which screens input for signs of danger but is not particularly bright—it is like a barking dog whose response to a threat is "better safe than sorry." If the amygdala detects danger, it initiates a series of emergency reactions even as the neocortex and the rest of the brain attempt to comprehend what is going on. The amygdala (there are two, one for each hemisphere of the brain) can initiate a rush of adrenaline, causing an increase in heart rate and associated flushing and panting, even if the neocortex subsequently determines that the threat is inconsequential. During what is now often called the fight-or-flight response, the nervous system fires more energetically, the blood's composition is altered so that it can coagulate more rapidly, muscles involuntarily contract, and digestion stops, all of which increase readiness for sudden action. When the neocortex starts talking, it is usually trying to slow things down. Survivors who recall hearing a voice inside them telling them what to do, or even a voice from beyond, may be experiencing the struggle of the neocortex to rein in responses triggered by the amygdala. Gonzales described emotion—the primary currency of the amygdala—as like a race horse quivering at the gate, and reason—which originates in the neocortex—like the jockey.

All this mental sorting takes place quickly, often in milliseconds; but because the outcome may be irreversible, it is extremely important to strike a balance, to know when to draw from your own experience—your own model of the world—and when to abandon it in favor of a new perspective. Conflicting responses from the amygdala and the neocortex may be nature's way of hedging its bets, but they can result in the kind of disastrous confusion that beset Summerville's 2nd cavalry during a patrol in rural Tennessee, when they were part of a larger force that encountered Rebels under Brigadier General John Morgan and simultaneously was attacked from the rear by the notoriously effective cavalry of Confederate General Nathan Bedford Forrest. As Union General R.W. Johnson later reported, the encounter went south very fast. "Soon some horses were wounded, riders killed, and confusion began to appear," he wrote. "Regimental and company organizations were lost, and without any apparent cause at least half of my command precipitately fled, throwing away their arms, &c. Many of the men, after getting a thousand yards from the enemy, wildly discharged their revolvers in the air." Without warning, previously brave soldiers had panicked. Their neocortexes had lost control. Unable to rally his troops, Johnson was forced to order a retreat. "I regret to report that the conduct of the officers and men as a general thing was shameful in the lowest degree," he wrote.

Lieutenant Colonel Edward McCook, who was in command of the nearby 2nd Indiana, lamented the loss of nerve that prompted the retreat, and noted that the men of the 5th Kentucky, in particular, had fled like "a drove of stampeded buffaloes . . . There appeared to be a question of rivalry between officers and men for which should outvie in the disgrace of their cowardly scamper."

A panicked amygdala can prompt good or bad decisions as a result of the same stimuli, and sometimes the results are not evident until later, such as when the soldiers compared notes around the campfire or mentally revised their personal narratives. Survival almost always involves a series of crucial choices that are influenced by luck and the ongoing dialogue between animal instincts and reason. A mindless rush of adrenaline, force-fed to the body's potent army of emotions, can save a person's life or cause a fatal overreaction. In this case, after the high-tailing Kentuckians passed through McCook's ranks, he managed to restore order among his own men, who waited until the enemy was within twenty-five yards and then "opened a volley which broke the rebel line and threw them back in confusion some 500 yards. In the meantime General Johnson's whole command, save the Second Indiana, had left and taken up a hurried retreat." At this point, McCook wrote, "General Johnson rode up to me and asked what he should do. I replied that no officer could command those damned cowards, pointing toward the Fifth Kentucky retreating."

Johnson's neocortex then made its own bad call. He told McCook he wished to surrender and asked to borrow a white handkerchief— a request McCook refused in disgust. McCook and his men found it necessary to retreat toward Nashville along a road littered with discarded rifles, pistols, sabers, saddlebags, canteens, curry-combs, brushes, and hats, all abandoned, as he put it, "in helter-skelter style."

If the 5th Kentucky's aim had been to stay alive at all costs, the argument could be made that they had succeeded. But in a time of war, staying alive usually means disabling or killing the enemy. In that regard they had failed miserably, and it would not be forgotten.

Fear that he might run was Henry Fleming's abiding fear in *The Red Badge of Courage*. Though Fleming was said to be a fictional composite of numerous veterans whom Crane—who never went to war himself—interviewed, his characterization was clearly on target, based on the book's popular reception by veterans. Fleming yearned for courage and grace, for himself and from others, which was crucial both during the conflict and afterward.

Armies are a diverse farrago of men with different backgrounds and motivations. But on the whole, soldiers tend to be young, volatile, and impressionable, and—at least in the beginning—are not likely to have ever experienced being shot at by anyone else. Under the circumstances, it is natural to feel that every gun in the opposing army is aimed specifically at you, and during the Civil War, new recruits such as Tolbert and Maddox soon found that their fellow soldiers brought to the battlefield a multitude of potentially lethal subtexts: Cowardice, vindictiveness, and all sorts of ulterior motives. Among the more common threats within their own ranks were men known as bounty jumpers, who joined the army only for the monetary reward, then bolted at the first opportunity. Bounty jumpers might leave their comrades in the lurch and so could be as menacing to the whole as enemy soldiers who donned blue uniforms to blend in until they could escape with horses and guns. There were also soldiers who bore grudges against comrades or officers, or who sought to discredit their peers to curry favor with their superiors. There were tricksters, frequently veteran soldiers who knowingly gave bad advice to green soldiers for sport. One soldier recalled a new recruit being encouraged to climb a tree in a hilltop orchard to pick high-hanging fruit, which attracted the attention of an unseen enemy battery on an opposing ridge. The unwitting recruit was startled by the sudden crash of shells through the branches, dropped from the tree, and scurried for cover, enabling others to gather the newly fallen fruit. Sometimes another soldier's bad judgment or simple mistake rippled through the lines, with disastrous consequences. In extreme cases, a perpetrator was drummed out of camp, or even shot.

Most Union soldiers were laborers—farmers, like Tolbert and Maddox, or industrial workers, with only a small percentage in commercial or professional pursuits. Within those categories were thieves, child molesters, religious zealots, patriots, tagalongs, leaders, overall good guys, and countless others whose personal integrity had not been tested or proved, and whose personalities were exaggerated by the stress of military life. Helping a wounded comrade to the rear was a popular way to avoid fighting, and desertion was a common problem on both sides. Some soldiers fled because they were scared, sick of war, never intended to fight, or had pressing concerns back home. The listing was occasionally in error, as occurred when a soldier was unaccounted for after being captured, killed, wounded, or cut off from the army.

As Dave Grossman wrote in *On Killing: The Psychological Cost of Learning to Kill in War and Society*, many Civil War soldiers—the vast majority, by some estimates—never fired their guns. During the unimaginable intensity of battle, preconceptions about long lines of men firing in orderly formation quickly evaporated, "And in the midst of the confusion, the smoke, the thunder of the firing, and the screams of the wounded, soldiers would revert from cogs in a machine to individuals doing what comes naturally to them," Grossman observed. Some loaded guns for others; others tended to the wounded, shouted orders, or wandered off in the smoke to find a convenient hiding place. A New York private wrote in a letter, "When you read of the number of men engaged on our side, strike out at least one third as never having struck a blow."

Even the behavior of those who fought was frequently erratic and wild. A person might lose all fear, all sense of time and place and self-consciousness as cognitive thought was interrupted by responses from another comparatively primitive part of the brain, the hippocampus. The brain's neocortex, the seat of language and reason, is where active memory operates. The amygdala, keyed into the nervous system, is the source of emotional responses, and it is where related memories are processed and consolidated. The hippocampus is where the information is put into context and, in many cases, stored. The three work in concert to determine how a person reacts to events and later reconstructs them, and they influence how he will react in the future. When a person faces a survival threat, the result can be a perfect aria or a discordant and dangerous racket.

In his book *Surviving the Extremes*, Kenneth Kamler, a physician with extensive experience treating people in survival situations, wrote, "The hippocampus flips some switches off, maintaining circuits essential to life, such as breathing and heartbeat, but shutting down stimuli to the higher centers that are less important for immediate survival. With incoming signals blocked, the frontal cortex receives no stimulation and loses its awareness of the individual self." A person in such a state may experience tunnel vision and lose track of time. The world may seem to move in slow motion, not unlike the way climactic battle scenes are depicted in movies, and the person may have an out-of-body experience triggered by fear, low oxygen or blood sugar, or fatigue.

"In a battlefield environment, if a person does not simply turn tail and run, the highly developed frontal lobes of the brain—the seats of judgment, thought, and will—command the body to embrace hostility, suppressing the survival instinct and protecting itself from the results as best it can," Grossman wrote. "This is otherwise known as discipline, and it is the only way a person can be made to wage offensive war, to seek out a threat to [his] own life. Once a person enters this realm, he becomes—at the behest of the part of his brain that normally subdues such tendencies—animalistic and aggressive."

A Massachusetts lieutenant wrote in a letter to his mother of one battle, "during that terrible 4 or 5 hours that we were there I had not a thought of fear or anything like fear, on the contrary I wanted to rush them hand to hand . . . and yet will you believe it? all day before the battle I dreaded it." Likewise a Texas artilleryman referred to "that wild hallucination which none but those in the brunt of battle can feel." An Iowa sergeant wrote similarly of "a strange unaccountable lack of *feeling* with me . . . Out of battle and in a battle, I find myself two different beings." Reconciling the two selves was crucial both to survival and to framing personal experiences afterward. Typically, the stress of battle increased with each engagement. Soldiers were bolstered by the hope of reaching the end, by a sense of honor, by peer pressure, by discipline, or by coercion. After the fighting ended, they often collapsed or became ill.

Some soldiers experienced battle fatigue and were plagued by nightmares, regardless of their ability to overcome their natural revulsion to killing. Others developed callous disregard. One Indiana soldier, William Blufton Miller, wrote that after overwhelming a Rebel force, "We captured about a hundred prisoners and killed about thirty of them. It was fun for us to see them Skip out. I seen one old Reb lying along the road (quite an old man) that had been a Saber stroke across his back and was not dead yet but mortally wounded and under other circumstances his grey hairs would have appealed to my heart for simpathy but we are not here to Simpathize and our orders is not let them cross the River." Otherwise sensible men tortured and killed captive enemies, mistreated women and children, and tore though private homes, smashing mirrors, pianos, and china, and rending someone's precious jacquard. Such behavior not only stoked desire for revenge but often disturbed fellow soldiers. A person who breaks free of his moral constraints poses a potential danger to everyone.

Soldiers naturally sought out others with whom they had an affinity. Perhaps they exchanged small photographs of each other and shared blankets and treats from home. But sometimes what a soldier expected from others turned out to be dead wrong, and it was never more obvious than when they were put to the test on the tattered, bloody fringes of morality. As Indiana soldier Jacob Bartmess wrote in a letter to his wife, it was not always enough to be on the same side. "I always was in favor of the administration and the war, and am yet, but there is a great evil right at the heart of the whole thing," he wrote. "That evil is, the war is carried on and led, principally by wicked and God dareing men."

THERE ARE FEW RELIABLE BYWORDS of war. It can be hell, as Sherman famously said, but it can also be boring, exciting, liberating, inspiring, and at times fun. In the downtime of the Civil War, there were snowball fights, sing-alongs, cannonball-bowling matches, stag dances, gambling tournaments, and what might be described as freestyle arts and crafts. On the basis of evidence unearthed by modern relic hunters, more than a few soldiers whiled away the quiet hours whittling lead bullets into frivolous items such as tiny penises.

A soldier's behavior during war is an extreme extension of his civilian life, and while the war stories most of them like to tell typically involve violence and deprivation, most of the tests are far less dramatic. John Maddox learned right away that serious danger could develop inside his own body and that, moreover, there was never a good time to drop your pants in the presence of your enemies. This was not a matter of mooning a distant column or debasing a conquered foe, both of which have occurred in other conflicts, but of enduring a sad pageantry of pit stops brought on by chronic diarrhea.

Of the more than six hundred thousand men who died during the Civil War, the majority succumbed to intestinal disorders brought on by bad water, rank food, and poor medical attention. The war was thoroughly toxic, and the stress it placed on the soldiers' bodies could quickly transform an ordinary bug into a fatal *coup de grace*. To make matters worse, "the troubles," as they were sometimes called, presented an inauspicious way to die, whether on the march, in camp, in a hospital, or on a suddenly, exponentially more complicated battlefield. Death by diarrhea would not likely be memorialized in heroic terms back home. There would be no news item in the *Courier* paying tribute to valiant digestive casualties among the ranks of the local boys.

For soldiers cut loose behind enemy lines, as Tolbert, Maddox, and Summerville were in the fall of 1863, even a minor case of diarrhea could be deadly. Some men wasted away; others were shot by snipers while squatting behind bullet-riddled trees. There were few options other than letting the sickness run its course, even if it meant the death of the host. The most common remedy was quinine, "whether for stomach or bowels, headache or toothache, for a cough or for lameness, rheumatism or fever and ague," as Union veteran John Billings noted in his book *Hardtack & Coffee: The Unwritten Story of Army Life*. Quinine, a bitter drug obtained from the bark of a tropical tree, was considered the cure-all; unfortunately it did not cure all. Although personal hygiene might play a role in determining whether a soldier got sick, in many cases luck played a greater role in influencing his survival than all the other variables over which he had a measure of control, including physical fitness and mental outlook.

In established camps, there was a special bugle call each day summoning ill soldiers, and while some men jumped at the chance to escape duty, true sickness was serious business. To make matters worse, even a relatively mild case of diarrhea was a source of quiet shame because it prevented soldiers from pulling their weight. They fouled their uniforms, made messes all over camp, fell behind on marches, and were frequently troubled by related hemorrhoids. Ohio soldier John Clark Ely wrote in his journal of his fear that the fort in which he was camped would be attacked while he was incapacitated by diarrhea, and of his sadness at not being able to uphold his duties. "Not feeling better yet," he wrote in one entry, "do wish I could feel well and get over this constant run of the sh-ts."

Maddox got caught in the intestinal crossfire in October while on a series of reconnaissance missions in northern Alabama. Though he had been in the army only a few weeks, it would have been obvious that the list of potential killers was long. The microcosm of camp was as hot as any battlefield, with weakened soldiers playing host to a raucous swap meet of excited and deadly pathogens. The soldiers' only hope was that a bout would last a few days and be gone, though the troubles had a way of coming back.

Diarrhea is caused by a variety of opportunistic microbes, most of which thrive where people are crowded together in unsanitary conditions. Civil War camps had no conventional bathrooms or access to clean water and nutritious food was limited. As the men shod their horses, wrote letters home, played cards, or flicked lice from their clothes, legions of germs, bacteria, and viruses met, coupled, feasted, and fought inside their digestive tracts. Perhaps the men joked about it at first, but as the sufferer took on a dangerous pallor and began having trouble walking, the laughter died away.

The troubles got comparatively little play in the written record, aside from official tallies of casualties, in which diarrhea was sometimes identified as dysentery. Even in private diaries it was rarely discussed in any detail. What was there to say? *I'm tired of watching my life dribble away into the stinking leaves.* A soldier might record in his journal the number of times he was stricken that day, as a way of charting the progress of the malady, but more often he simply noted that he was "still sick." Even today, nearly a century and a half later, when Civil War reenactors stage cinematic mock battles and encampments, diarrhea is not a prominent feature of the historical play. The reenactments lack the awful details of rotting horse carcasses, camps ringed by cesspools, fistfights, and other troubling facts of life for men who endured being crowded together in a succession of rank and hostile environments for months at a time. There are no piles of amputated arms and legs outside the faux surgeons' tents, no disturbing stains on the seats of the soldiers' pants, no reenactors salving saddle sores or high-stepping to the woods. Somewhere, out of sight, there is toilet paper.

Civil War soldiers were accustomed to many privations that

people today would consider intolerable, but faced with the prospects of thousands of men exchanging parasites, germs, and diseases, the army had to institute at least rudimentary sanitation measures to keep its soldiers functional. At the start of the war, the camps tended to be reasonably clean. Tents were pitched in orderly lines, with designated latrines drained by hand-dug ditches. There were regimental guidelines for just about everything. Each man carried half a tent—a rectangle of white cotton canvas to which his mate adjoined a complementary piece to assemble a shared shelter. The day began with a bugle call summoning them to reveille, or roll call, though typically the men were still pulling on their boots and stuffing in their shirt tails as they fell in line. After roll call there was a mass exodus to the latrines, which were not pleasant places but were at least situated and engineered logically.

In long-term camps, the soldiers sometimes built small log huts to replace their tents, complete with stick-and-mud chimneys, and arranged their possessions inside just so, perhaps with a candle mounted on the butt-end of a bayonet stuck in the ground by which to read and write letters. This was all done with the knowledge that their lodgings were temporary. As John Billings observed, "It *was* aggravating after several days of exhausting labor, of cutting and carting and digging . . . to have boot-and-saddle call blown, summoning the company away, never to return to that camp, but to go elsewhere and repeat their building operations." During the long marches, when skirmishes and chance encounters with the Rebels were common, camps were established hurriedly wherever the men found themselves, and they were likely to be struck with equal haste. Formerly essential items were often left behind, and there was no time to dig even crude latrines. A soldier might "wash" his knife and fork by running them into and out of the dirt a few times.

Clothes went unchanged for months at a time, seldom washed because there was neither the time nor the means. Opportunities for thorough bathing likewise became increasingly few and far between. The result was that even short-term camps quickly grew foul, and as the war intensified, order became harder to maintain, never more so than on extended marches and raids.

Army life is notorious for its rampant testosterone, which during the Civil War occasionally led to fights and attracted camp followers, who brought their own ingredients to the already volatile epidemiological mix. By bringing together men and sometimes women from different backgrounds and regions in the crowded, generally unsanitary environment of camp, the war helped spread disease and enabled the formation of explosive new combinations of the sort that nature seems to love. The mix of stress, squalor, and occasional violence both contributed to and exacerbated the problem. Maybe a soldier was playing cards, or riding with the column through unfamiliar terrain, or on solitary picket duty when he suddenly felt the stabbing pain in his gut and thought, *Not now. This is not a good time.* In fact, there was never a good time, though some times were worse than others, such as when a soldier was stuck in the saddle on a long foray through hostile territory.

Maddox got sick while the 39th Indiana was camped at a temporary fort near Stevenson, Alabama, a small rail crossing on the Tennessee River. The 39th was then mounted infantry—basically foot soldiers who traveled on horses—and the men spent most of their time roving the countryside in the vicinity of Chattanooga, guarding railroads and river crossings. Sometimes they chased the Rebels; sometimes the Rebels chased them. The fighting was sporadic, unpredictable, and amorphous, shifting randomly back and forth through forests and fields. The men camped in remote bivouacs and subsisted mostly on stale hardtack, beans laced with weevils, and salt pork and beef that were tough as leather yet laden with parasites and germs. One night Colonel Harrison observed long lines of lights among the distant trees, from the fires and lamps of an army camp. He heard the movements of horses and artillery but could not tell if the lurking figures were enemies or friends. It would not have been a good time to wander off into the trees alone.

In late September and early October, the 39th was dispatched on a manhunt through east Tennessee in pursuit of the Confederate guerilla Champ Ferguson, whose men were reviled by Union troops as ruthless cut-throat raiders. Ferguson and his men had allegedly murdered a group of black Union troops and their white officers as they were recuperating in a military hospital, and they ceased the slaughter only after a band of Cherokee Indians and highland vigilantes arrived to drive them away. Bizarre rumors circulated around Ferguson—that he decapitated prisoners and rolled their heads down hillsides as a joke, that he killed elderly, bedridden men. If Harrison's men encountered him he was to be executed on the spot. A soldier would want to be in fighting trim when he went after a man like Champ Ferguson. In the end, the manhunt turned out to be a wild goose chase. The 39th roamed a network of inscrutable switchback roads, past hardscrabble farms, through the deceptively beautiful mountains, without ever finding Ferguson or his men. Eventually the 39th was summoned back to Nashville to receive its new designation as the 8th Cavalry and to take on two companies of new recruits. From there they headed south, past Chattanooga, deeper into enemy territory.

Harrison set up his first field headquarters in a tavern at a place called Poe's Crossroads, where he awaited further orders. While there, his men contended with bands of Rebels who stole horses, menaced the guards posted at the all-important river crossings, and destroyed railroads that provided the Union lines of supply. Harrison's troops were hungry and in many cases sick, and he was reluctant to press farther until he had been issued more rations and replenished his lost wagons, horses, and mules. It took tons of food to support seven hundred fifty men and horses and more than a hundred mules, and the logistics of transporting even minimal supplies, including medicine, were complex. Often there was not enough loot to sustain them in the countryside. In one report Harrison lamented, "We are now 50 miles from rations and 25 miles from forage. We cannot ration our men and forage ore' horses with the transportation on hand. The discrepancy is becoming serious."

The day after Harrison filed his dispatch, he was ordered to a ferry crossing on the Tennessee River known, coincidentally, as Harrison's Landing, where his men lingered in nervous ignorance, interrogating any civilians who came their way, sinking all the boats they could not use, and wondering what would happen next. The region was conflicted about the war, and that resulted in frequent guerilla and revenge attacks. At Rankin's Ferry a young black boy was caught transporting Rebel mail and arrested as a spy. At Harrison's Landing a local white woman arrived in camp to provide information about the movements of Confederate troops. The soldiers were fearful of being overpowered, and it was often difficult to tell who was on their side.

The 39th had been in the vicinity of Harrison's Landing the previous summer, before Maddox and Tolbert arrived, doing much the same thing, though the circumstances were serene by comparison. John Barrett, a soldier with the 39th who was present during the previous picket, wrote to his brother to say the Rebels were camped directly across the river and that he and a few fellow Union soldiers had gone bathing there one evening and conversed with one of them as he sat on the opposite bank. At night the bands of the two armies battled it out in song, and at one point four Illinois soldiers surreptitiously crossed the river and allowed themselves to be captured and released on parole, which meant that according to the rules of war they were prohibited from fighting until they had been officially exchanged. "They were tired of the service," Barrett observed.

By the fall of 1863, however, encounters between the opposing armies were uniformly hostile, and when Harrison's men were sent to guard the river crossing at Stevenson, their base was a rudimentary fort—a ring of earthworks on a hill within firing range of the local supply depots, warehouses, and the two railroads that intersected in the small town. The site of the fort would one day become a popular spot for mountain bikers, then a police shooting range, and eventually a city park, but in October 1863 it was a lonely, dangerous outpost, and it was where the war got inside Maddox for the first time.

As a boy Maddox had suffered through typhoid fever, which was arguably a greater threat than diarrhea, but he was now far from adequate medical care, in a hostile land. He had no choice but to tough it out. When the troops were ordered back to Nashville, he was admitted to a military hospital, and his diarrhea eventually ran its course. But as often happened, his recovery was more of a remission. The troubles would haunt him not only during the rest of the war but off and on for the rest of his life.

Chapter Four

THE
RAIDS

F ROM THE LATE FALL OF 1863 THROUGH THE FOLLOW-
ing spring, the soldiers of the 8th Cavalry got to know the
area between Chattanooga, Tennessee, and Ringgold, Georgia, perhaps better than they wanted to. They were assigned to courier duty,
which meant ferrying messages and supplies, foraging, and serving
as sentinels. Now and then they engaged Rebel cavalry. Travel was
difficult over roads that became muddy and rutted once the winter
rains set in, and they had little protection from the elements other
than their rubber blankets and, for some, broad-brimmed hats.

Summerville's 2nd Indiana followed a similar routine, and by
Christmas the two cavalries were operating in tandem through north
Georgia. Twice they visited the farm of Champ Ferguson, where
they captured supplies that his men had confiscated from the Union
Army. They caught a few Confederate stragglers and stripped them
of their mounts, arms, and clothes before turning them loose. There
was not much notable action, aside from one fight that earned the
8th accolades. After watching a small detachment overwhelm forces

under the vaunted Confederate General Joseph Wheeler in February, Union General William Carlin wrote in a dispatch, "On arriving within 500 yards of the town, Colonel Harrison, with only 25 men, charged on the enemy and put him to a most disgraceful flight ... This was the most gallant and handsome exploit of cavalry I ever witnessed. Had it occurred in the early days of the war it would have immortalized the gallant men engaged in it."

Such encounters presaged even more intense cavalry engagements the following summer. In April and May, the 8th was furloughed, which gave the men a brief respite before the most rigorous work detail many of them would undertake during the war: A series of exhausting raids into western Georgia aimed at disrupting the lines of supply to the Confederate stronghold in Atlanta. During the raids the men would ride for days, shifting from one haunch to the other, stomachs growling, eyes caked with dust, dry-mouthed and saddle-sore, alternately anxious and bored. The raids were about as far as an organized force could get from formal warfare, which was both exciting and uniquely taxing.

In the campaign leading up to the siege of Vicksburg, Union General U.S. Grant had learned that his infantry could operate without a fixed line of supply by living off provisions confiscated from the local residents. It had been a radical concept at the time, but Grant's success proved that it could be done. By the time the 8th and other associated troops departed on their Georgia raids, living off the land—in the most brutal way—was an established practice in the Union cavalry. But being cut off so far behind enemy lines, and meanwhile attracting the attention of Confederate troops by raiding arsenals, towns, and farms, they faced new and pressing dangers. Their most reliable lifelines proved to be their horses, which enabled them to get into and out of trouble quickly.

Horses have been used to wage war for thousands of years, and during the Civil War they were used extensively by the cavalries of both armies for reconnaissance, marches, delaying actions, and raids. Superior weapons had reduced the effectiveness of traditional cavalry charges, and during organized battles most cavalrymen, like mounted infantry, fought on foot. But during the marches and raids, the men were still likely to engage the enemy from the saddle. Horses enabled them to cover broad expanses while pursuing and eluding their enemies, and good mounts were prized for their ability to endure hunger and thirst, to remain manageable during violent encounters, and to survive long, grueling marches.

The Confederate cavalrymen were considered superior to their Northern counterparts in the early years of the war because the Rebels tended to have more personal experience with horses, having raced them for sport and grown accustomed to riding them for long distances. Rebel cavalrymen were also more familiar with the terrain they were passing through. General Sherman made no secret of his lack of confidence in his own cavalry. By the summer of 1864 they were learning the ropes, though the added mobility of a horse could become a liability if a soldier got lost, which happened fairly frequently.

During marches that lasted for weeks, often for twenty hours a day with only brief rests, the column traveled at a rate of about four miles per hour—fast enough to be "killing to horses," as Massachusetts cavalryman Charles Adams put it. "An officer of cavalry needs to be more horse-doctor than soldier, and no one who has not tried it can realize the discouragement to Company commanders in these long and continuous marches," Adams observed. "You are a slave to your horses . . ."

More than a million horses died or were killed during the war.

In addition to being shot or hit by cannonballs, they broke their legs on rough terrain and died of exhaustion, infection, and disease. Aside from his gun and his own life, a cavalryman's mount was his most valuable possession; yet, few kept the same mount from beginning to end. A few soldiers took their own horses to war, accepting the risk because they were confident of the animals' behavior, but most, including Tolbert and Maddox, had to make do with whatever mounts the army (or unfortunate local civilians) provided. A good cavalry horse could be ridden hard, fast, and long and performed to its utmost, whether out of excitement over the chase or in blind obedience to its rider. It was not unusual for a horse to run itself to death. A good horse anticipated its rider's needs and could respond to his shifting weight and the changing stimuli of a fight with minimal reining. Losing a good horse was a major setback, but it happened often, and cavalry soldiers had no choice but to find new mounts and press on. The heavy behind-the-scenes work was usually done by mules, which were famously durable and less finicky than horses but more temperamental, prone to kicking and biting, and averse to conflict. Horses had a steadier disposition and "under fire behaved better than men," Billings wrote.

When horses flagged, the soldiers had two choices: To send them to the rear or to force them to continue until they dropped. "I do my best for my horses and am sorry for them," Adams wrote, "but all war is cruel and it is my business to bring every man I can into the presence of the enemy, and so make war short. So I have but one rule, a horse must go until he can't be spurred any further, and then the rider must get another horse as soon as he can seize on one."

"Every few weeks a veterinary surgeon would look over the sick-list of animals, and prescribe for such as seemed worth saving or within the reach of treatment, while others would be condemned, led off, and shot," Billings wrote. Burying dead horses was among the more loathsome tasks in camp, not only because of the stench but because the pits had to be so large and the carcasses had to be manhandled into them. Not surprisingly, dead horses were not buried on the march, and particularly after skirmishes and battles, the roads were often littered with their carcasses for miles.

The U.S. military operated its own central supply agency for replacing lost horses, and the cavalry stole others along the way. Harrison was issued nine hundred horses in the summer of 1863, but by the fall he was asking for more, and with the Confederate Army also commandeering private stock, horses and mules were increasingly hard for Southern civilians to come by. Abandoned, unhitched wagons and carriages were a common sight along rural southern roads.

Billings recalled one incident in which Rebels began shooting his army's artillery horses, each bullet striking a horse's flesh with a sound he described as similar to a pebble hurled into mud, yet seeming not to cause the animals much alarm. When a bullet struck a bone it made a hollow, snapping sound, and the horse promptly went down. "In cavalry service they knew their place as well as did their riders, and it was a frequent occurrence to see a horse, when his rider had been dismounted by some means, resume his place in line or column without him, seemingly not wishing to be left behind," Billings wrote. As the eyes and ears of the army, cavalry soldiers developed specialized survival skills, and they usually had more information to work with than foot soldiers who were left in the dark between engagements and sometimes during them. But to utilize those skills, the rider and his horse had to work in concert and respond effectively to sudden changes.

Cavalrymen sometimes wore specialized boots of plain or elaborately stitched, enameled leather, which reached to the knee and were stylish and protected the riders' legs as they rode through woods and brambles. But more often, the boots were eschewed for brogans, which were far more utilitarian on the ground. Most cavalrymen embellished their caps with the number or letter of their company and regiment, along with two crossed sabers, the cavalry emblem. New recruits wore "boiled" white cotton or loud, checked woolen shirts, leather gauntlets, and indigo jackets embellished with yellow piping, and wore an array of headgear, from floppy slouch hats to squat kepis.

Maddox and Tolbert were of average height and slight build, and perhaps fell short of the romanticized image of the lavishly costumed cavalryman, waving a sword from atop a rearing horse as the wind ruffled the plumes of his hat. Their duties, too, were usually more prosaic. Aside from random encounters with Rebels, they spent most of their time standing on picket duty, tearing up railroad tracks, and looting farms. On long marches they were more like human baggage than gallant equestrians; men sometimes fell asleep in the saddle, remaining upright only by instinctively squeezing their mounts between trembling, fatigued legs. Still, the threat of violence loomed around every curve of the road, and without warning the 8th became embroiled in one skirmish that continued for so long and with such intensity that the men ran out of ammunition, and the decision was made to charge the Confederate line rather than face capture. A Kentucky colonel who was there described it as "the most terrific, yet magnificent, charge ever witnessed." The mounted men trampled the Confederate lines with few injuries, even though, as the officer noted, "The saber and the horses' hooves were about our only weapon."

As the 8th roamed rural Alabama and Georgia, the men knew little about the local geography or which enemy forces were nearby, which put them at a disadvantage even when they outnumbered the Rebels. Unlike foot soldiers, who typically fought over specific ground, or artillerymen, who operated from relatively distant, stationary positions, cavalrymen were free ranging. The last thing any of them wanted was to find himself alone, behind enemy lines, without his comrades or his horse.

SOUTH OF CHATTANOOGA, the Appalachian Mountains slowly dissolve into the red clay hills of northwest Georgia, a thin and rugged landscape that today is steadily disappearing beneath the hundred-mile sprawl of Atlanta. The landmarks of the past are falling by the wayside, and those that remain have a disenchanted look: Galleried mansions, many of them empty; forgotten cemeteries with tilting monuments and rusty, cast-iron gates; remnants of historic trace roads that no longer lead anywhere. A holdout like the Owl Rock Church, a simple clapboard structure with a mossy graveyard out back, is basically a footnote that few people read. The contemporary story is playing out across the highway from the church, where a blistering wound of cleared and flattened hills marks the beginning of yet another real-estate development.

But among the landmarks that survive is a one-lane gravel road a few miles east of what was once the town of Campbellton, which parallels the Chattahoochee River, then passes through a narrow, deep gap carved by wagon wheels and hooves, and curves blindly into the wooded bluffs. This is the spot where Romulus Tolbert's life took a momentous turn on September 10, 1864. Tolbert would probably still recognize the road, with its narrow bed and high banks edged by forests of oaks and beech trees, though a short distance beyond, it crosses a creek on an antiquated one-lane wooden bridge and comes up hard against a towering manmade hill of dirt, which resembles a landfill but is actually the site of another new development. For now, the site of Tolbert's wartime capture remains intact, though it is hard to imagine that it will hold out for long.

Tolbert arrived here in the fall of 1864 after spending the summer traveling along a network of similar roads, all of which were far better known by the Rebels, who could discern the movements of Union troops using information from captured soldiers, stragglers, malingerers, and slaves. Sometimes the commanding officers of the various Union cavalries might try to throw off the Rebels by intentionally taking a wrong fork, but more often they were the ones who were confused and misled; they were a thousand miles from home, their maps were unreliable, and they tended to get bad directions.

Lieutenant Colonel Fielder Jones, who led the 8th for much of the summer either under Harrison or in his absence, lamented in one dispatch, "Owing to the extreme darkness and the carelessness of some person unknown, the column was broken and my command got lost; it was nearly daylight before we succeeded in extricating ourselves from the labyrinth of roads and reach Vining's Station." Brigadier General George Thomas, whose vast command of about sixty-five thousand men included two-thirds of the Union forces involved in the Atlanta campaign, wrote of traveling roads with countless unmarked intersections, through impenetrable woodlands that lent themselves to ambush. To make matters worse, Thomas wrote, he "could procure no suitable guides. All intelligent persons had left the country, or had been driven out by the enemy."

The troops who participated in the marches carried little besides their guns. They had been required to leave their tents, blankets, and other personal possessions behind, for safekeeping and to lighten their loads, the assumption being that when supplies ran low they could steal food and forage from farms and towns along the way. For many, the summer's forays proved to be the most grueling experience of the war, mixing the occasional rush of battle with the physical, mental, and emotional challenges of an endurance run.

The towns they passed through—places such as Vining's Station, Smith's Ferry, and Campbellton—were strange not only because the men were behind enemy lines but because most were eerily empty, the residents having evacuated in advance of the action. By then the South was starting to unravel, and the penetration of the Union Army so deep into Georgia, toward the rail and industrial center of Atlanta, sparked a frenzy of mass migrations. Over the course of the summer the troops torched cotton mills, depots, and foundries; they looted private homes and stores, occasionally bumping hard against the limits of wartime honor and sometimes running roughshod over them. Literally and ethically, the raiders were all over the map. Some Union officers tried to restrain their men, to limit their pilfering to necessary supplies, but others tacitly endorsed outright theft. William Blufton Miller, the 75th Indiana infantryman who wrote of his pleasure in shooting captive Rebels, was among the thieves in the Union ranks and boasted of the jewelry he "foraged" from private homes.

But if the raids at times seemed reckless, they were deliberate. Their nexus was a June attack in which the troops of Union Major General Lovell Rousseau destroyed a mill producing Confederate contraband, after which the employees, including many women, were sent north to prison. As a result of his success, Rousseau was ordered to Selma, Alabama, to raze the Confederate ironworks there, and he took along the 8th Indiana, under Harrison's command. Again the mission was a success, so General Sherman ordered Rousseau to undertake a more ambitious campaign—a long raid through Georgia, with twenty-five hundred "good cavalry," to destroy the Montgomery & West Point Railroad, one of the main supply lines to Atlanta. Rousseau had been impressed by the 8th on the Selma run and so decided to take them again. This time Harrison would command several regiments, and the 8th would be led, under his direction, by Fielder Jones.

According to historian David Evans, author of *Sherman's Horsemen: Union Cavalry Operations in the Atlanta Campaign*, Rousseau was a self-taught soldier, a robust, charismatic man who exerted great personal influence over his troops. He was known to hoist his hat atop the tip of his sword while urging his men on during a fight. He rarely studied maps, and he usually galloped across the field on his thoroughbred to deliver his orders himself. He was just the sort of leader the soldiers would need on a long, exhausting, and occasionally terrifying raid.

Assembling the troops proved to be a greater challenge than Rousseau expected, because so many men had fallen ill or lost their horses, but he managed to assemble more than twenty-five hundred, including Tolbert, Maddox, and about six hundred others from the 8th Indiana, in Decatur, Alabama, in early July 1864. The 8th had traveled from Nashville to Decatur by train, and the cars had been so crowded and hot that many had chosen to ride on their roofs, a decision they regretted when the clouds burst open with torrents of rain. Arriving across the Tennessee River from Decatur, the cavalrymen were subjected to typical army delays—the usual hurry-up-and-wait as Rousseau struggled to outfit and find enough horses for them. Some took the opportunity to cool off in the river. A day later they were at the depot vying for good horses and to be issued saddles, blankets, and reins. They were instructed to pack only two changes of clothes, five days of rations, minimal ammunition, and their rubberized blankets, sabers, and guns.

The actual departure from Decatur was disorganized. A herd of braying pack mules bolted and ran, and a short distance from town the column encountered Rebel bushwhackers, though everyone managed to escape uninjured. None of the enlisted men knew where they were headed. Rousseau's adjutant, Captain Thomas Williams, later wrote that "all, however, felt that the expedition was of more than ordinary importance, and that it was intended to penetrate farther into the interior of the Confederacy than any similar expedition had reached. Hazardous it might be, but there was a smack of daring and dash about it, which was captivating, and gave to officers and men an inspiriting feeling different from that of an ordinary march."

On their first night in camp, a private who had been given the unenviable task of leading a troublesome pack mule (and who had trouble keeping up with the column as a result) arrived late. The men heard him swearing at the mule, then call out, "Cap Boyer, what will I do with this mule?" Seeing an opening, a soldier called out a response that was later described as a suggestion for what he might do with the mule, to which the private answered in kind. .Mule jokes were legion in the army, often a sort of verbal crotch grab, as in, I got your mule right here. After this particular exchange, laughter and cheers echoed through the darkness of the ridge. As one soldier recalled, "we just made those jack-oak bushes tremble with our noise." Soon a regimental band played on the lawn of the plantation house where Rousseau made his headquarters, "Taps" was sounded, and the men bedded down beneath the stars.

At dawn the next day, Rousseau surveyed his troops and noticed that some had brought tents and blankets, despite his prohibition, and that the 8th Indiana was overburdened with ammunition. It was important to travel light on a raid; the Roman army had good reason for calling military gear *impedimenta*. Rousseau ordered his army's extra baggage and munitions loaded into wagons and sent back to Decatur. The men began moving out at 5:30 a.m., with the 8th in the lead. The morning was quiet until about eight o'clock, when the column flushed out a few Rebel scouts, whom they fired upon but who got away. Soon the terrain grew steeper, and the going became rough. The soldiers, now powdered with dust, managed to confiscate a few horses, mules, and supplies of food from bewildered farmers along the way and to capture a Confederate soldier on furlough. Hearing of the capture, Rousseau rode up in a commandeered carriage and told the man he would be hanged as a spy, though he eventually let him go. The 8th captured a few more Rebel soldiers later that day in a mountaintop village, but they were released, too. Rousseau did not want to be slowed down by prisoners.

The first day's march covered about fifteen miles; the second, thirty. If there had been any doubt, it was now obvious that the raid was going to be rigorous. Each morning the troops that led the column the previous day moved to the rear, giving everyone a chance to be first to encounter the enemy. At one point on the third day, Rousseau moved ahead to check on the advance guard of the column, and in his absence a group of soldiers began vandalizing farmhouses and hauling away valuable nonessential items. Coming upon one such scene, Fielder Jones, of the 8th, approached the farmer and his family, who were watching in dismay from their porch. An elderly woman was at that moment shouting at the looters, and Jones intervened and apologized for their behavior. When he mentioned that he was from Indiana, the woman told him she had a son there. In a strange coincidence, Jones knew the man, and so he offered to provide the family a letter so that they might receive provisions from the army in Decatur. The family politely declined, saying it would cause trouble with their neighbors.

Late in the afternoon the column began threading its way through a mountain gap, and night fell before they emerged on the other side. As they pressed on under a sliver of moon they found the road descending so steeply that at times they had to dismount and lead their horses. The wagon brakes squealed. The guns were unlimbered and belayed down the slope. At 11 p.m. they finally halted and fell asleep on the ground without unsaddling their horses. They were under way again at 6 a.m., stiff and sore, riding into a valley that glistened with dew, and continued on until they reached the town of Ashville, where Rousseau stopped to have the horses' shoes inspected. As the farriers did their work some of the soldiers ate or dozed. Others looted the local post office and freed prisoners from the jail. Rousseau accompanied a group that broke into the newspaper office, where they printed general orders for conduct of the march, instructing the men to take good care of their horses and prohibiting them from straggling or entering private houses. They then set about altering the news for the next day's paper, which had already been typeset. The front page article now carried the headline "Distinguished Arrival" and reported, "Maj. Gen. L.H. Rousseau of U.S. Army, paid our town the honor of a visit this morning, accompanied by many of his friends and admirers. The General looks well and hearty. It is not known at present how long he will sojourn in our midst."

The troops rode out of Ashville in the early afternoon and by sundown had reached the Coosa River at Greensport, where they saw two steamboats chugging upstream, just out of range of their guns. Crossing the river, which was deep and about three hundred yards wide, turned out to be one of the major challenges of Rousseau's raid. While the 8th Indiana waited on the bank, Confederate guerillas attacked the far end of the column and shot two men, one of whom, Captain William Curl of Princeton, Indiana, was the first Union cavalryman killed on the raid. While waiting to cross, Rousseau concluded that three hundred or so of his horses were no longer fit for service, and he organized a group of sick or injured men to be diverted to the Union garrison at Claysville, forty miles to the north.

As night fell the men watered their horses, cooked supper, and prepared to camp. Some picked blackberries in the moonlight. At about 10 p.m., Major Thomas Graham, whose forces included the 8th, was ordered to cross the now-darkened river with plans to camp on the other side and, after daylight, move four miles downstream to cover the crossing of the rest of the command at the Ten Islands ford. Tolbert and Maddox, along with four companies of the 8th, saddled up. At the landing they met an officer and two soaked scouts, who had retrieved a ferry boat from the far bank. The remainder of Rousseau's raiders, including the other companies of the 8th, then led by Fielder Jones, moved on to the Ten Islands ford.

The ferry could carry only ten or twelve men and horses at a time, and the first group to reach the far side learned from scouts that the Rebels were already close by. The four companies of the 8th took cover near a group of cotton warehouses while the rest crossed with the wagons and mules. Once everyone was across, they settled in for a nervous night. There were no fires, and the men spoke in whispers, listening to the rustling of cornstalks for any indication that the Rebels were on the move. They slept on their arms.

Lying in wait were two hundred Alabama cavalrymen under the command of Brigadier General James Holt Clanton, who had received word of Rousseau's advance from Ashville that afternoon. Clanton, a tall, muscular man who had served in the Mexican War and in the Alabama legislature, was variously described as gallant, rash, and "a perfect demon in appearance when aroused." Though his men were dramatically outnumbered, he decided to attack at dawn.

At 5 a.m., Graham led his four companies of the 8th down the road from the ferry crossing, and soon those who had been left behind heard the crackle of gunfire and scrambled onto their horses. Clanton's men had attacked the 8th about half a mile from the river, with the Rebel general himself charging around a curve of the road, pistol in hand, leading the 6th Alabama on foot. Clanton's clothes were riddled by bullets from the Yankee guns, but he somehow escaped injury. His men were not so fortunate, and they proved no match for the 8th Indiana's repeating rifles. Those who were not shot soon broke and ran. Several were captured, including one who lingered, kneeling over the body of a friend. It was an almost bloodless triumph for the 8th, with the only serious casualty a private named John Matz, of Tolbert's company. He had foolishly worn a Confederate hat that he had pilfered the day before and was shot in the face by not-so-friendly fire.

The rest of Rousseau's men heard the shooting as they prepared to cross the ford at Ten Islands, and soon they too were fired upon from an island in the river, and their advance was halted. Fielder Jones asked Rousseau to let him take the rest of the 8th upriver to reinforce Graham, and after much deliberation Rousseau agreed. Jones and his men splashed across the ford at a safe distance from the Rebels lurking on the island and headed north. Jones was known as a fighter. He had returned to combat after recuperating from gunshot wounds to his liver, arm, and thigh, and at the battle of Stone's River he had engaged in hand-to-hand combat with the Rebels using his pistol and sword.

Once Rousseau's men managed to drive the Rebels from the vicinity of the ford, they too crossed unmolested. "The passage of the river was a beautiful sight," wrote his adjutant, Captain Thomas Williams. "The long array of horsemen winding between the green islands and taking a serpentine course across the ford—their arms flashing back the rays of the burning sun, and guidons gaily fluttering along the column, formed a bright picture, recalling the days of romance, and contrasting strongly with the stern hardships of every-day life on the duty march."

When the troops were reunited near Greensport, Jones and Rousseau learned that the 8th had whipped Clanton's brigade of Rebel cavalry, killing one officer, wounding a large number, and capturing about twenty, whom Rousseau promptly paroled—again because he did not need prisoners slowing him down. The column then turned south and marched about fifteen miles into the night. The road was dry, and the column produced a cloud of dust, which made it difficult for the men to breathe. After the moon set at about 2 a.m. and it became too dark to see, Rousseau called a halt.

The next day the raiders occupied the town of Talladega; burned the railroad depot, several train cars, and a gun factory; and captured food stocks earmarked for Atlanta. When they departed Talladega they took with them a group of liberated slaves and a few fresh horses. Private Jack Wilson, who was with the 8th Indiana, wrote that the region around Talladega was "the most beautiful and fertile portion of Alabama I have yet seen, many splendid, commodious and tastefully decorated dwellings studding the road on either side."

At every house they passed, he wrote, slaves approached them with questions, such as where they were from and what they did when it rained. Another soldier wrote, "We found the niggers everywhere to be our friends, they all have an instinctive idea that some how or other they are to be set free in spite of the terrible teachings of their masters to the contrary." Many slaves followed the column, though they had difficulty keeping up on foot with the rapidly marching horses.

From Talladega, Rousseau directed the column toward the state capital of Montgomery—a ruse designed to confuse the Rebels, when his actual aim was the Montgomery & West Point Railroad, west of Atlanta. It certainly confounded the local residents, many of whom fled with their valuables from the area around Montgomery, only to end up in the path of the raiders. The route now became a treasure hunt, with men discovering caches of silver and gold hastily hidden in bushes around abandoned plantation homes, but soon the men were fatigued, and over the course of the long, hot afternoon, most slumped in their saddles, staring blankly ahead. It would be two more days before the column reached the railroad, and the gambit began to pay off. By then they had forded two rivers, marched two hundred forty miles, and won a significant skirmish, and they had reached Confederate General Joseph Johnston's lifeline to Atlanta. Once there, they set about prying loose the tracks, using fence rails as levers, and building bonfires of wooden ties to melt and twist the steel.

The Rebels were regrouping, and as Rousseau's men worked at their destruction near the tiny town of Chehaw, a ragtag force, including men who had lately been patients at a Confederate military hospital in Auburn, arrived by train. The Union troops easily repelled the attack. Rousseau reported forty Confederate casualties, and he captured the train. The next day his men marched all day and night, during which they were forced to navigate a zig-zag ford of the swift-flowing Tallapoosa River in the dark, and many men and horses lost their footing and nearly drowned. Once they made it across, the opposite bank was so slippery that some had to dismount and hold on to their horses' tails and be pulled to the top. The last of the troops made it across at about two or three in the morning. This, their third major ford, would be remembered as a particularly trying episode. Ohio Colonel Douglas Hamilton later noted, "Ever after, we referred to the crossing of that river, in that night, with a shudder, for the thought of it was as unpleasant as any battle we were ever in." Remarkably, the only casualty was a young slave who drowned when his mule was swept away by the currents. Farther down the road, the raiders encountered a Rebel company of twenty old men and boys. They killed one and captured two.

By eleven the next morning, a Sunday, they reached the town of Dadeville. Fearing an ambush, the 8th Indiana charged onto the square and down the side streets, capturing a handful of Rebels. They also unhitched horses and mules from buggies and wagons transporting women and children to church, then went to work tearing up the tracks again. In their zeal they nearly burned the entire town. First, sparks from their bonfires ignited the depot, and the fire threatened to engulf a nearby hotel and several commercial buildings. Horses tied to fences and hitching rails began to stamp and whinny, and a few broke loose and galloped away, troopers chasing after them. Men began frantically gathering up guns and ammo that were imperiled by the spreading flames. Eventually the blaze was contained, but the effort to fight it sapped the men of what little strength they had left. No doubt some wondered why Rousseau bothered to put out the fire, anyway.

The presence of Rousseau's raiders was now widely known. Church and plantation bells raised the alarm, and Confederate cavalry troops began to descend on the area from as far away as Mississippi—on foot, on horseback, by boats and trains. Remarkably, as Evans wrote, "Rousseau's men were only vaguely aware of the widespread consternation and confusion they were creating." Still, this much was clear: The work of destroying the railroads was complicated by the necessity of defense. General Sherman had warned Rousseau that the point of the raids was destruction, not engaging the Rebels, and Rousseau was concerned that holding the enemy at bay was diverting too much manpower from the task. According to Evans, Rousseau confessed during a moment of weakness, "I shouldn't have got into this affair. I'm very much afraid this isn't judicious."

When his forces arrived at Auburn on July 18, the men and horses were seriously fatigued. The marching was stressful and exhausting, and the raiders' chief task—destroying the railroads—was hot, dangerous, and backbreaking. They were perennially short of food and water and exposed to both the blazing sun and occasional thunderstorms. It was not as if they were unused to being exposed, but now they were at large for an indefinite period of time, without even tents. Further complicating matters, more Confederate troops, bolstered by local volunteer forces, were arriving from all directions.

Faced with the Rebels' renewed strength, Rousseau decided to withdraw, believing his efforts had achieved the desired result. In addition to railroad tracks and telegraph lines, his men had destroyed a Confederate locomotive and several train cars, thirteen depots and warehouses, two gun factories, an iron works, a conscript camp, more than a thousand bales of cotton, several tons of tobacco, at least four wagons, and huge quantities of military supplies. They had also commandeered about three hundred slaves, as many horses, and four hundred mules. And they had done it while losing very few men. Though the Confederate Army repaired and reopened the railroad a little over a month later, there was no discounting the damage done. If nothing else, the Union cavalry now knew what it could do.

The 8th Indiana led the returning column as a regimental band played, of all songs, "Dixie." The men plodded along until 2 a.m., stopped for two short hours, and then took up the march again. They halted briefly at noon the next day to rest and forage for supplies, and then continued into the night. After another brief rest they resumed marching at 5 a.m. and did not stop until they encountered pickets from General George Stoneman's cavalry about three miles north of Villa Rica, Georgia, where they were finally safe within Union lines. They entered camp triumphantly, standing in their stirrups, holding their hats aloft, and cheering themselves.

The jubilation was short lived. After traveling more than four hundred bone-rattling miles, the men were informed that they were scheduled to embark upon another raid—disappointing news, to say the least. As Fielder Jones cheerlessly noted in a later dispatch, "We had just returned from the long and fatiguing Rousseau expedition, and both men and animals were sadly jaded."

McCOOK'S RAID WAS LARGELY a disaster. Sherman had decided to send Edward McCook, by now a brigadier general, and Colonel Harrison west of Atlanta, and Generals Kenner Garrard and George Stoneman east, with plans to rendezvous south of the city on the Macon & Western Railroad after they had destroyed railroad and telegraph wires and cut off General John Bell Hood's avenues of retreat. Things did not go exactly as planned. After accomplishing the destruction east of Atlanta, Stoneman wanted to liberate Andersonville prison, and Sherman agreed to let him try, but only as a secondary goal. Stoneman made a unilateral decision to undertake the attempted raid, with disastrous results. Confederate General Wheeler sent three brigades after Stoneman and captured him and many of his men. The officers ended up in the nearby Camp Oglethorpe prison, and the enlisted men were marched to the dreaded Andersonville stockade.

While Stoneman was on his way to prison, the companies of the 8th Indiana under Fielder Jones, which included Tolbert and Maddox, and which had been reduced by sickness and exhaustion to four hundred men, got lost. When they finally caught up with the rest of the regiment under Colonel Harrison, they rendezvoused with McCook, who was not the inspirational leader Rousseau had been. In April 1864, after getting his commission as brigadier general, McCook had written, "I am so tired of taking my share of this fight in little skirmishes and scouting parties that I would cheerfully risk the lives of and wind of the few anatomical steeds I have left for the purpose of getting my proportion of the glory, if there is any for the cavalry, in this campaign." Not surprisingly, McCook's mounts took a beating. Eighteen pack mules dropped dead in their harnesses during the twenty-six-mile trek from Turner's Ferry to Campbellton alone. And on his beleaguered horses rode equally vulnerable men.

To make matters worse, McCook's raiders were hampered by inferior equipment supplied them by opportunistic government contractors. In a survival situation, such details mattered: A soldier could die if his reins broke or his saddle slipped. The saddles,

McCook wrote in one dispatch, were "utterly worthless. The raw-hide covering upon the saddle-trees is green, part of the wood green, and the whole construction imperfect . . . This fraud that is being practiced upon the Government by either Government contractors or Government inspectors, or both, is certainly sufficiently gross in its character to demand prompt investigation. The frauds of a set of unscrupulous speculators are rendering one of the most impor-tant and efficient arms of the service a burden instead of a benefit." Here, then, was another disturbing survival lesson: A soldier's life could be imperiled not only by inept officers but by greedy contrac-tors counting their wartime profits in distant cities.

The Rebels were meanwhile marshalling their forces again. Confederate General L.S. Ross reported on August 1 that he had tracked down and engaged a group of Yankees near the Owl Rock Church: "About noon we came upon the trail of the foe clearly de-fined by smoking ashes of burned wagons and the sad havoc and destruction of property everywhere visible, and the eagerness of all to overtake and chastise the insolent despoiler was increased two fold."

After crossing a pontoon bridge downriver from Campbellton on July 28, McCook reported that his men encountered Confederate snipers at "every hill on the road." Leaving troops behind to dis-tract the Rebels, he moved toward Palmetto, where he found and destroyed a commissary wagon train and killed at least four hun-dred Confederate mules. Some accounts put the number of slaugh-tered mules even higher, but however many it was, running sabers through hundreds of mules must have been grisly and sad. From there the men pushed on to Lovejoy's Station, on the Macon & Western Railroad, where they cut the telegraph lines; burned the depot and the water tower; and destroyed cotton bales, stores of tobacco, bacon, lard, salt, and ordnance, and a mile of track. Harrison's men reached Lovejoy's Station later the same day and also began tearing up the tracks. Confused by Stoneman's no-show, McCook eventually gave up on him and headed west.

There was also confusion over McCook's intended route, and the column made slow progress because of the bounty of their raids, occasional Rebel attacks, and the fact that the men had not bedded down for sixty hours. Reaching Newnan, the exhausted soldiers happened upon Rebel cavalry preparing to depart by train for Atlanta, who fired upon them from the train windows and nearby cellar doors and rooftops. "Yonder comes the Yanks now," one surprised Rebel shouted over the wail of the locomotive. The 8th Indiana was outnumbered ten to one and fled after exchanging a few shots, then returned with reinforcements, at which point they were met by the similarly reinforced Rebels, under Generals Wheeler and Ross, the latter of whom reported, "Friends and foes were mixed up in the struggle, without regard to order or organization, and frequent hand-to-hand encounters were the consequence. Many instances of capture and recaptures occurred during the day, the victor one moment becoming a captive to his prisoner the next." Ross proudly proclaimed the capture of nearly six hundred Union soldiers and flags from the 2nd Indiana and the 8th Iowa, the latter of which raised the white flag of surrender. He also reported capturing numerous pieces of artillery, ambulances, horses, and arms—none of which, notably, were mentioned in the Union dispatches. Eventually the 8th fled, leaving behind its beloved Colonel Harrison, who was separated from his command and found himself alone, without his horse. Unable to run because his calves were cramped from exertion, he was cornered by the Rebels and, like Stoneman, ended up in prison in Macon.

After fleeing Newnan, the 8th was again surrounded by a superior Rebel force, and Colonel Fielder Jones called for a withdrawal. Amid the confusion, his mule trains and led horses stampeded, and once he managed to restore order and reclaim his troops, the men lost their way. One of his officers reported finding "an obscure road, but he could not ascertain where it led to." Jones decided to follow it anyway. They soon ran up against a solid line of Rebels, at which point McCook, in command of the overall Union force, seems to have lost his nerve. "What shall we do? What shall we do?" he asked one of his officers, who told him contemptuously that he should fight. McCook ordered the officer to take command and "do the best you can." The 8th attempted to cover the rear and left flank of the column, but to no avail. As Rebel reinforcements continued to arrive McCook reportedly told his officers, "We must get out of this!" but his men were determined to fight, if only to prevent being captured. For no obvious reason, someone let loose the mules and horses, and there was a stampede. When some semblance of order was restored, Jones led the 8th in a charge of the Confederate lines and later reported, "We moved out at a brisk trot, and so well were our forces in hand, and so sudden the movement, that nearly one-half the Eighth Indiana got through the lines without receiving a single shot, and, although the remainder of the column ran the gauntlet of a heavy fire of musketry, yet, strange to say, but 1 man was wounded, although the enemy was in some places near enough to almost touch the horses."

After passing through the Confederate lines, the men hurried on, burning bridges behind them. At the New River, Jones was forced to leave many of his precious horses behind. "Several attempts were made to swim the animals, but they were so thoroughly exhausted that the attempt had to be abandoned," he reported. Soon after daylight his troops were again attacked by Confederate cavalry, and Jones was "compelled to leave 15 men, about 200 horses and mules in his hands. The most of the animals were unserviceable." He escaped with the Rebels in close pursuit. Many of his dismounted men were exhausted and barefoot and could not keep up, so he ordered them to break off from the column and hide in the mountains while the rest advanced toward Rome, Georgia. "I must say that the physical powers of the men were pushed to the very verge of human endurance," Jones later observed. "Five days and nights of almost constant duty in the saddle, added to the fourteen days' rapid marching with Rousseau, would shake even the most robust constitution. Men fell asleep on their horses, and the most persistent efforts of their officers could not keep them awake."

The column arrived in Marietta, Georgia, on August 3. Jones reported one hundred of his men killed, wounded, or missing and said that three regimental doctors had "voluntarily remained in the hands of the enemy to care for our wounded." No doubt many of the soldiers wished they had left well enough alone after Rousseau's raids. This time there were no self-congratulatory cheers, and some of the soldiers were reduced to riding cows back to camp, where one of them collapsed and died of exhaustion.

It took the Rebels only two weeks to repair the damage to the railroad. By then the 8th was on the road again, on yet another raid, this time under General Hugh Judson Kilpatrick, whom Sherman described as "a hell of a damned fool." The routine was becoming familiar: Another inept general, another series of towns and dangerous roads, another set of tracks to destroy. At Jonesboro, the challenge was compounded by darkness and rain. "Everything calculated to confuse men we had here to contend with—an utter ignorance of the formation of the ground, the darkness of the night, with heavy rain, and the only information of the enemy's position was gained by receiving his volleys of fire," Jones wrote. Forced to withdraw, they marched on, continually skirmishing with the Rebels. On and on it went. Like McCook's raid, Kilpatrick's raid proved to be nothing to write home about, unless to decry his ineptitude.

When he reported back to General Sherman, Kilpatrick exaggerated the accomplishments of his raid, claiming he had destroyed the Macon & Western railroad—though even as he spoke, a Rebel locomotive could be heard chugging into Atlanta along the line. The raids did have the effect of preoccupying Confederate forces, who might otherwise have helped defend Atlanta against the Union infantry and artillery. The former included the 22nd Indiana, in which Tolbert's brothers Silas and Daniel fought. Notably, the officer commanding the 22nd fired off a dispatch requesting that several of his men be cited for bravery and heroic conduct, including one whom he identified only as "Tolbert."

On September 2, the isolated and besieged Rebel garrison in Atlanta surrendered, and the largest Confederate industrial and rail center in the deep South fell into Union hands. The aggressively amoral William Blufton Miller observed, "It was a grand sight from our camp to look down on the burning city." At that point, Silas Tolbert was camped just outside Atlanta with the 22nd Indiana. Daniel Tolbert had been hospitalized with a gunshot wound to his left hand, which would result in the loss of three fingers and his discharge from the army.

Though the news of Atlanta's fall caused elation in the Union ranks, it was not as if Romulus Tolbert, Maddox, Summerville, and the rest of the cavalrymen in the area could let down their guard. There were plenty of Rebels still out there, and they were more desperate now. About forty-five hundred Confederate troops under the command of Nathan Bedford Forrest continued to assail the Union supply lines after the fall of Atlanta, and occasionally they overtook Union outposts and captured Union soldiers on patrol. Most of General Hood's army had escaped, leaving an estimated forty thousand Rebels at large.

Jones and his men continued to roam the countryside, building a succession of barricades along rural roads and camping behind them at night. When they again arrived at the Owl Rock Church, they were relieved to find that the baggage and camp equipment they had left behind two months before had been shipped south and caught up with them, though for Tolbert, his possessions would be of only temporary use.

The Owl Rock Church was to be the last stop of Tolbert's military career. On September 10, he departed the church in his newly issued uniform on a patrol of fifty 8th Indiana cavalrymen led by Major Graham, headed toward Campbellton. As they rounded the blind curve about a mile east of Campbellton they came face to face with Rebel cavalry. Before any of them had time to think, they were being fired upon. Tolbert wheeled to escape, glancing over his shoulder, and took one bullet in the back and another in the neck. Blood splattered his new uniform and ran from the corners of his mouth. The first bullet, a ball from a Navy revolver, entered behind his left ear, passed through his mouth, and lodged in the opposite side of his jaw. The second passed cleanly through his shoulder. About half of his patrol managed to get away and raced back toward the Owl Rock Church. Three of the men, including James Taylor, Tolbert's boyhood friend from Saluda, were killed. Twenty-two others were captured, eight of whom were wounded.

Tolbert was now gravely wounded and depended for his survival on a group of highly agitated enemy soldiers, sweating in their wool uniforms on a hot September day, who moments before had wanted him dead. He had also lost his horse.

When Graham delivered the news to the men back at the Owl Rock Church, Maddox was no doubt particularly disheartened. He was now separated for the first time from the friend who had accompanied him into the army, through his sickness, and along hundreds of miles of inscrutable, dangerous roads. He had no way of knowing whether or when he would see him again.

Chapter Five

SOMEWHERE, THE LITTLE BROTHER

S AMUEL TOLBERT WAS THIRTEEN, SMALL FOR HIS AGE and "fleshy," as one of his officers described him, when he enlisted in the 22nd Indiana Infantry in March 1864. Samuel was the last of the six Tolbert brothers to join, and his father was dead. The argument could be made that despite his age he had no real choice but to go. He had to contribute, to prove his worth before the war was over. At the time he was living with his sister's family, and for whatever reason his mother acquiesced.

He mustered in at Indianapolis, as his brothers had, and followed the same route to the war, through Nashville. His troubles began along the way when he came down with measles. He was hospitalized in Nashville, got better, relapsed, and was sent to a convalescent camp—basically quarantine. He caught up with the 22nd near Atlanta in September 1864, about a week after his brother Daniel had been shot in the hand at Jonesboro and subsequently discharged, and a day before Romulus was captured near Campbellton.

Underaged boys were often allowed to join the army as drummers or fifers, but Samuel enlisted as a regular soldier and so had to lug the heavy and cumbersome accoutrement of war: A gun, forty rounds of ammunition, a haversack, a knapsack, and a canteen. By the time it became apparent that he was not up to the task, it was too late to turn back. Whether from general weakness as a result of the measles or the weight of his cartridge belt, or some combination, he developed a hernia in his left side and suffered what appears to have been a growth deformity in his still-developing ribs, also on his left side. Some of his ribs subsequently fused together, and he was unable to expand his chest cavity on that side and so had trouble breathing.

The problem would grow continually worse during Sherman's March to the Sea. As he later wrote, his side became inflamed and "these pains and hurting grew worse day by day. After we traveled back from Savannah Ga.—Feb. 65—my hurting in side grew worse, so great was the paining that I could not stand to have my belt around my body, and my comrades, as also did my captain— A.C. Graves—carried my belt and other things for me." His physical condition deteriorated as the 22nd marched north through the Carolinas toward Washington, D.C., where he was put on "light duty."

"I remember that this boy gave out on march somewhere between Raleigh N.C. & Richmond Va. and my attention was called to him by finding him by the road side crying like a child," Joseph Stillwell, a surgeon with the 22nd, recalled. "He then told me that he was given out, said he could not carry his things; that they hurt him, and that his feet were sore. He seemed to feel that he was disgraced by giving out and having to report to Surgeon. I remember that I, appreciating his feelings, did not put him in Ambulance but got down off my horse and let him ride." In hindsight, Stillwell would conclude something that should have been obvious to others all along: "This soldier was too young, and should not have been put in service." On the other hand, "He was very gritty and was ready to do his part."

W.H. Snodgrass, who served with Samuel Tolbert in the 22nd, saw him as "a tenacious fellow, and disposed to do what he could and what was right." In fact, according to Snodgrass, "All of said Tolbert boys were ready soldiers." Another soldier called him "the baby of the company"—a description that could cut both ways.

Before joining, Samuel was "a stout healthy boy," according to his friend and uncle, George Dickinson. "He was a heavy, square made fellow." An acquaintance, a musician in the 22nd named Thomas Sample, said that Samuel first showed signs of serious physical distress during a forty-mile march immediately before the March to the Sea, when he struggled to keep up with the command and often straggled behind. He was "a mere boy," Sample said, "not old enough to perform the duties and endure the hardships of soldiering at that time."

Graves later remarked, "I had no idea when I saw Tolbert in the Comp'y that he was the mere child that he was." But, Graves added, "I noticed that he looked as though he had just come from a sick bed; he was thin and emaciated, and I thought, at the time, that his place was at home; and I said so to him, when he first joined the Company: 'You had better staid at home with your mammy.'" Graves said Samuel "was an ambitious boy and was proud of the privilege he enjoyed. He was always prompt in the performance of every duty imposed." But he also observed that when loaded down with his gear, "the little fellow would sink under it." Sometimes he would unbuckle his cartridge belt and let it swing from the end of his bayonet, to take the pressure off his side, "and march wearily, but pluckily, along with us."

During the March to the Sea, Graves often carried Samuel's gun and other equipment. "He would come to me, to the head of the line, and complain that his side and breast hurt him, that his cartridge box hurt him, and he would ask that I let him have them hauled in a wagon," Graves remembered. "I used to say to him: 'Sammie, I will carry your gun and accouterments, and you carry my sword. And I have carried the little fellow's gun all day long. I used to pity Sammie, on account of his youth, and the claimant's brothers—He had three brothers in my company—complained very much because the Recruiting Officer had accepted him." That recruiting officer, James Benham, who later commanded the company, said he had known Samuel "since he was a babe." A local resident recalled that after hearing that Samuel and another boy had joined, "it was re-marked by someone that the recruiting officer ought to take a cow along to give these boys milk."

Graves wrote, "I have seen and known him to have been ex-hausted from the fatigue of the march, and I often wondered what kept the boy up, and used to encourage him by telling him that he had more courage and grit than half of the big men of the company," adding that Samuel "was generally very fond of being where I was; and, like a child would do, he usually confided to me his troubles."

Samuel would make it to the end of the war, but would never get over the physical damage it caused.

Chapter Six

CAPTURED

T HE WAGON AND ITS UNWANTED CARGO BUMPED ALONG
the road, flexing and bouncing through the ruts like a crude
float in a parade of tired and dusty horsemen. Romulus Tolbert lay
among the wounded prisoners in the crowded wooden bed. By then
someone had stanched the bleeding; otherwise—with two gunshot
wounds, one to his neck—he would have bled to death. Field treatment of wounds during the Civil War was simple: You stuffed the
wound with a rag.

The Rebel entourage, encumbered by its twenty-three insolent
despoilers, was headed for Fairburn, Georgia. After driving away
the rest of the 8th Indiana patrol, the Rebels had loaded their prisoners and loot, including thirty rifles (some of which were the coveted repeating Spencers), in the wagons and hastened away, leading
a pack of captured mules as they passed through Campbellton.
Little of importance was left in the town now, other than the ferry
crossing on the Chattahoochee River. Campbellton had been in decline since before the war as the result of a local vote to prevent the

Atlanta & West Point Railroad from passing through on account
of the expected noise. Only a scattering of empty houses, barns,
and stores remained, along with a gutted brick courthouse. Campbellton was an empty stage set in a hotly contested war zone—a
place no one wanted to be for long. The railroad had been routed
to the south, through Fairburn, which boomed as a result. Though
the Union cavalry spent much of the summer tearing up the tracks,
Fairburn was still securely enough in Confederate hands that later
in the month Confederate President Jefferson Davis would visit to
try to boost the morale of the troops, who were discouraged by the
fall of Atlanta.

In saving Tolbert and the other gravely wounded men, the Rebels
followed the rules of war, though soldiers on both sides were known
to occasionally shoot prisoners. Perhaps their anger had been muted
by Tolbert's helplessness and misery. It is one thing to take pride
in being able to bring down an enemy, and another to disregard
someone's suffering, even if that someone had been trying to kill
you a few minutes before.

Confederate General L.S. Ross, who had been fighting the Yankees in the area for much of the summer, was now in charge at Fairburn. One of his officers, J.M. Taylor, had led the ambush in which
Tolbert and the others were captured. Upon their arrival in Fairburn, the Rebels unloaded their captives as soon as they could, and
Tolbert, who was too badly injured to travel farther, was placed in a
private home. There were no real hospitals nearby, and it would have
been apparent to anyone that his chances of survival were slim. He
was now essentially alone. Everyone who knew him, who thought
the way he did or understood why he thought the way he did, was
gone. His blood-soaked shirt, his knapsack, his gun, his saber, his
horse—all were gone. He could not eat.

Tolbert left no account of his stay in Fairburn, so there is no way to know whether he awoke in a stranger's bed and wondered where he was, with his head and shoulder bandaged and throbbing with pain; whether the women were compassionate or resentful or the doctors attentive or uninterested. But he likely drifted in and out of consciousness for days, his mind floating to the surface like a fish in a stream, then sinking back into the depths. Severe trauma frequently leads to shock, and during the Civil War a soldier who survived his wounds almost inevitably faced some degree of infection, usually accompanied by fever and delirium. Jesse Hawes, a private from Illinois who went through a period of disorientation after being similarly shot and captured, observed that "the fever that follows a gun-shot wound fills the mind with the wildest fancies." Hawes, who was also shot in the neck near his ear, recalled that he was placed in a Confederate ambulance with three other injured men who had difficulty not getting in each other's way and aggravating each other's wounds. "But I was soon oblivious to all around me," he wrote. "That awful faintness over-powered me, and I unconsciously went to sleep."

A person in such a state typically becomes confused, unsure whether it is day or night, alternately fearful, suspicious, and angry, not unlike someone with dementia. There is always a degree of hubris involved in going into battle, but once a bullet penetrates flesh, the hubris bleeds out. The dynamic changes. A captive soldier in such a state has few survival tools other than the ability to enlist sympathy. As his body struggles with trauma and perhaps infection, he may feel the urge to give up one moment and fight the next, then to escape, then to acquiesce. Tolbert's trials had suddenly escalated. He had endured the energy-sapping marches only to be ambushed. He had survived the ambush only to face the potential for death from his wounds or from infection. Each time he survived, but each time he faced a new and different challenge. Given the level of medical care a Civil War soldier usually received, the struggle that followed would be just as easy to lose. Infected arms and legs could be amputated—and often were, even unnecessarily, but amputation was not an option for someone who was wounded in his trunk and in the head, as Tolbert was.

In his condition, he was certainly a source of consternation for his hosts, and perhaps a curiosity. Patience James, a Fairburn resident who was compelled to care for a wounded Yankee at another time (when the Rebels were away), recalled that the local women were accustomed to keeping plenty of food on hand for their own soldiers, for marauding Union troops, or for men whom they were compelled to nurse. As James told her granddaughter, who wrote it all down, she had been pressed into nursing service after a nearby battle, when Fairburn was in Union hands, and, "the Yankees took an old empty house across the street from me for a hospital. They placed straw over the floor and it was where they placed their wounded. The women had to care for them. I did not wait to have one sent to me, but went to select mine. There was a large German soldier shot in the stomach who died soon afterwards. There was a young soldier who claimed to have a broken back whom I selected. He said he couldn't walk. I believe there were only five men left in Fairburn at that time, so I had to get a little negro boy to help me carry him to my house."

Once she got her injured soldier home, James placed him in a bed and, she said, "I made the little negro boy, Mont, a pallet by the side of the bed, telling the soldier that if he needed anything during the night to call Mont." She did not say whether she was relieved when the injured soldier turned up missing the next day, along with

Mont's coat and shoes. She assumed he had lied about his broken back and escaped. Perhaps he became a straggler—what would one day be referred to as AWOL.

Jesse Hawes, whose injuries during his capture were similar to Tolbert's, was also treated in a private home. After his capture, the Rebels temporarily left him in a wagon with other wounded captives, and he escaped and made his way to a log cabin, where two women helped him inside and put him in bed after laying his rubber blanket across it so as not to soil the linens. The women then brewed coffee for him on the fire. The elderly woman who took charge of his care treated his wound, though as Hawes recalled she mostly just picked at it, rubbed some herbal remedy into the parts that were not violently tender, and talked to him. When Rebel soldiers arrived at the cabin, Hawes officially became an enemy captive again.

Tolbert's captor-caregivers managed to keep him alive long enough to get free of him, too. After a week in the private home, he was sent to a Confederate military hospital in Montgomery, where he remained for six weeks. Along the way, someone dug the ball out of his jaw. That was necessary, though it amplified the risk of infection, the chief cause of death during recovery from a gunshot wound. Gunshot wounds are uniformly nasty, and during the Civil War they were typically contaminated, such as by a dirty hand raked across them or a rag used to stanch the flow of blood. Flies were a problem, too, bringing with them traces of whatever filth they had recently tracked through, such as feces or carrion. Tolbert's doctor may have done his best to clean the wound and to remove any related debris, but he would have done so with his fingers and whatever surgical tools he had at his disposal, which were probably not fully sterilized. Before such surgeries patients were given opium or laudanum if it was available, and chloroform if they were lucky.

After the largest bits of debris were removed, Tolbert's wound would have been sewn up with a needle whose thread had been wetted with saliva, then wrapped in gauze overlaid with plaster. Debris was almost always left behind: Bits of cloth, lead, dirt, gunpowder—even pieces of thread, skin, or bone from other soldiers, if the bullet had passed through them first. Such alien particles were anathema to the body. Even if the wound did not become infected, a fragment of debris could easily move into the bloodstream and cause an aneurysm in the heart, lungs, or brain. When the soldier awoke from surgery—assuming he had been put under, and perhaps even if he had not—he likely suffered from severe headaches, fever, vomiting, and painful swelling. Either way, by the time he was fully conscious, Tolbert would have been acutely aware that major things were going wrong in his body.

As an enemy soldier in a military hospital Tolbert probably received treatment only after the injured Rebels. One woman who served as a nurse in the Union Army reported that after the battle of Gettysburg, "It took nearly five days for some three hundred surgeons to perform the amputations that occurred here, during which time the rebels lay in a dying condition without their wounds being dressed or scarcely any food." The injury to Tolbert's neck, mouth, and jaw was clearly the more serious, but the wound to his shoulder was dangerous, too. Minié balls—thimble-sized cylindrical bullets of soft lead that were commonly used during the Civil War—were particularly damaging because they spun during their trajectory and tumbled and deformed inside the victim after impact. If the injury did not kill the person outright, or cause brain damage or paralysis, the ragged wound soon began to enlarge and swell, sometimes to many times the size and depth of the original point of entry.

Bandages were changed infrequently and sometimes reused, which added to the potential for infection. Infected wounds generated copious amounts of pus and sometimes became infested with maggots. Civil War surgeons referred to draining wounds as producing "laudable pus" because of their misunderstanding of bacterial infection, knowledge of which would be developed only a decade or so later—too late to benefit the wounded of the Civil War. In some cases they allowed maggots to remain because they consumed dangerously rotting flesh, a process believed to promote the growth of new tissue. One surgeon recalled treating a wound scarcely larger than the bullet that made it, which become larger and larger until, as he described it, he could have inserted his fist inside. Gangrene also spread rapidly through hospitals, particularly after a few days of cold rain, which required windows and doors to be closed, and one surgeon reported observing a wound on the inside of a man's upper thigh become enlarged so dramatically that it exposed the femoral artery "until the pulsating vessel stretched like a red rope across the chasm." Treatment of hospital gangrene called for isolation and exposure to fresh air, which was not always possible, as well as local application of nitric acid, nitrate of mercury, or bromine if they were available. If a patient survived and the infection was arrested, the tissue would slowly grow back. One Wisconsin soldier who was captured and held in the officers' prison at Macon endured three successive amputations from one leg as a result of spreading infection before he died.

In Hawes's case, by the time an actual surgeon arrived to tend his wound, it had become so swollen that "one could easily lay his hand in the opening. The surgeon proceeded to sew it up, which operation was a good deal like trying to draw the mouth of a well-filled sack together, and caused me the greatest pain and agony." Hawes was then loaded onto an ox-drawn wagon, part of a caravan of injured prisoners, each wagon driven by an old man. "At almost every house we came to a halt was made and more wounded added to our number. The heat was intense. The sun poured down its burning rays upon our unprotected bodies like a ball of liquid fire, while the green flies swarmed around our festering wounds like bees around a hive." Hawes and his fellow prisoners were eventually loaded into a boxcar, but because the railroad tracks were in such bad repair, the train derailed. The car he was traveling in overturned, throwing the injured men against the ceiling, and rolled down an embankment. Men began to wail as a result of new injuries and reopened wounds. "Help was slow in coming," he wrote, "as the guards had their own killed and crippled to attend to first." Finally a surgeon and his assistants began working on the injured prisoners, "but when the car was opened some were already past all help, while others soon bled to death from having their wounds torn open."

Hawes and his fellow survivors were put aboard another train bound for the Confederate prison at Cahaba, Alabama—the same pen where Tolbert ended up after he was released from the military hospital in Montgomery.

The fact that Tolbert was in the hospital in Montgomery for six weeks indicates that he was not doing particularly well, and he had to be stabilized before he could be transferred to Cahaba, where blockades and raids—by men such as him—led to periodic shortages of food and medicine. Clearly, his situation was going to get worse before it got better.

Tolbert's conditioning, his youth, and his spirit may have helped prepare him for the challenge. If nothing else, he was still alive. There were possibilities.

THREE DAYS AFTER TOLBERT'S CAPTURE, a group of foragers from the 2nd Indiana Cavalry ran into a similar ambush near Stilesborough, Georgia. Perry Summerville had enlisted in the 2nd three years before, at age fifteen, and had seen battlefield action in Alabama, Georgia, Kentucky, Mississippi, Tennessee, and Virginia, including some of the bloodiest conflicts of the war: Shiloh, Perryville, Stone's River, and Chickamauga. The 2nd had also participated in McCook's disastrous raid and a few drowned in the frigid river when a ferry overturned in Tennessee. Summerville had come through each trial to fight another day, but on September 13, 1864, as his cavalry patrol fled a Rebel ambush, he jumped from a speeding wagon and into the abyss. He fell beneath the wagon wheels, felt his leg snap, and was unceremoniously left behind. He then became a prisoner of war.

Summerville was an alert and affable young man, with hawkish eyes and a musing, slightly frowning mouth. He reacted to captivity by drawing upon both his personal charms and his powers of concentration. After his capture the Rebels put him on a mule, which he rode for a few hours in what must have been excruciating pain, until he was loaded into a wagon. Two days later the wagon pulled to a stop in Jacksonville, Alabama, where Summerville was placed in a hospital for a few more days, and where his physician took pity on him. As Summerville later wrote, "The man at the hospital gave me a fine comb, which was the means of catching at least fifty thousand inmates at the prison, and his lady gave me a ten dollar bill." The "inmates" were the scourge of Civil War soldiers—body lice, which were a nuisance in camp but a plague in the prisons, where the crowded, filthy conditions provided an especially productive habitat.

Throughout much of the war, prisoners were routinely paroled in the field, pending an official exchange. Technically, they were not to fight again until a corresponding enemy prisoner was released, and sometimes their captivity lasted only a few hours. But not everyone was paroled, and the prisoner exchanges had been suspended by the time Summerville was captured. Most soldiers, including Summerville, had been on the other end of the transaction, having captured their share of enemy soldiers, so everyone knew the drill. The prisoners were stripped of their weapons, their mounts, and their personal possessions, which often included items of no monetary value that their captors kept as souvenirs. As soon as possible they were sent to a holding camp. Sometimes the prisoners were treated roughly; at other times they conversed with and even befriended their captors. They were almost always robbed, which was not only an affront but limited their ability to bargain or even to perform routine tasks such as keeping a supply of drinking water on hand.

After being captured in North Carolina, Thomas Newton wrote that he and his fellow Yankee prisoners were "deprived of all that was on our horses, including haversacks, blankets, canteens, tin cups, etc. so we had no cooking utensils or anything to get water in." This forced Newton to be resourceful. "While marching through Goldsboro, I saw an oyster can in the street and stepped out to get it. The guard, not knowing my intention, ordered me back to my place, but I requested the next guard to get it for me when he kindly went and brought it to me, and still farther along I picked up a piece of wire to make a bail for it, all of which seemed to be providential, for undoubtedly the little pail was the means of saving my life."

Newton was aware of one of the basic truths of surviving captivity: You had to start from scratch. Men who bemoaned their circumstances and failed to adapt typically did not fare well. Those who made use of their limited control did better. Some men wasted away in the dirt of the prison yard, nearly naked and starving, while others set up rudimentary business enterprises, carving utensils from roots to trade, cutting soldiers' hair on barter, hoarding and then selling food. At his next stop on the way to prison, Newton secreted the pail he had fashioned from the oyster can, along with a few other possessions he had managed to conceal from the guards. "They took everything in the shape of money and valuables that they could find or thought was worth something, with some exceptions," he wrote. "One of the boys had a good watch that he refused to give up. He told the guard he could not have it unless he was stouter than he. Mr. Reb gave it up saying he would see the lieutenant about it after examination, but we heard no more about it." As for himself, Newton wrote, "I had a watch, jack-knife, wallet and two or three dollars in money, all of which I put in my little pail and slid under the cell door, which was open at the time, so he did not find it."

After arriving at a temporary prison in Charleston, South Carolina, Newton and the other prisoners received nothing to eat for sixty hours (he apparently timed the lapse with his treasured watch). "We had become so weak it was with difficulty we could walk across the floor; in making the attempt we would be so dizzy that we would almost fall over. I never knew what hunger was before, but thought I knew then." In fact, as was the case with many prisoners, the worst was still ahead. Soon Newton was sent to Andersonville, the most notorious prison in the Confederacy.

Jesse Hawes had been captured the first time near Guntown, Mississippi—the result, he later said, of his troops' "overweening confidence" in their repeating Spencer rifles. Advancing hurriedly through a dense bramble, Hawes had tripped on a vine and simultaneously "a thousand bullets flew hissing into the thicket." Trees began to splinter around him, and smoke from the Rebel guns blew into his face. He realized that his fall may have saved his life. Many of his comrades were killed or injured. Soon he was on his feet again, rushing toward the Rebel line, but when he emerged into the open he found himself alone in the face of the enemy, with perhaps a hundred guns leveled on him. "For a moment I stop in confusion," he recalled. "A score of Confederates yell, 'Don't shoot that man; surrender, d—n you, surrender!'" So he did. "Running so actively that hot day, for a few moments I was breathless and a passive subject in their hands while they stripped me of my arms, a dozen men swearing at me most roundly during the act. The instantaneous change from a pursuing, exultant freeman to a roughly handled, roundly cursed, humble prisoner, presented a ludicrous side to my mind, and as soon as I could get breath suggested to my captors that the change was a rough joke to their unwilling guest. But they were in no joking mood. Indeed, they were never more serious in their lives." He later escaped, was recaptured, again escaped, and was again recaptured.

There was no hope of escape for Summerville, since his leg was broken. After Jacksonville he was taken to Talladega, where he was locked in a small cell with a dozen Rebels, who, he assumed, were captured deserters. At some point he was given a pair of crutches, and a few days later he was transferred to a jail in Selma, then moved to Cahaba prison. It was now the end of September 1864. He would spend Christmas and his eighteenth birthday there.

Cahaba was an unfinished cotton warehouse, partially roofed, on the banks of the Alabama River, surrounded by a small wooden stockade. As Summerville entered the stockade gates he heard other prisoners hollering "fresh fish," the army slang for new arrivals. He spent the day scoping out the situation and looking for an older man named Brown with whom he had been taken prisoner in Georgia. At nightfall he had no blanket to ward off the cold and fell asleep on the ground, using his crutches for a pillow. The next morning he spent several hours trying to clean the dirt from his uniform, unwilling to give in to the squalor of the prison. Meanwhile his leg was getting worse. He was taken to the Confederate hospital housed in the nearby Bell Tavern Hotel, a few blocks from the prison, where he managed to surreptitiously fashion a knife from a piece of iron hoop he had found. He was unable to mentally endure the hospital, though, writing, "to see the dead carried out every morning was too much for me and I went back to the stockade." He eventually found Brown, and the two formed an alliance, Summerville with his knife and Brown with a railroad spike, which they used for splitting wood. This meant, he said, "We were better fixed than the average prisoners."

It would not be long before wood became scarce and Summerville was reduced to whittling away one of his crutches for firewood, to stay warm and to cook the meager rations the prisoners were issued raw. He burned all of the first crutch and started in on the second, which left him with a cane. When the cane was stolen, he observed, "That left me in a bad fix."

FOR J. WALTER ELLIOTT, the pivotal event of the war came around the time Tolbert and Maddox were setting off on Rousseau's raid, in early July 1864, when he was promoted to captain in the 44th regiment of the U.S. Colored Troops. Elliott, who had

graduated from officer's training school six years before, finally got
the recognition he wanted, but it carried immense challenges and
risks. Racism was common in both armies, and the use of black
troops was controversial. The white officers who commanded them
were often ridiculed within their own army, and the troops were
typically undersupplied and given few opportunities to prove themselves in battle. They were also largely unschooled and received less
pay than their white counterparts. More significantly, according to
Confederate law they and their white officers were subject to execution as illegal combatants if captured.

In the movie *Glory*, which is based upon the journals and letters of Robert Gould Shaw, the protagonist accepts a promotion to
lead the colored troops of the 54th Massachusetts Infantry. His best
friend reacts incredulously, saying, "I know how much you'd like to
be a colonel, but a *colored regiment?*" A contemporary article in the
Indianapolis Journal was even more blunt, observing that the practice of arming blacks was tolerated only because "no white soldier
could be found who would not sooner see a Negro with one arm off,
than to have one off himself."

Elliott's promotion unleashed a series of calamities. Though he
did not mention his black soldiers by name in his numerous wartime accounts, nor the fact that almost all of them were returned to
slavery after capture, he used their shared travails to portray himself as a brave, well-connected leader who endured great adversity.
Like the majority of officers in the U.S. Colored Troops, Elliott was
white, though his dark complexion perhaps opened him to insults
along the way. The Elliotts were a staunchly Unionist family. His
uncle Robert was involved in the Underground Railroad, and two
of his younger brothers, Simeon and John, also served in the Union
Army. One of his cousins, James H. Elliott, served alongside him

initially in the 10th Indiana Infantry. While in the 10th, Elliott was involved in some of the war's bloodiest conflicts. He participated in the siege of Corinth, Mississippi, in the pursuit of Confederate cavalry under General Braxton Bragg into Kentucky, and—more or less—in the battles of Stone's River, Chickamauga, and Missionary Ridge. After joining the 44th U.S. Colored Troops he was posted to Chattanooga and saw limited action, mostly in and around Dalton, Georgia, and Nashville, Tennessee. At Nashville his troops came out on the short end of one engagement, though not, apparently, for lack of trying.

The 44th was organized in Chattanooga in April 1864 by Major General George H. Thomas and placed under the command of Colonel Lewis Johnson. After the fall of Atlanta, the 44th was primarily used for manual labor and picket duty. Like other black regiments, the men were aware of the special perils they faced, but their willingness to fight was bolstered by a profound fear of capture. On September 24, 1864, soldiers of the 110th Colored Infantry were captured by forces under the command of Confederate General Nathan Bedford Forrest near Athens, Alabama, after their commanding officer, Colonel Wallace Campbell, set fire to his own supply stockpiles and ordered his troops to seek refuge in a blockhouse, or stockade, beside the railroad tracks. Campbell had sent two couriers with a request for reinforcements, one of whom was captured and killed, while the other escaped, injured, and returned to the fort. Just after dawn the next day, the Rebels began shelling the fort, and after a few hours Campbell received a surrender ultimatum from Forrest.

"I have a sufficient force to storm and take your works, and if I am forced to do so the responsibility of the consequences must rest with you," Forrest wrote. "Should you, however, accept the terms, all white soldiers shall be treated as prisoners of war and the negroes returned to their masters. A reply is requested immediately." After Campbell sent a message declining to surrender, Forrest replied, "I desire an interview with you outside of the fort, at any place you may designate, provided it meets with your views. My only object is to stop the effusion of blood that must follow the storming of the place."

Campbell wrote that Forrest subsequently informed him that "if he was compelled to storm the works it would result in the massacre of the entire garrison. He told me what his force was, and said myself and one officer could have the privilege of reviewing his force. I returned to the fort, when, after consultation with the commanders of various detachments in the fort, it was decided that [if] after reviewing the force of General Forrest I found he had 8,000 or 10,000 troops, it would be worse than murder to attempt to hold the works."

Campbell agreed to surrender on the condition that all of his commissioned officers would be permitted to go to Meridian or some other point in Mississippi, and from there to Memphis for parole, and that they would be allowed to keep all their personal property, including horses, saddles, sidearms, and clothing, while the enlisted men—about three hundred fifty of whom were black and one hundred twenty were white—"shall be kindly and humanely treated and turned over to the C. S. Government as prisoners of war, to be disposed of as the War Department of the Confederate States shall direct."

Forrest agreed to the terms, but many of Campbell's own officers and men did not. Though they argued that the fort was strong enough to withstand a Rebel attack indefinitely (and a group of his officers afterward requested that Campbell be investigated by the military), they were overruled. In their request for an investigation, the officers wrote, "We also feel it our duty to make mention of the bearing and disposition of the soldiers in the fort, both white and black. It was everything that any officer could wish of any set of men." When told that the fort had been surrendered and that they were prisoners, the officers wrote, "they could scarcely believe themselves, but with tears demanded that the fight should go on, preferring to die in the fort they had made to being transferred to the tender mercies of General Forrest and his men."

The 44th, in which Elliott served, met a similar end. The men saw their first real action at Dalton, Georgia, on October 13, 1864, and it resulted in their capture. They were part of a Union garrison in Dalton that was surrounded by Confederate troops under General John Bell Hood. Colonel Johnson, who commanded the 44th, occupied the garrison with about seven hundred fifty men, as many as a hundred of whom were unarmed and more than six hundred of whom were from the 44th. A few soldiers had gone "foraging" or "recruiting" and so escaped capture, but Elliott was not among them. He and the other officers of the 44th were captured and paroled in the field on October 15.

The surrender at Dalton was remarkably similar to the one at Athens. Johnson reported that his scouts had observed the Rebels destroying the railroad within five miles of the town and burning the connecting bridges. He had requested reinforcements and received about fifty white troops from Illinois. By the time his cavalry returned, the Rebels were in close pursuit. After some brief skirmishing, Hood delivered an ultimatum under a flag of truce, demanding that Johnson surrender. Hood promised that the white officers and soldiers would be paroled but said, "If the place is carried by assault, no prisoners will be taken." In other words, everyone would be killed.

Johnson responded that he could not surrender, "whatever the consequences may be." After another half-hour of skirmishing, the parley was repeated. Then Hood began to prepare for battle in earnest, forming what Johnson described as "a very long and dense line of infantry, about two miles in length," with artillery emplacements. "In short," Johnson reported, "we were surrounded." He sent three white officers out under a flag of truce to demand an inspection of the Rebel troops and said that if their numbers proved overwhelming, and if Hood would guarantee safe conduct to the next military post, he would evacuate his garrison. Hood refused. Johnson's men had seen what they needed to, however: An overwhelming force, in a far more commanding position. "General Hood told me that I must decide at once; that I already had occupied too much of his time; and when I protested against the barbarous measures which he threatened in his summons he said that he could not restrain his men, and would not if he could; that I could choose between surrender and death," Johnson wrote, a bit breathlessly, adding, "To fight any more than had been done was madness, in the face of such barbarous threats, which I was fully satisfied would be carried out, as the division of Cleburne, which was in the immediate rear of the rebel general and his staff, was over anxious to move upon the 'niggers,' and constantly violated the flag of truce by skirmishing near it, and to fight was also hopeless, as we were surrounded and could not be supported from anywhere."

Unwilling to submit his nearly eight hundred troops to possible slaughter, Johnson surrendered on the condition that his black enlisted men would be treated humanely, that his officers and white soldiers would be paroled and allowed to retain their swords and whatever personal property they could carry, and that they be allowed to remain with their black troops. The latter request was denied. "I was told by General Hood," he wrote, "that he would return all slaves belonging to persons in the Confederacy to their masters; and when I protested against this and told him that the United States Government would retaliate, and that I surrendered the men as soldiers, he said I might surrender them as whatever I pleased; that he would have them attended to, &c."

Despite the threat, "The colored soldiers displayed the greatest anxiety to fight," Johnson reported, adding, "It grieved me to be compelled to surrender men who showed so much spirit and bravery." After the surrender, the black soldiers "were immediately robbed and abused in a terrible manner. The treatment of the officers of my regiment exceeded anything in brutality I have ever witnessed, and a General Bate distinguished himself especially by meanness and beastly conduct. This General Bate was ordered to take charge of us, and immediately commenced heaping insults upon me and my officers. He had my colored soldiers robbed of their shoes (this was done systematically and by his order), and sent them down to the railroad and made them tear up the track for a distance of nearly two miles. One of my soldiers, who refused to injure the track, was shot on the spot, as were also five others shortly after the surrender, who, having been sick, were unable to keep up with the rest on the march." As his white officers were being paroled Johnson entreated his captors to free the black "servants and soldiers" in the regiment who came from the free states of Indiana and Ohio, but to no avail. "From the treatment I received, and what I observed after my capture, I am sure that not a man would have been spared had I not surrendered when I did, and several times on the march soldiers made a rush upon the guards to massacre the colored soldiers and their officers," he wrote. "Mississippians did this principally (belonging to Stewart's corps), and were often encouraged in these outrages by officers of high rank. I saw a lieutenant-colonel who endeavored to infuriate a mob, and we were only saved from massacre by our guards' greatest efforts."

Johnson and his officers were paroled and released at a place called Dug Gap, but their black troops were sent south into slavery or to work for the Confederate Army. John Leach, a sergeant with the 44th, later reported that they were put to work in the vicinity of Dalton, then marched to Selma and Corinth, destroying railroads along the way. "During the time I was in the hands of the rebels there were about 250 men of the Forty-fourth delivered to their former masters, or men who claimed to own them, thereby returning these men to slavery," Leach wrote. At the time he managed to escape to Union-held Memphis on Christmas Day, about one hundred twenty-five men from the 44th were "still laboring on these railroads, the remainder having either been sent to the hospital to die, or turned over to civilians as slaves, or effected their escape."

Elliott later said that after being paroled, he and the remaining officers of the 44th returned to Nashville, where they reorganized and moved south to Chattanooga to join the army of General William Tecumseh Sherman, though they were subsequently ordered back to Nashville and placed under the command of Colonel Thomas J. Morgan. On the way to Nashville, the train on which the 44th and two companies of the 14th Colored Infantry were being transported was disabled by fire from Confederate General Nathan Bedford Forrest's batteries at about 11 a.m. on December 2, 1864.

The train on which Elliott and his troops had been riding was "the hindmost one," and during the night of December 1, the train ahead of them had derailed. Thus delayed, they had received what Elliott later concluded were bogus orders, fabricated by the Rebels, to return to Nashville. "We went forward, and when on the bridge over Nine Mile Creek at Block-house No. 2, Gen. Forest opened fire on us with a battery, at short range, from the curve just in advance of the train," he wrote. The train was crippled on the bridge. Elliott and company leaped into the creek, waded to the bank, drove the Rebels back, and then made their way to a small blockhouse, where they continued fighting until dark. "Soon after dark a council was called by our colonel, Louis Johnson, in the block-house, & as the result was sent 4 several parties to try to pass Hoods line to . . . the Cumberland to reach Gen. Thomas & seek his aid for our rescue."

At about midnight, Elliott recalled, the men concluded that Hood had invested Nashville, preventing Thomas from coming to their aid, and "that our only safety lay in stealing out thro' the darkness and then some must remain to maintain the line and keep up the spasmodic night firing. That duty fell upon myself and my 2nd Lieutenant H.C. Knowles."

Johnson reported that the Confederate batteries were delivering relentless fire upon the stockade and had destroyed the lookout tower, caved in the roof, and injured or killed numerous men. "My position was quite desperate, and when I took into consideration that my stock of ammunition was almost expended, the stockade so much used up that a few shots would have knocked it down, and having lost one-third of the men, I resolved to abandon the stockade and fight my way to Nashville," Johnson reported. "I knew that should the place be surrendered or taken by assault a butchery would follow, and I also knew that re-enforcements would have been sent to me if it had been possible to send them. I therefore left the block-house at 3.30 a.m., and, contrary to my expectations, got through the rebel lines without much trouble. I arrived at Nashville about daylight." The 44th's troop surgeon and chaplain remained behind with the wounded men and raised the hospital and truce flags above the blockhouse.

Elliott, Knowles, and a small squad of soldiers meanwhile crept away into the darkness and "began the task of stealthily passing two lines of Forest's and thro' Hoods lines to Nashville, an almost hopeless undertaking, but I & Knowles had all to win & nothing to lose by the experiment. Capture meant death, shot like dogs by the Southern chivalry while prisoners of war, and no living comrade to tell our friends of our end." They managed to pass through the first line of pickets but soon encountered mounted squads of Rebels and "had some lively, active firing experiences in bush, briar, brambles and streams of water," which scattered his men.

In the early light, Elliott found himself alone with Knowles, and they were forced to do some "zigzag running and dodging" to try to escape. Once they passed out of the line of fire, they hid behind a fallen tree, "concealed by a dense growth of weeds that lapped over the log." They could see pickets about seventy-five yards away and decided to lie quietly, wet, hungry, and shivering from the cold, to "watch & pray for night, when we might hope to crawl thro' Hood's army. Foragers passed so close I could have touched them with my hand as I lay there in the wet earth." Sometime after noon, Elliott fell asleep and was awakened by a whisper from Knowles, who told him the Rebels were advancing toward them. Glancing up, Elliott realized that "discovery and capture was inevitable. We were alone & might escape identification as 'nigger' officers and recognition. It could be no harm to try & we had life to gain by success & could be no worse off by a failure, so quick as thought, in that supreme moment of capture thought and action were simultaneous. I whispered to Lieutenant Knowles, 'My name is Capt. David E. Elliott of Co. 'E' (I now think it was) 75th Ind. V.I. & yours is Lieutenant Henry Clay of Co. 'F' 16th Ill. V.I.' the co. he was promoted from. About two minutes afterward Knowles & I advanced on a brisk walk to report to Col. or Gen. Ross of Forest's command, having by then been discovered by one of the Rebels." Elliott had met David Elliott the first night of the organization of Company E of the 10th, back in Indianapolis, and the two, he later recalled, "became friends & I loved him for his gentlemanly & soldierly qualities."

Despite his fears, Elliott wrote that the first Rebel to interview him was "a very courteous gentleman." When General Ross demanded Elliott's name and command, he unfurled his lie and introduced "Clay," who, he said, "seemed scared and to lose his wits." Asked why they were separated from their command, Elliott said they had been cut off after Sherman "took one of his crazy fits and took French leave of Atlanta & left a few thousand of men & officers on leave at home and as we returned to join him we found ourselves cut off and were stopped at Chatta. & when you uns got to kicking up such a hell of a racket here General Thomas sent us straglers a very pressing invitation to join him, but while on the way General Forest took charge of the train & we took to the woods."

Ross sent Elliott and "Clay" to Forrest's headquarters "at the first toll-gate out from Nashville." En route they passed through Franklin after a two days' march, subsisting on two ears of corn per man. Elliott said he "kept up a merry fusilade with the long haired jesters," all the while fearing he would be recognized by his fellow prisoners and outed as an officer of colored troops.

The remaining colored troops under Johnson continued to fight, and in a subsequent report he observed that they suffered the greatest casualties. During one particularly brutal skirmish, he reported, "I was unable to discover that color made any difference in the fighting of my troops. All, white and black, nobly did their duty as soldiers, and evinced cheerfulness and resolution such as I have never seen excelled in any campaign of the war in which I have borne a part."

George Fitch, a lieutenant with the 12th Colored Infantry, reported that later in the month he was captured and shot, along with two other black officers, one of whom was with the 44th. After their capture by Forrest's scouts, the men were robbed, stripped, and marched toward the Rebel headquarters. "After leaving the road about half a mile, as we were walking along through a wooded ravine, the man in advance of us halted, partially turned his horse, and as I came up, drew his revolver and fired on me without a word," Fitch reported. "The ball entered my right ear just above the center, passed through and lodged in the bone back of the ear. It knocked me senseless for a few moments. I soon recovered, however, but lay perfectly quiet, knowing that my only hope lay in leading them to believe they had killed me. Presently I heard two carbine shots, and then all was still. After about fifteen minutes I staggered to my feet and attempted to get away, but found I could not walk. About that time a colored boy came along and helped me to a house near by. He told me that the other two officers were dead, having been shot through the head. That evening their bodies were brought to the house where I lay. Next morning they were decently buried on the premises of Col. John C. Hill, near by."

Fitch continued: "The shooting occurred on the 22d, and on the 23d, about midday, one of Forrest's men came to the house where I was lying and inquired for me; said that he had come to kill me. The man of the house said that it was entirely unnecessary, as I was so severely wounded that I would die any way, and he expected I would not live over an hour. He then went away, saying that if I was not dead by morning I would be killed. After he left I was moved by the neighbors to another house, and was moved nearly every night from one house to another until the 27th, when I was relieved by a party of troops sent from Columbia and brought within the Federal lines."

Chapter Seven

CAHABA

A MISERABLE TABLEAU MET AMANDA GARDNER'S EYES each time she looked out her upstairs windows. Below her, on the flatlands along the Alabama River, three thousand thin, dirty men milled about inside the crowded stockade of Cahaba prison under a perpetual pall of smoke. Many of the men were sick. Some of them died as easily as fog rose from the river on a cool morning, and their friends had to touch their bodies to make sure they were gone. Others died hard, thrashing on the ground.

Gardner lived in an otherwise comfortable house in the town of Cahaba, Alabama, an enclave of columned mansions, storefronts, and shanties that spread across the floodplain of the Alabama and Cahaba rivers. The town had been the state capital in the 1820s but, like Campbellton, Georgia, had been sliding toward obscurity since before the war, primarily because it was prone to floods. The local railroad had gone bankrupt, and the Confederate Army had torn up the tracks to repair more important lines elsewhere. But in June 1863, the town took on one final momentous role as a portal into the darkest underworld of the war. Gardner's house stood next door to the prison, providing her with an unenviable box seat.

By late October 1864, Gardner could see the prisoners hugging their shoulders against the chill of autumn. The weather was invigorating and brisk for anyone who had only to pull cloaks, blankets, and gloves from the cedar chest, pick the last of the season's roses, and lay a cozy fire on the hearth. But the prisoners were dangerously exposed, and the halcyon sky, open to the cool, clear air pushing down from the north, was a harbinger of the deadly chill to come.

The prisoners' suffering was not a significant source of concern for most of the people of Cahaba, who had problems of their own. The Confederacy was running short of food and supplies; the rebellion was not going well; and the women's husbands, sons, and brothers were fighting and dying on distant battlefields. The prisoners' countless small fires sent smoke through both the stockade and the town, and everyone within range could smell the stench of sickness, of death, and of the god-awful latrines. Occasionally, the report of a guard's rifle echoed across the river. The muffled chatter during the day, the occasional moans and cries at night, provided the background noise at every table. But the prisoners themselves were largely a faceless, nameless mass. On Sundays, when the church held services next door, the parishioners' singing drowned them out.

Gardner did not have the luxury of living in studied ignorance. She saw the prisoners meting out their last reserves of energy, lying in the dirt, hovering over their tiny fires, waiting in line at the awful latrines, stepping over each other and the accumulation of filth. Sometimes they fought. They were tormented by mosquitoes, maggots, and flies.

Somewhere amid the rabble was Romulus Tolbert, who arrived at Cahaba in October from the military hospital in Montgomery, after the Rebels had done all they could for his throbbing shoulder and jaw. By a strange twist of fate, his friend John Maddox arrived at about the same time, after being captured near Draketown, Georgia, as did Perry Summerville, hobbling on his swollen, unset broken leg. For Tolbert and Maddox it must have been a bittersweet reunion. They were in prison, but they had each other for support as Tolbert nursed his wounds and both were afflicted with diarrhea (Maddox eventually came down with scurvy, too). A man who had a friend at Cahaba, or a company of fellow soldiers, was comparatively fortunate. Friends could look out for each other, watch over whatever possessions they could still claim while the other waited in line for rations or at the latrines, help defend against the depredations of thugs, and tend to their respective needs when they were sick. A lone man was completely dependent upon the kindness of strangers and vulnerable to predators, who were numerous in the prison population.

Cahaba was run by Captain Howard H.A.M. Henderson, a Methodist minister, who maintained generally good relations with the prisoners. As winter set in Henderson arranged for a steamboat load of clothing, blankets, medicines, and other supplies from the United States government to travel to the prison under a flag of truce. Its cargo included two thousand coats, hats, and pairs of pants, shoes, and socks; fifteen hundred blankets; medicine; envelopes and writing paper; and one hundred cooking tins. Unfortunately, most of the clothing was soon traded off to the guards for food, leaving the men almost as bereft as before. A far less compassionate man, Lieutenant Colonel Sam Jones, headed the military post at Cahaba and was second in command of the prison. By late 1864 Jones was in charge most of the time, as the comparatively benevolent Henderson was frequently away, procuring needed supplies or trying to effect a prisoner exchange.

According to Jesse Hawes, who ended up at Cahaba after his third and final capture, "It was often in the power of Henderson to extend kindnesses and courtesies to prisoners, and we are glad to note that the opportunity was not infrequently embraced." Henderson even bought a pair of shoes for a barefoot young prisoner whom he escorted to Memphis to be exchanged, and he openly wept over the death of another young Union soldier.

Jones was another story. A bitter man who scoffed at the prisoners' suffering, he had been assigned to Cahaba after being court-martialed for falsifying military records, and he was later suspected of the murder of a prisoner alleged to have been behind a failed uprising. Jones would be remembered darkly by the prisoners.

At Cahaba, as at other prisoner-of-war camps in both the North and the South, a man could die of almost anything. Hawes wrote in his journal of the death of "a tall young boy" from Illinois of chronic diarrhea, the result of "miserable, polluted surface water, the coarse meal, poorly cooked, the exposure to the cold rains." He watched the boy make frequent trips to "the sinks," as the latrines were called, and noted a few days later that "his journeys were fully as frequent, but his steps were slower, his face more hollow, his eyes more dull. He growled at first, then complained in a hollow voice; the lines of pain and long-suffering deepened upon his face; his steps grew slower, weaker, sometimes staggering; he neglected to fasten his clothing; faeces ran from the bowels as he slowly dragged himself to the 'sink.' A day later he sat all day resting his chest upon his knees, his head falling forward. The next day he lay upon his side on the ground; some one gave him all he had some boughs of pine for a bed. He was too weak to go to the 'sink' now. The drawn, haggard, suffering face showed less of the agony he manifested a few days before, and more of weakness, dullness. The eyes grew more sunken, the discharges from the bowels were only a little bloody mucus. He could answer questions if one asked him anything; he asked occasionally for a sip of water, never for food. He was getting more and more stupefied. During the day we placed over him whatever we could to render him as comfortable as possible. I went to him in the night he was only a few feet away from us and found him dead."

The next day, Hawes wrote, "A cold rain started in before morning, and at daylight some one pulled off his ragged garments to cover his own suffering limbs." A detail of the boy's friends was permitted to remove him from the stockade for burial.

That was the way it sometimes worked. Of the nearly two hundred thousand Union troops held in Confederate prisons during the war, more than thirty thousand died. The rate was only slightly better among Rebel prisoners held in the North: More than twenty-six thousand dead among the more than two hundred thousand incarcerated. The fatalities at Cahaba were a fraction of the total—a few hundred. But for people like Amanda Gardner, each one was a sadness and an affront.

Cahaba, sometimes known as Castle Morgan, was the most crowded prison in the Confederacy, perhaps of the entire war. Despite Henderson's efforts, medicine, food, clean water, and firewood were sometimes in short supply. Captive officers fared better than enlisted men; they were housed in town and were free to move around upon their pledge not to escape. But the stockade was dismal. Originally designed as a holding pen for Union soldiers captured in battle or cavalry raids who would ostensibly be transferred to established prisons elsewhere, it quickly became overcrowded after the two armies' exchange program broke down. Afterward, men continued to arrive even as other prisons filled, which meant there was no place for them to go. Confederate General Nathan Bedford Forrest's cavalry was particularly adept at catching Yankees and was largely responsible for the Cahaba overflow. Soon the population swelled to the point that each man had, on average, only about six square feet of space during the day, and even less at night, when the prisoners were sequestered within the warehouse. By the time Tolbert and Maddox arrived the place was starting to implode.

It is hard for anyone who has never experienced loss of freedom to fathom the insult of it: The deep disappointment, the uncertainty, the claustrophobia, and the fear—to be locked up by a stranger who cares little about you and may even loathe you, to finally lose control. At meal time hundreds of prisoners crouched in the bare dirt, cooking mush in tin cups and broken pans over their fires. Smoke shrouded the compound and burned their eyes as they tried to cook, so that they had to bury their faces in their sleeves or call for someone to relieve them. Many of the men wore ragged blue uniforms that had gone unchanged for months and were stained with sweat, shit, and blood. Some were barefoot. The sick lay on the ground drawing the thin warmth of the sun, clutching pained bellies, or nursing fantastic, infected wounds. Many were oblivious—moaning, groaning, talking to themselves, cursing at anyone who stumbled over them. Here and there men sat with their shirts in their laps, methodically picking lice for hours, their sunburned arms and heads mismatched to their bony white torsos. Now and then a prisoner would go high-stepping through the crowd toward the privy, where there was always a line because there were only six stinking holes for three thousand men. Maddox, and eventually Tolbert, ended up spending their share of time there, too.

Gangs of criminals roamed the stockade, many of them bounty jumpers, the majority purportedly from New York City. There was

little policing of the prison by the guards, aside from the no-go zone
known as the deadline, which extended around the inside perimeter
of the stockade, so for long periods of time the muggers ruled. Hawes
wrote that solitary prisoners—the most vulnerable to the raiders, as
the thugs were called—were fortunate when the man known as Big
Tennessee arrived. Big Tennessee, whose exact identity would later
be debated (though there was general agreement that his last name
was Pierce), arrived at Cahaba at about the same time as Tolbert,
Maddox, and Summerville and made his presence known almost
right away. A blue-eyed, illiterate farmer, he was nearly seven feet
tall and a "mountain of muscle" before he grew emaciated like the
rest of the prisoners, his arms and chest "enormous even for a man
of his gigantic dimensions. He brought to mind old pictures of
gladiators," Hawes recalled. In one perhaps embellished scene—for
Hawes, like J. Walter Elliott, was sometimes prone to exaggeration,
though he had a remarkable eye for detail—he described Big Tennessee dispatching two muggers with a right and a left hook, then
grabbing two more by their hair and cracking their heads together.
After the initial fight, all Big Tennessee had to do was show up to
right a wrong, according to Hawes. When prisoners went to him to
report a robbery, he would escort them to the perpetrator, confront
the man, and force him to make amends.

Big Tennessee could not be everywhere, though, and fear of the
raiders led the prisoners to form their own police force and eventually to seize and try a group of offenders, after which the ringleader was sentenced to be chained to a log each night. The police
force became less effective after its leaders were transferred to other
camps, and eventually the raiders infiltrated its ranks. Some semblance of order was restored only after the bulk of the raiders joined
the Confederate Army and left en masse.

Hawes observed a group of raiders molesting a young man, stripping him naked and dousing him with cold water. The episode drew the attention of Big Tennessee, who pulled the men off and helped the young man back into his clothes. Afterward, Hawes recalled, the boy was allowed to return to "his little nest in the sand," though he died the next night. Hawes also recalled a "smooth-faced, handsome boy, a gun-boat man belonging to the monitor Chickasaw," whose eyes "were large and full" and whose manner was "pleasant and captivating." The handsome young man attracted attention, some of it unwelcome. According to Hawes, a prisoner informed a randy ruffian named Perry—who had deserted the Confederate Army and joined the Union Army, only to be captured and sent to Cahaba—that the young man was actually a woman in disguise. This may have been a euphemism—sex was never openly discussed in the accounts of Cahaba survivors—but for weeks afterward, Hawes said, "the boy, who was informed of the fraud, was the recipient of numerous gifts and more numerous smiles from his uncouth admirer, his reticence and coyness when speaking with Perry only adding to the ardor of the suitor."

Sickness, hunger, cold, and the attention of greedy and occasionally horny thugs were not the only menaces. The men faced soul-sapping ennui and aggressive, even sadistic guards. The compound was surrounded by a wall of wood, which blocked out everything but a rectangle of sky. The prisoners might catch the scent of the river or the murmuring of the town, the occasional neighing of a horse, the ringing of a bell, the passage of hushed voices or shouts, or the singing in the church on Sunday. Now and then a few were allowed outside to gather wood, or on some other supervised detail, or to be treated for what ailed them at the makeshift hospital in the nearby Bell Tavern Hotel. But for the most part, the prisoners suffered from a lack of mental stimulation. The days were marked by the changing color and light of the square of sky, which brightened and dimmed, glared or crackled with lightning, and was traversed by clouds and the arcing sun and moon and stars.

Melville Cox Robertson, a prisoner who was also from Jefferson County, Indiana, wrote in his diary that "prison life is rather the most monotonous thing yet. But where there is so many together as there is here it can hardly be dull to most of those confined but to myself it sometimes becomes almost intolerable. There is so little of congeniality of spirit among those with whom I am associated that I often feel myself almost completely alone in the midst of 500 men."

Jutting into the sky above the stockade, alongside the gables of Gardner's house, were guard towers where old men and boys watched with guns resting on the rails, waiting for a prisoner to step across the deadline. Anyone who set foot across was subject to being shot, and many were. In one diary entry, Robertson wrote, "A shade of gloom is cast over all this evening by the sudden death of one of our beloved prisoners. Shot by the guards for stopping a moment in the passage from the entrance to the yard." Less than two weeks later Robertson wrote that another prisoner was shot by the same guard.

The number of prisoners ebbed and flowed as new captives arrived and others died or were shifted to different camps, and exchange was such a perennial subject of discussion that some prisoners eventually found it tiresome.

Robertson, who was assigned as a nurse at the Bell Tavern Hotel, wrote in his diary, "I am sensible that the best thing I can do is to make the best of my condition and I am trying to do it. I eat my corn-bread, smoke my pipe and look forward to something better."

The hotel, whose bar, elaborate ballroom, billiard hall, and poker room had, before the war, been a favorite meeting place for area planters, politicians, and river travelers, was appropriated by the Confederate government and outfitted with cots. When the number of patients grew to two hundred, additional beds were set up in a neighboring house.

A report by Confederate surgeon R.H. Whitfield on March 31, 1864, when Cahaba contained only about six hundred fifty men, noted that the spring that provided water to the camp was polluted before it entered the stockade by "washings of the hands, feet, faces, and heads of soldiers, citizens, and negroes, buckets, tubs, and spittoons of groceries, offices and hospital, hogs, dogs, cows, and horses, and filth of all kinds from the streets and other sources." As a result of Whitfield's scathing report, Cahaba was ordered closed and its inmates transferred to Andersonville. Many were transferred, but Cahaba never closed, partly because of the halt in prisoner exchanges. Soon the population of inmates began to grow again, by leaps and bounds.

The U.S. Army burial records list ten deaths among the Cahaba prisoners from gunshot wounds or other injuries, which could have been inflicted by guards or by soldiers before or during their capture. The roll lists only two men dying of scurvy, the disease that killed hundreds at Andersonville. Because fruits and vegetables were also scarce at Cahaba, the lower toll probably stemmed from better treatment of the disease. In general, the prisoners appeared to have had decent access to medicine most of the time, because Cahaba was situated between Alabama's medical supply depots at Demopolis and Montgomery, but there were periodic and significant interruptions. The disruption of the supply lines deprived everyone, including the citizens of Cahaba, their slaves, and the Rebel army, of food and medicine, and when the precious commodities were being doled out, the prisoners were last in line. Extended deprivation weakened everyone. Weakness and parasites rendered them vulnerable to disease. The proliferation of disease begot more disease. Dysentery flowered. When a person is measuring out his last remaining energy, something as minor as an infected mosquito bite can drain away the last of it like water from a busted barrel. By then the body has burned all its fat and begun consuming muscle and tissue. It is only a matter of time until vital organs begin shutting down. The greatest causes of mortality at Cahaba were pneumonia, dysentery, and diarrhea. Some prisoners during the Civil War died of simple homesickness, or "nostalgia," which surgeons actually listed as a cause of death.

Many of the problems associated with Cahaba and other prisons, both in the Confederacy and in the Union, were brought on by lack of planning for such large numbers of captives. In many ways, conditions were better at Cahaba than at other camps in either the North or the South, and the inmates' chances of survival were only slightly worse than on many battlefields, but that would have provided cold comfort at the time. They were enduring the worst living conditions they could have imagined, and no one knew how or when it would end. For the most part, their world consisted of the same dirty prisoners corralled inside the dreary compound, which alternated between dusty and muddy, depending on the weather, and was filled with smoke day in and day out. As Hawes wrote: "I had entered the prison in the most vigorous health, and blessed with an appetite that made no discrimination among foods that were edible. Like the rest, I divided my day's ration into equal parts, consuming them one in the morning, the other in the afternoon; but as soon as I had gone to sleep I nearly always began to dream of being home, and as soon as I would enter the house I at once went to the pantry and began to eat . . . Oh, what delightful lunches I used to get in those dream journeys to the home pantry!"

In later descriptions of the Bell Tavern hospital, Hawes judiciously left out that after being admitted there he was officially diagnosed with "nothing," apparently during a severe cold snap that made the prospects of a heated ward more attractive. Even in the deep South, the cold could be severe enough to give unprotected men frostbite. Hawes recalled one particularly cold morning when a popular young prisoner known as Little Eddie failed to show up for roll call. When Hawes asked about Little Eddie, he was told that the boy was breathing his last, so he and a group of five friends went in search of him. They found Little Eddie curled in a fetal position in the dirt, shivering and unable to speak. It was not the first nor would it be the last time they observed a prisoner wasting away, but Hawes and his friends were not ready to give up on Little Eddie. They gathered him in their arms and dragged him from the shadows into the warmth of the sun, wrapped him in blankets borrowed from more fortunate prisoners, and took his hands and feet in their own hands and exhaled their own warm breath onto them, rubbing them and holding them close to their bodies. They dribbled warm water into his mouth, trying, as Hawes recalled, "to coax back the ebbing tide of life." Slowly, Little Eddie came around. His friends had bought him some more time.

Initially, the prisoners slept in bunks in the warehouse stacked up to five tiers high—essentially shelves of rough boards spaced about thirty inches apart, with no bedding. There were only enough bunks, or roosts, as the prisoners called them, to accommodate four hundred men, so the rest had to sleep on the ground unless a roost came open as a result of a transfer or the death of its former occupant.

Because there was no way to heat the partially walled and roofed building, aside from a single fireplace, the prisoners had to build their own open fires if wood was available, and the resulting smoke was suffocating on cold nights. There was only one wheelbarrow to be used in removing rubbish and waste, and the stench was horrendous. The entire stockade was filthy, like the men, and overrun with lice, fleas, flies, and rats, which buzzed or nosed around them and kept them awake at night. Hawes found the lice particularly disgusting and wrote that they "crawled upon our clothing by day . . . crawled over our bodies, into the ears, even into the nostrils and mouths by night." He was also disturbed by the rats, which he wrote "were a source of much annoyance to us who slept upon the ground." He was at first fearful the rats would bite him, but over time he became mostly annoyed that they kept waking him up.

When food ran short, the men were reduced to consuming ever-shrinking portions of cornmeal—delivered raw and riddled with partially ground-up cobs—and rancid meat. Bad as the food was, it was not unusual for prisoners to trade articles of clothing or interesting trinkets to the guards for extra rations. A prisoner had hope as long as he kept his mind and body comparatively sound, and hope had enormous potential to keep a person going. Even when circumstances were bleak, it was possible to nurture hope, to feel a kind of camaraderie peculiar to people enduring shared travail, and to benefit from the kindness of strangers.

No stranger was kinder to them than Amanda Gardner. Though she was a staunch Rebel and had lost a son to the Yankees at the battle of Seven Pines in Virginia, Gardner could see firsthand what was going on inside the stockade and found it impossible to stand idly by. When the prison's rations ran low, she emptied her pantry and sent her daughter Belle to pass food through the stockade wall to a group of cooperative guards. When she saw jaded prisoners staring blankly at the sky for days on end, she opened her late uncle's library to them, lending them Dickens novels, world histories, biographies, poetry, travelogues, and scholarly works on science, philosophy, and religion. Occasionally prisoners sent notes to her by the guards requesting specific books, including accounts of inspiring, legendary wars and comparatively quaint travails. Gardner also donated all her extra bedding and clothes, and after those ran out, she had her draperies and carpets cut into squares for blankets. She also enlisted items from some of her neighbors. Melvin Grigsby, a prisoner from Wisconsin, described Gardner as "of good family and in every sense a lady of culture and refinement. She is a fluent talker and uses elegant language." She was, he also noted, "a thorough rebel."

Hawes wrote that an unfriendly guard eventually saw Belle Gardner passing something through the stockade and reported her to Jones, after which the gifts of food were halted. Amanda Gardner, who saved all the notes written to her by the prisoners, likewise irked Jones by protesting the cruelty of disciplinary actions against some of the prisoners, which she could see from her windows. By the time her second son entered the Confederate service late in the war, her role at Cahaba was well known, and he was returned to her unharmed after his capture by Union troops. But as conditions worsened, Gardner's ability to help diminished. By then, she lamented in a letter to her daughter, everything was going wrong.

Still, as Melville Cox Robertson observed, "I have my seasons of light and shade here as I have had under more favorable circumstances." On the last day of December 1864, when Robertson had been in the hospital for most of the month, he noted that the patients were given a turkey dinner for Christmas, which made him long for home. "The end of '64—an eventful year—to me at least what will '65 bring forth?" he asked in his journal. "Will I see home before it ends?" In another entry he wrote that after attending a sermon delivered by another prisoner, he felt hopeful that better times lay ahead. "Then came thoughts of *home*, followed by a flood of pleasant memories of old associations."

———————————

IF ANYONE HAD WHAT it took to survive, it was George F. Robinson. Cocksure, with a reputation as a bit of a rogue, he had a stylish sweep of auburn hair and what one friend described as "a small mustache." His defining trait was independence, which did not dovetail with captivity.

Robinson had served in various arms of the military, starting with the infantry, then as a second lieutenant in the Corps d'Afrique, part of the U.S. Colored Troops, with which he sailed to New Orleans aboard a ship named the *Wild Gazelle*. While stationed on a malarial island for six months he had caught fever, resigned his commission, and returned to Charlotte, Michigan, to live with his brother-in-law. After a few months he joined the 2nd Michigan Cavalry and fought across the deep South until his capture at the age of nineteen during a skirmish at Shoal Creek, Alabama.

Robinson endured his share of close calls as a soldier, but he went into true survival mode as a prisoner of war. In his first stop, Meridian, Mississippi, a fellow captive stole his stash of rations from beneath his head as he slept, which Robinson later wrote was "experience No. 1 as a prisoner." He said he was "much surprised" by the theft and within two weeks decided to cast his lot with five others in an escape attempt. The men tunneled out of the camp and made

it sixty miles before being cornered, as Robinson wrote rather petu-
lantly, "by an old woman and fifteen dogs." He was returned to the
Meridian pen, covered in mud.

A month later he was on his way to Cahaba when the train derailed and he and a friend, John Corliss, escaped through an open
window. They may have actually been thrown through the window—Robinson's account is not clear—but either way they were
presented with an opportunity and they took it. As he tumbled
down the rail embankment Robinson became "badly mangled" and
received a serious cut on his head. The weather was cold, and he
was wearing only a shirt, underwear bottoms, and now one shoe.
For the next five days he and Corliss eluded the hounds that tracked
them, eating raw corn and wallowing through a swamp where icicles
hung from the trees. They were recaptured, shivering and hungry.
Sent back to Meridian, he and Corliss were transferred to Cahaba,
from which they escaped after only a month by cutting a hole in
the stockade wall. They were recaptured near Selma and held in
an elevated building, from which they escaped by digging through
the soft brick wall with a knife and a piece of an old poker. Again
recaptured, they were returned to Cahaba, where they remained for
four months, until the end.

There were few escape attempts at Cahaba, and Robinson's attempt was among the more bold. The stockade was closely moni-
tored, and the men were crowded together in public view, which
made it hard to do anything without detection. Remarkably, most
of the prisoners who tried to escape, including Robinson, came
through the episodes unscathed. The glaring exception was Captain
Hiram Hanchett of the 16th Illinois Cavalry, who was alleged to be
a spy at the time of his initial capture, and later as the ringleader of
an attempted uprising at Cahaba. Although Hanchett and his men

overpowered nine guards, the prison was quickly locked down and the uprising quelled by a cannon trained on the compound. The cannon was never fired, and no one on either side was killed, but afterward Jones forced the prisoners to pass naked between two files of guards, holding their clothing above their heads, in the hope that a man reportedly injured by a bayonet during the uprising could be identified (he was not). In his report of the incident, Henderson described Hanchett as "an exceedingly dangerous and bad man." After languishing for a while in the dungeon of the county jail, Hanchett vanished. It was said that he was told he was being paroled, escorted out, and never heard from again. Most of the prisoners believed he was murdered, and they pointed the finger at Jones.

Hawes also escaped Cahaba with two other prisoners by squeezing under the floor of the privy and following the sewer ditch to the stockade wall, which they scaled while a companion distracted the guard. In his account, Hawes wrote that he hatched the scheme with three prisoners, one of whom—a man whose name he gave only as Grimes—was a hotheaded, poorly educated, but otherwise likeable Virginian. Grimes had deserted the Confederate Army following an altercation that left a fellow Rebel dead, changed his name when he reached the Union lines, and joined the other side. He had a similar altercation with one of his Union compatriots, deserted again, and joined the Missouri cavalry. Not surprisingly, after his capture he was terrified of being identified by either side. "The quality that commended Grimes as a companion in a contemplated escape was his unchanging, earnest determination to secure his freedom," Hawes wrote. The other two conspirators were both from Ohio: E.A. Gere and D.E. McMillan. Gere was a restless spirit, who chafed more than most under the constraints of prison life, and Hawes considered him courageous, vigilant, prudent, and tough. McMillan was much younger than the rest, the greenest of the bunch, and ended up backing out at the last minute.

The group concluded that tunneling out of Cahaba was not really a viable option. Rumor had it that the Rebels had planted torpedoes outside the stockade, and in any event, there was no way to dispose of dirt without being noticed, either by the guards or by the prisoners, some of whom would betray another for an extra ration of food. So the decision was made to escape through the sewer.

Guards stood sentinel at the privy as well as over the space between the brick wall of the warehouse and the wooden stockade, so Hawes and his crew persuaded sympathetic prisoners to distract the two who might see them escape. One engaged the guard stationed at the wall with negotiations for the trade of a fancy knife; another did the same with the guard at the latrine, using an embroidered blue-and-gold band from Hawes's hat. "If one thing more than another was pleasing to the eyes of the Confederate guard, it was some such gewgaw as that band," Hawes observed. They had to wait until no one was coming or going from the privy—no small feat considering that it served three thousand men. The idea was to slip into the eroded gully beneath the front of the privy, but with the guard only a few feet away, Gere decided it would be safer to slip through the toilet hole, which proved a bad idea. Not surprisingly, the Rebels had ensured that the hole was too small for a man to go through, so Gere got stuck. A frantic moment followed, but Hawes and Grimes succeeded in extricating him, and they went back to their original plan. "It was but the work of a second for Grimes to glide as noiselessly as a cat to the opening, to glance eagerly at the guard, to place his feet in the opening, to glide under the floor on which Gere and I were standing," Hawes wrote. He and Gere followed. There, in the muck beneath the privy, they listened for a moment to see if they had been observed, but heard the hat-band negotiations continuing uninterrupted. They then crawled into the open area between the privy and the stockade wall. Peering nervously up, they saw the guard still dickering with their accomplice over the knife. Without further hesitation they scaled the wall. "When we jumped to the ground we observed a negro a few rods away looking at us; but we were each dressed in gray, and sauntered along leisurely through the portion of town nearest the prison." Hawes assumed the man thought they were Confederate soldiers taking a shortcut over the wall.

From there they strolled through the town before slipping into the Alabama River, hoping not to leave tracks that a bloodhound could follow. Their plan was to find a boat and paddle to Mobile, then into the open Gulf of Mexico to Pensacola, Florida, which was held by the Union. It was a far-fetched scheme, but they were desperate. The never found a boat and so traveled cross-country, intentionally stepping in cow manure to confuse any hounds that might pursue them—a Grimes suggestion. They encountered a few slaves, who were bewildered by their presence but chose not to get involved. They told the slaves they were lost Rebels on their way to Cahaba. At night they slept in the woods.

Eventually they encountered a black plantation overseer, who was clearly suspicious of them. "He was very obsequious," Hawes wrote, adding that "his fawning, servile manner made Grimes suspicious of him." After they departed, Grimes wanted to go back, waylay the man, and either make him accompany them or tie him up for the night, but Hawes and Gere disapproved. They were faint from lack of food and sleep, confused about where they were, and increasingly uneasy, but they felt they had no choice but to forge on.

Apparently the overseer reported them. "Just as we had nearly passed through a large field of corn, Gere halted and listened; he said he could hear the cry of hounds," Hawes recalled. Everyone's hearts dropped. Soon the sound seemed to grow more distant, and they resumed their march. Then the sound was suddenly close, and the men, "pale with fear and sickening despair," began to run. The cries of the dogs grew more excited as they burst on the scene. The three men ran as hard as they could across the cornfield and barely managed to climb atop a tall fence before the dogs were upon them, barking and growling. A short distance behind they could hear the voices of men on horseback. When the first man arrived, he pointed his gun at them and asked if they were armed. He did not seem to believe them when they said they were not, and asked again. Then he ordered them down from the fence. They hesitated until he shooed away the dogs. "Did you come from Cahaba?" the man asked. Hawes began his spiel about being lost Rebels, but he was interrupted by Grimes, who admitted they were fugitives from the prison. "That put a full and irreversible quietus on my story," Hawes lamented, though he had to admit that their accents would have given them away.

After two days of freedom, Hawes and company headed back to Cahaba, arguing with their captors along the way about the war, their respective equestrian skills, and no doubt whatever else came up. That night they were inside the stockade gates, where they were welcomed back by their disappointed friends, less one fancy knife and Hawes's blue-and-gold hat band.

Chapter Eight

ANDERSONVILLE

DURING THEIR IMPRISONMENT IN AUGUST 1864, COL-onel Harrison, General Stoneman, and Colonel Joseph Dorr, all of whom had been captured during McCook's raid, wrote to President Lincoln to give "a heartrending account of the conditions of our private soldiers now prisoners of war at Andersonville, Ga." The letter asked Lincoln "to use every honorable effort to secure a general exchange of prisoners, thereby relieving thousands of our comrades from the horrors now surrounding them."

About thirty-three thousand Union soldiers were held inside the twenty-six-acre stockade at Andersonville, and the three officers estimated that perhaps twenty thousand had no shelter of any kind, or even shade. "Thousands are without pants or coats, and hundreds without even a pair of drawers to cover their nakedness," they wrote.

The United States government had ceased its prisoner exchange program after the Confederacy refused to trade U.S. Colored Troops, although there was believed to be an ulterior motive: The desire to reduce the beleagured Confederacy's manpower, even at the expense of Union prisoners of war. Harrison and company alluded to the impasse, writing, "We were told that the only obstacle in the way of exchange is the status of enlisted negroes captured from our armies, the United States claiming that the cartel covers all who serve under its flag and the Confederate States refusing to consider the negroes soldiers, heretofore slaves, as prisoners of war . . . Is it not consistent with the national honor, without waiving the claim that the negro soldiers shall be treated as prisoners of war, yet to effect an exchange of the white soldiers?" Captured black soldiers, the three contended, were routinely distributed by the Confederates as slaves and so were rarely imprisoned, and "their slavery is freedom and happiness compared with the cruel existence imposed upon our gallant men."

Lincoln, apparently, was unmoved. Official exchanges did not resume. Harrison, Stoneman, and Dorr, who did not likely spend much time at Andersonville before being quartered in the Macon officer's prison, were transferred to a Confederate military prison in Charleston, South Carolina, and in late September paroled.

IN THEIR LETTER TO LINCOLN, the three officers may have exaggerated some aspects of Andersonville. There is no evidence to support their contention that thousands of prisoners were kept naked. But conditions there were undeniably bad. Everything that was wrong with Cahaba was worse at Andersonville. Every threat was amplified. The sickness, hunger, and ennui were more intense than in the most desolate army camp, the environment was hopelessly defiled, and violence was common. It would have been bad enough if all the prisoners had to contend with were bad food, diarrhea, and hostile guards, but the stockade walls delineated more than the limits of their freedom. They also described the boundaries of their physical, mental. and emotional stamina, and their willingness to do what was necessary to make it out alive. Men who put their trust in God, who persevered because of concern for loved ones back home, who steeled themselves with anger or pride or honor or even greed—for all of them there were limits, and the odds were that they would reach them at Andersonville.

Andersonville existed on the far fringes of human civilization. It was overcrowded, contaminated, poorly supplied, and often brutally violent. Law and order, food, and medical care were in perennially short supply. Most of the prisoners were enlisted soldiers or captive officers of black troops; other officers, including Elliott (on account of his ruse), were held in Macon. No one had it all that good, but officers of black troops, along with their enlisted men, were in many cases treated more harshly. As New Jersey Private George Weiser observed, "There were four or five hundred colored prisoners in this prison and nearly all of them were lame or wounded." Black prisoners also suffered the highest death rate: Of the approximately eight hundred held at Andersonville, two hundred eighty-four died— about 35 percent.

Elliott may have spent some time inside the stockade for brief periods, because it was not unusual for prisoners to be shunted around to more than one prison camp. Tolbert's brother Mathew, who was captured at Chickamauga and reportedly spent eighteen months at Andersonville, was eventually transferred and released in North Carolina. In his published accounts after the war, Elliott wrote that following his capture he was transported to Chattanooga; then to various holding pens in Mississippi and Alabama, including

Cahaba; and finally to Andersonville. He wrote of being confined to a crowded boxcar ankle-deep in horse dung for a day and a night, during which "indignities and humiliations" were heaped upon him. "Shall I tell of the march over ice and snow; the wading of deep streams from Nashville to Dixon ... suffering from cold and exposure in the dead of winter, and from hunger ..." he plaintively asked his readers.

Reading between the lines—always a good idea with a carefully crafted memoir—one can surmise that Elliott spent most of his time at Camp Oglethorpe, the preferable prison on the south side of Macon, about sixty miles away. He avoided the stockade because no one knew his identity. Not that the Macon prison was comfortable. Elliott recalled "the stench of rotten meat, of which we had not half enough to eat" and "the bitter, bitter feeling that our country had abandoned us to our fate." Still, for the men who were incarcerated at length inside the stockade, the horrors superseded everything that had preceded them, perhaps even in bloody battles such as Gettysburg and Chickamauga.

Why would anyone claim to have been inside the stockade if they had not? Clearly, no one wanted to be there at the time; yet, many prisoners would later make much of their experiences at Andersonville, which represented a survival saga of epic proportions.

Of the more than forty-five thousand prisoners who passed through the stockade, about thirteen thousand died—almost one in three, the highest rate of any prison during the Civil War. Formerly healthy men died of malnutrition or easily treatable illnesses and wounds, and the underworld of criminal raiders within the prisoners' ranks was entrenched and at times murderous.

The stockade's physical boundary was a wooden palisade fifteen feet tall, inside of which ran a deadline extending nineteen to twenty-five feet into the compound. Prisoners who stepped across the deadline were shot. Thomas Newton recalled that, "About my second day there, without doubt my head would have been pierced with a bullet, but for a comrade's timely jerking me from the scene of danger. I was not aware that in stooping over, my head extended a few inches beyond the 'dead line.'" In some cases, men who were within the safe zone were shot by stray bullets aimed at violators. Another prisoner recounted how a crippled soldier nicknamed Chickamauga, who was in the habit of approaching the guards to talk or trade, retreated to the space inside the deadline because he feared a group of fellow inmates, and asked to be let out of the stockade. When his request was denied, he refused to return to the safe zone. Prison commandant Captain Henry Wirz then rode up on his horse and ordered him back. Although Chickamauga initially complied, he later returned, and Wirz ordered the guard to shoot him, which he did.

For some the deadline represented more than a restriction on their freedom. Numerous accounts tell of prisoners who gave in to the temptation to end their own suffering by intentionally stepping across the line to be shot. Andersonville was also an incubator of psychiatric disorders ranging from acute depression to abject, raving lunacy. Men kept their distance from the crazed among them out of fear of injury, such as being bitten. A great many more suffered loss of hope, and now and then someone quietly ambled across the line to embrace death. After having survived the war and months inside the worst prison anyone could then imagine, they had finally reached their limit.

If there was one overarching factor influencing a prisoner's chances of survival, it was luck, but there was no accounting for it. Even if a man was lucky, he had to know how to take advantage of it. The factor over which the prisoners had most control was the ability to maintain presence of mind, and in that regard they made countless crucial decisions every day. Upon his arrival, Newton recalled feeling "the most intense agony I have ever experienced"—so much so that he had trouble catching his breath. At that moment his mind reeled at the specter of his life's dreadful new context: A world of dispossessed soldiers, some of whom were "literally rotting alive, limbs dropping off with scurvy and other diseases." Another arriving prisoner reported observing "living skeletons, with sunken eyes and long matted, tangled hair, dirty and filthy, many of them with not enough clothing to cover their nakedness." Once Newton caught his breath, he felt overpowering bitterness toward his captors, followed by resolve to survive despite them. As a survival mechanism, it worked. He was able to remain focused.

Still, there was no guarantee that firm resolve would carry a prisoner through. If the men learned anything during their captivity, it was that death was not always heralded by alarums and excursions, with the blast of bugles and the booming of cannonades. It could begin with quiet despair, with a covetous stare from a raider, or it could hop unseen onto a man's skin and inflict a tiny, fateful bite. It was possible to die as a result of almost anything. Men became dangerously sunburned, suffered heat stroke, were driven by overwhelming thirst to drink water contaminated by feces and parasites. They suffered from the relentless summer heat with little or no shade, and in winter they endured teeth-chattering nights, often without so much as a blanket. As soldiers they had experienced profound discomfort before, but never with such intensity, for so long, with so little hope of relief.

A small barracks was eventually built at one end of the stockade, but for the most part the men slept in the open or in the prison's signature "shebangs"—crude shelters cobbled together from whatever materials the prisoners could find, including pieces of tents, sticks, and other debris, over holes dug in the ground. When William Jellison first arrived and stood surveying the scene, he was relieved to hear someone call his name and turned to see a member of his old company, who had also been captured in Stoneman's raid. "He invited me home with him," he recalled. "I asked where he lived, and he led the way to his abode, which was a hole in the ground." The interiors of the shebangs were filthy and cramped. Weiser wrote that he slept each night "in a sitting position with my knees drawn up and my head and arms resting on my knees."

Meanwhile, Stockade Branch, the prison's primary water supply, was contaminated by runoff from the guard camps and livestock pens before it entered the compound. Once inside it was used for everything—drinking, washing, and the discharge of human waste. Theoretically, those uses were segregated: Drinking at the beginning of the stream, then washing, then the latrines. But in practice the system broke down. Eventually the entire branch was coated with scum. Because the muddy ground around the latrines was so difficult to traverse, many men relieved themselves where they were and, by convention, buried the waste. The holes, Weiser wrote, "thousands of them, would get full and by the effect of the hot sun and rain they would boil over and run down the hill. This was the cause of creating millions of maggots, and when we would lay down to sleep hundreds of maggots would crawl over us. Some of them would crawl in our ears and in our mouths."

Cleanliness was all but impossible. In addition to the filth they walked through, and their own accumulated sweat, the men burned pine branches in their cook fires, which created black soot, "and not being furnished any soap, we could not keep our persons nor scanty clothing anything but filthy," Newton wrote. "There were serious disputes sometimes whether a person was a negro or white person, which would be decided by the hair, being straight or curly."

In such an environment a body develops its own wild and fecund ecosystem, and the period of transition for a previously sanitary man was tough. On Jellison's first night he crawled into his friend's hole and was immediately overwhelmed by lice. "The whole pen was literally alive with crawling vermin," he wrote. "I lay about thirty minutes, but could stand it no longer; got up and attempted to walk around, but the darkness was so intense that I could not see where I was going; so I had just to stand and stamp and shake myself for hours, and each hour seemed an age. I thought morning would never come."

Lice were so prolific that many prisoners felt compelled to strip and spend hours picking them from their bodies and clothes each day, "or they would kill us," George Weiser wrote. "From the fourth of July until the first day of September, every day in those two months, I killed three hundred lice and nits. When I got up to this number I would stop killing until the next day."

A man who could spend hours not only picking lice but count-ing them does not have much to do, which was another problem at Andersonville. The prisoners were for the most part idle. In a typi-cal entry from his diary, William Farrand Keys wrote, "Hot, Show-ery. Passed like many more, lying in my kennel like a dog. It would be far better for our health if we had something to do that would offer muscular exercise and I often start for a walk within our prison walls but the sickening sights and smells to be met with everywhere are harder to bear than dull activity."

The atmosphere was so self-contained, miasmic, and stifling that one of George Hitchcock's friends volunteered to carry a body to the dead house—a shelter of bowers outside the stockade where cadavers were held for burial—just to get some fresh air. "When he returned, after a stay of some ten minutes, he seemed greatly refreshed," Hitchcock wrote. Later, Hitchcock had a similar experience. "Rourke, of our squad, died to-night," he wrote in his diary, "and I was detailed to carry him out to the dead-house. This is the first time I have been outside these horrid gates since I came in three months ago, and 'tho' outside less than three minutes, I caught a breath of fresh air which gave me a new lease on life."

Small changes could be pivotal in a man's struggle to survive. A seriously despondent, failing man could be brought around by a friendly sing-along. But a summer storm that brought a respite from the heat, and an opportunity to capture fresh water or bathe, could impose a final intolerable stress upon someone who was extremely weak, particularly if he had no shelter. To make matters worse, there was no real hospital to turn to as a last resort. What passed for a hospital was a cluster of crowded, unsanitary tents and sheds outside the stockade, which served more as a halfway house to the cemetery than as a medical facility. Not only was the hospital ill-equipped, it was vulnerable to theft by soldiers assigned as nurses and by unscrupulous or desperate prisoners. In a report for the Confederate Army, Andersonville surgeon Joseph Jones wrote that the diseases his overworked staff treated in the hospital were myriad, but all were exacerbated by "seclusion from society, long-deferred hope, a lack of cleanliness, insufficient supply of nourishing food, a want of proper exercise of both body and mind." Once weakened, Jones wrote, the prisoners tended to suffer oxygen deprivation, which led to a variety of both physical and psychiatric ills. Stockade Branch was so contaminated that it emitted "a sickening stench"—one of many olfactory assaults Jones referenced in his report. In fact, the odor of Andersonville was so vile and pervasive that people complained about it in Americus, Georgia, more than ten miles away.

The hospital itself was a breeding ground for contagious diseases, and sponges and bandages were routinely reused. The most common diseases Jones treated were diarrhea, fevers, respiratory infections, sexually transmitted diseases, scurvy, and skin ulcers, the latter of which, he wrote, "are produced from the slightest causes imaginable. A pin scratch, a prick of a splinter, a pustule, an abrasion, or even a mosquito bite are sufficient causes for their production." Even the inoculation of prisoners for smallpox caused some to develop deadly ulcers, he wrote. The only solution to unchecked gangrene was amputation, and there was more to fear than loss of a limb when a man was operated on in such an environment. During August and September 1864, Jones reported performing thirty-two surgeries, after which eighteen of the patients died. Medicine was hard to come by, and Jones often had to rely upon "such other indigenous remedies as we can obtain from the woods." Sometimes the only remedy was "one ounce good whisky" every six hours.

Initially the dead were buried in caskets, but the graveyard details soon became overwhelmed, and the bodies were interred en masse in long shallow trenches that sometimes received more than one hundred cadavers per day. Dying became so commonplace that men expected it, though they never truly got used to it. "One poor wretch died this morning within a rod of our tent, he had been suffering some time with diarrhea and scurvy," William Farrand Keys wrote in his diary. "Last night I heard him crying out calling on his mother and incoherently wandering in his speech. When the sun had fairly risen he calmly died. Requiescat."

Henry Devillez recalled "one poor fellow who was wasted to a mere skeleton by a long and painful disease, when at last he was unable to longer move around, he retired to his burrow in the ground, and without hat, coat or vest lay down there, and in his miserable louse-infested kennel resigned himself to die. Being unable to partake of one morsel of the course and unwholesome food dealt out to the prisoners, he welcomed death as the means of ending forever his miserable existence. But death was slow to answer the summons. And thus he lay day after day in a semi-comatose condition, too weak to move either hand or foot, while the lice, fleas and musquitoes could be seen crawling from his nostrils, his ears and his mouth. Each morning for many days his comrades would go to his burrow expecting to find that death had closed the scene, but on their near approach, his stertorous breathing would announce to them that life was still there. It was not till after the vermin had actually eaten into his flesh, creating great sores where innumerable maggots found a burrow, did his spirit take its flight."

Lucius Wilder noticed that soon after arriving at Andersonville, several of his friends began to fail for no obvious reason. "There seemed to be no disease particularly, but a sort of despondency," he wrote. "A man would lie there, and would groan and look up at the sky, and think of home and the old farm. He soon passed away."

The dead wagon, which arrived inside the stockade each morning, was at its busiest in August, when more than three thousand prisoners died. Some mornings Henry Harman stood near the gate and watched the bodies being removed. Most were brought there by their surviving friends and had been stripped of their clothing and possessions, often "before the breath had left the body," as he put it. "It was pitiable to view the naked dead as they were pitched like cord-wood into the wagon preparatory to their ride to the deadhouse or cemetery. They were thrown in indiscriminately. It was horrible to see the heads, arms and legs as they swung back and forth with the jolting motion of the wagon. This wagon was made to do double duty, for it not only carried the dead out in the morning, but it brought in our rations of bread in the afternoon, not as much as being swept out."

Weiser sometimes stood at the gate and counted the bodies, and occasionally he observed fights breaking out over claims to their tattered and filthy rags. It happened most frequently when the arrival of the wagon coincided with the morning sick call—an ugly combination—which was announced by a drummer boy at 10 a.m. Sick call was a chaotic event, with hundreds of prisoners typically rushing toward the gate. "Very often when the fight was over one or the other of the sick men would be dead," Weiser wrote. "This surely was a sad sight."

But if the dead wagon presented a gruesome sight, it also spurred men to survive. Some attempted escape during work details or through tunnels dug in secret from the shebangs to beyond the stockade wall, or joined the Confederate Army. Others came up with their own diversions. They played cards, staged plays, formed debating societies, and held religious meetings, chess matches— even classes in foreign languages. Drawing from captive members of the estimated forty thousand musicians employed by the Union Army, an 8th Indiana cavalryman formed a glee club.

With all this activity, the stockade was normally a noisy place, quiet only in the predawn hours, when the silence was punctuated by the moaning of the sick and dying and the hourly calls of the guards. But with no real focus other than survival, there were a lot of hours to fill. The men who fared best were those who conceded that Andersonville was now their world and made the most of it.

Remarkably, among the core functions of civilization that survived in the prison was property ownership. More fortunate prisoners had access to one of the fifteen or so hand-dug wells, from three to thirty feet deep, which were "owned" by communal parties. "Anyone who was not an owner was not allowed to use this well water, without which they bought it at a rate of one cent a quart," Weiser wrote. With three friends, Weiser also bought a twelve-foot-long board from another prisoner for $2 and used it to build a frame for a tent. Their shebang was so renowned that Weiser claimed a few prisoners made drawings of it to copy.

When Wilder first arrived, he was surprised to be approached by a prisoner offering to sell him a place to live. "I replied, 'Do you sell the land here?' 'Well,' he said, 'there is no rule, but all of my friends have died and I am heir to the estate,' and he smiled." Wilder and a friend paid the man $5 for the lot. They had one blanket between them, for which they had traded a haversack to a Rebel officer, and joined it with a shirt and extra pair of pants to make a tent. Because Wilder was part of a larger group, the men took turns using the shelter. When they slept, they lay "spoon fashion, one turn, all turn."

The prison was roughly divided into neighborhoods, some better than others. According to William Marvel's *Andersonville: The Last Depot*, sailors, black prisoners, and criminals gravitated toward the south side of town. There were also ethnic ghettos, including German, Irish, French, Scots-Irish, Swiss, Russian, Spanish, Portuguese, Slavic, Italian, and Native American sectors. So many immigrants were incarcerated at Andersonville that Wirz, who was himself Swiss and spoke three languages, employed translators in his office and in the hospital.

Eventually craftsmen began to ply their wares, trading with other prisoners, guards, and even civilians outside the stockade for extra rations, wood, and clothing. Some traded brass buttons from their uniforms. Marvel noted that Andersonville at its height was the fifth largest city in the Confederacy, and that "Hardly an occupation could not boast of at least one representative inside the palisade." Among them were barbers, merchants, at least one dentist and doctor, two watchmakers, bakers, tailors, cobblers, and real estate speculators. Newton sold wood. "Rather small business," he recalled, "but it diverted the mind in a measure from our extreme misery." The value of everything was increased at Andersonville. Even a bone could be fashioned into a tool.

Weiser estimated that about $40,000 in U.S. money circulated within the prison. "This money was all the time in circulation, and some of it would get so black and dirty that we could scarcely tell the value of it," he wrote. The men used the money for transactions with each other, the guards, and Rebel sutlers. Local farmers also sold produce, though only for Confederate money and always outside the prison walls. "If a man had a barrel he started a beer saloon and his fortune was made, all he done was to throw in corn meal and water and dip out sour beer for five cents a pint," Weiser noted. "There were three of these saloons in the prison." Keys reported seeing a man "peddling fresh butter" at $15 per pound, and Hitchcock wrote in his diary that amid the malnutrition and starvation, "Water-melons, apples, eggs, doughnuts, berry pies, biscuit, etc., for sale in camp, but no one has any money."

"Tobacco was as hard to get as anything else; a quarter of my rations went daily for it," Henry Harman observed. "Although I never was accustomed to chewing until after entering Andersonville. I am satisfied that but for the use I should not have survived."

Trying to make the most of the situation was one thing, but ruthlessly exploiting it was another. Everyone was forced to decide the lengths to which he would go to survive, and the raiders epitomized the dangers of going too far. Many—perhaps the majority—were ruthless criminals and bounty jumpers from northern cities, but their strength metastasized as other prisoners allied themselves with them because they seemed likely to survive. Along the palisade wall stood sentry boxes, or "pigeon roosts" as the prisoners called them, at thirty-yard intervals overlooking the dead zone. Beyond the wall were eight small earthen gun emplacements, where artillery could be trained on the prisoners in case of a disturbance or turned to defend against a Union attack. But as at Cahaba, there was little policing within the stockade itself, and for a while the raiders ruled.

About a thousand men were associated with what became known as Mosby's raiders, and they were a malevolent force that preyed especially on the new arrivals, stealing their clothes, food, and few possessions, and sometimes beating or murdering them. Weiser saw one of the raiders steal a dog that belonged to a doctor who was visiting the camp, after which he killed the animal and cooked it in a stew that he peddled to other prisoners. "To counteract this 'raider force' the 'regulators' were organized, and in a pitched battle the latter came out ahead, and organized a police force to do duty night and day," Newton wrote. Prisoners who observed someone stealing would alert the regulators by crying out "Raider!" and if the man was caught he received ten to forty lashes on his bare back, often until he bled—something no one wanted to undergo in the fetid environment of Andersonville. Sometimes the perpetrators were tied to posts or forced to carry blocks of wood until they were exhausted, Newton wrote, adding that there were also "other punishments too numerous to mention." At one point Hitchcock observed several prisoners being paraded by the camp police, their hair and beards shaved on one side and a card attached to their backs bearing the word "thief."

As the regulators exerted their authority, outrage over the raiders found expression. Eventually the ringleaders were captured, after which Wirz held them until a tribunal of prisoners was organized. The trial was the highlight of the season in Andersonville. In addition to the prisoners, the guards and crowds of locals gathered to watch. The verdict was predictable: Guilty as charged. Of the twenty-four tried, eighteen received beatings and six were sentenced to death. The prisoners then built a gallows and, with Wirz's blessing, hanged the six. "The day was cloudy and gloomy and seemed to darken visibly as the time (5 PM) for the execution approached," William Farrand Keys wrote. "The view of the prison at that hour was one that will long remain pictured in my recollection but no language can describe it."

Heightening the drama, one of the doomed men attempted to escape, either before or after the rope was tied around his neck, depending on whose account you believe. He ran through the crowd, sank to his knees in mud, fell down, crawled on his hands and knees to solid ground, clambered to his feet again, and ran until he was brought down. During the resulting stampede, Indiana infantryman Eli Wamsley was shoved headfirst into a deep well and dislocated his shoulder. He later wrote that he missed the actual hangings but was extricated from the well by the same ropes.

Each of the ringleaders was given the opportunity to speak before he was hanged, and one claimed that he had felt compelled to join the raiders out of fear of starvation, while another, according to John Ransom, "said he'd have rather been hanged than continue to live in Andersonville as the others did, adding that Delaney was not his actual name," and "The last man, Rickson, 'did not care to say anything.'"

After the executions, Hitchcock wrote in his diary that the prisoners felt a greater sense of security, "but may I never witness another scene like that!"

The executions proved that the men could triumph over their own chaos, and many took it as a positive sign. Likewise, they were bolstered by a fortuitous event that came during the otherwise torpid month of August: The appearance of what became known as Providence Spring. The spring mysteriously began flowing within the stockade after a rainstorm, providing the only source of pure water within the stockade. Though it surfaced beyond the forbidden deadline, Wirz later allowed a sluice to be built to divert its flow entirely to within the safe zone. A drink of fresh water, after months without it, was a source of quiet ecstasy. "The man is a fool who doubts a kind and benevolent Providence after such a manifestation," Hitchcock wrote. Yet, the dying not only continued, it accelerated. Among Lucius Wilder's friends, one named Handy was the first to go. After him went Asa Rowe, then Ed Holt. As Wilder recalled, the men were cooking outside his shebang when he mentioned that his throat was sore. Holt replied, "So is mine." The next day Holt asked Wilder how his throat was feeling. "It is not any worse," Wilder said. "I think I am getting better." Wilder only had a cold, but Holt was not so lucky and came down with diphtheria. "The third day I walked him round the prison to see the boys," he wrote. "They spoke to him. He was like death, and he could hardly speak. He said he guessed he would go back and lie down. He went back and lay down. He looked up and said, 'Wilder, I never shall live to see the sun rise.' I told him I thought he might live to see the sun rise on many an occasion. He spoke to his friend Melvin, who did not give him much encouragement, and he strangled to death.

I went outside the tent and I shed tears, the only tears that I shed while I was inside that prison, for it did not do for a man to get despondent."

Amid such pathos, men occasionally found moments of succor that helped them survive. Despite his seemingly endless accounts of human travail, Hitchcock at one point was moved to write in his diary: "There is a beautiful harvest moon shining down upon us."

Chapter Nine

GOING OFF ALONE

Private Samuel Melvin, with the 1st Massachusetts Heavy Artillery, was captured at Harris's Farm, Virginia, on May 19, 1864, when he was twenty years old. In his struggle to survive captivity at Andersonville, he clung to his abiding love for a fellow soldier, Lieutenant John M. Dow, adjutant of their regiment, with whom he planned to move to London, England, after the war.

As he prepared to go into battle on May 14, 1864, Melvin wrote in his diary, "Orders for us to move. I am on guard as usual. Everybody is packed up. I got excused and went down to Ft. Craig and packed up my things, marked them for James and left them in charge of Sergt. Hayes. Wrote to Caroline. Page and I read letters. Saw Lieut. Dow in the eve. We are now going into rough usage, I guess, but let it come. But if we go, I should like to return." On May 18 he wrote that because he did not sleep with Page, he was very cold during the night. During the next day's fighting he was helping an injured comrade to the rear when, as William Marvel wrote, he "had to abandon his comrade to save himself, but in the smoke and confusion he must have turned the wrong way; soon he could see none but grey uniforms, and he threw down his rifle."

After his capture, sympathetic Rebels saw Melvin limping on sore feet and gave him a ride on a horse. That night, "I slept rough but was truly thankful for my treatment," he wrote. "The guards were everlasting kind to me." He soon grew weary with the hunger and pain. On May 25, en route to Andersonville, he wrote, "Don't I wish I could see Page and Dow?" He was eager to get to prison, where he assumed he would be well fed and soon released. As often happened, the train they were riding in (in hog cars soiled with manure) derailed on the way to Augusta, Georgia, killing one man and wounding many others. Melvin wrote again how much he wished he could hear from Dow.

On June 3, 1864, after arriving at Andersonville, Melvin and his friends Asa Rowe and George Handy immediately "bought a little lot on the hill for $4.50," where they slept the first night uncovered in the rain. They paid $5 for a rubber blanket and huddled beneath it in the downpour the next day while they watched a steady parade of prisoners carrying dead men across the ditch to the south gate. Melvin then wrote to his sister asking for any kind of box, "as did most of our boys," because they were prized possessions in the camp. He also wrote a letter to Dow. Melvin was particularly distressed that had he not been captured he would have fulfilled his service soon and could have put the war behind him. He mentioned this often in his diary. His stomach began to give him trouble right away, and he struggled to remain upbeat, writing, "Still, men have lived through rougher scenes than this, and if I take good care of myself, am very hopeful."

On June 6 he wrote: "Asa Rowe is in a bad state, and we are all in a deplorable condition, still I guess that by being prudent we will all get through it." On June 10, Melvin, Rowe, and Handy entered into a partnership for making money and trading to improve their food supply. "My principal thoughts and hopes and fears are that my friend Dow will get killed or not be able to fulfill his promises with me."

June 13 was cold and rainy, which inspired Melvin to record a little ditty: "When the birds cannot show a dry feather, Bring Aunt with her cans & Marm with her pans And we'll all be unhappy together."

June 14: His friend Handy had the shakes.

June 15: With the arrival of more than a thousand new prisoners came word that fifty-three men had been killed or wounded or were missing from Melvin's regiment in the May 19 battle in which he was captured. "O how glad I was to learn that Dow and Page were all right up to the 2nd of June. I was painfully grieved when they told me that Dow felt very badly when he learned my fate. He came to the Co. and enquired for me of Joe. There is a TRUE friend, & if he will go home in July and wait until I come, it will be the happiest moment of my life, and I pray to God that such may be the case. How I hope Dow will get my letter, but I am afraid he will not." He then reported that he had come down with diarrhea.

June 16: Handy still had the shakes, and his salt and spoon were stolen.

June 17: "My diarrhea is no better, but it is not very bad, so I am not alarmed about it yet," he wrote. Then, "Ten thousand times a day do I think of my engagement to go to England. If I can't enjoy life after this, I am not sentient."

June 28: "Had a good shower which made it quite comfortable for a season. A large lot of Yanks came in, about 1000. I am about discouraged. Only think, if we only had staid at the forts, only one short week from today our time would be out and that long wished for period would have come, and I should have been the happiest of men. Now I might say I am quite the reverse. Only one week more, oh how good it sounds! But now the future looks gloomy. Otherwise Dow and I would have been going home together. Now it will be otherwise, and perhaps one of us never will go home. But we will look as well as we can on the dark and gloomy picture."

June 30: "Only 5 days more, then I was expecting to enjoy life as hugely as any man could. Got out lots of raiders and tried them by court-martial."

July 1: "O dear! Ain't this a tough life? July has come, & instead of bringing its anticipated joys; woes as intense have followed it. But why keep sighing? Because I can't help it."

July 3: "Only think, tomorrow is the immortal 4th. If I were only in Boston my joy would be unspeakable. I can't imagine the joy if Dow and I were there, free and accepted, in all things as well as Masonry."

July 4: "This has been a curious 4th to me, and it has to us all, I guess. Not a sign of any celebration, but no rations. This is my 4th Fourth of July in the Army. 3 years ago today I was on guard for the first time in the tent at Fort Albany. I came out of the G.H. [guardhouse] for seeing Dow 2 yrs [ago] today. I was with Dow at Albany, went off berrying with him. Thus time has passed with me."

July 6: "Would not I like to be on my way home now with Dow? I guess yes. It would be the most intense joy I can think of or imagine. But I will be with him soon, I hope."

July 7: "I have got a very bad cold and a touch of the dumb ague, making this prison life not very pleasant. I dreamed last night of being paroled and seeing Dow, and the disappointment when I awoke & found myself still in Hell! I have given up all hopes of hearing from home, likewise of their hearing from me. But while there is life there is hope, and that consoles me."

Following the arrival of new prisoners, Melvin learned on July 9 that Page, from his regiment, had been slightly wounded but was all right and that Dow had been slightly wounded in the foot. "Dow still keeps in the field," he wrote. "I wish he would go home!" In closing, he wrote, "I am glad to hear that Page is safe, & I think Dow will now be out of danger."

July 10: "Today, sad news indeed I must record." Word came that his brother Asa had been shot through the heart while charging the breastworks at Petersburg. The man who delivered the news told him that he got to his brother just in time to prevent some officers from pilfering his pockets as he lay dead on the ground. "Corp. Wm. Hills died with the diarrhea. He was a good boy, and a friend to me. It is sad, but I still have faith in my belief, & find relief therein . . . I am mighty glad to learn that Dow has gone home & knows where I am."

July 12: "To have things go right, I shall get out of here this, or early next month, find Dow all right waiting for me, & then, after settling the things at home, I will start on our life's journey."

July 13: "How I would like to meet Dow in the Astor House or in Boston! God grant that things will work for our good & that we may be permitted to spend the life of pleasure and enjoyment together that we have doted on so much!"

July 14: Melvin's tempo was beginning to slow. He was weary with dashed hopes of an exchange, annoyed even to hear the subject discussed. He wrote, "O dear, has Dow patience to wait for me? If I have patience to wait in this pen, I think he ought to have."

July 17: He visited the doctor for his diarrhea and cough. "I am in a bad condition, nothing but water passes me, & no appetite for anything we see here at all. O God! The man that will take me out of this I will call him 'Prince of Kings & Lord of Lords.' He to me will be a true Redeemer, I think, in every sense of the word."

July 18: "Lay on my back in the tent all day, pretty sick. This is hard, indeed, but I don't see why we must stand it. How I wish Dow would come down to see me as he did in Albany when he heard I was sick. But I only live to see it through, I think it will be all right. The weather is quite cool today, with some rain."

July 24: He was feeling better, but "Emery is getting worse, and Handy, too."

July 26: Prisoners had the option of taking what was known as a parole of honor, by which they would work for the Confederates outside the stockade—a controversial choice. "Emery sent in an application for himself to go out shoemaking, and also for me," Melvin wrote. "I do hope we shall both be successful and get where we can enjoy life a little." He added, "If I can get out on parole of honor, I shall do it, & shall think it no harm. I wish I could ask Dow's opinion of it. I would abide by that."

July 29: He awoke with a strange paralysis that went away over the course of the day. He fetched salt for the ailing Emery. Another man cut his hair, and he "washed all over."

July 30: He began to fear that Emery would die. Then he got the shakes again himself. "I thought of Dow, I can assure you, and Page and every friend I ever had."

August 1: He was still suffering from chills, and his religious convictions were flagging. "The stories say we are not to stay here long, & if the Devil will get me out of this I will worship him, for I am discouraged."

August 7: His diarrhea came back with a vengeance. "I was called up 30 times in 24 hours," he wrote.

August 8: "Here I lie and wallow in the dirt from morning till night."

August 9: "Emery is very badly off and will not live but a short time, I am afraid. I do wish I could do something for him, but can't. My feet and face swell some, and what in the world is going to become of us is more than I know. Did not draw my ration. Some of the stockade fell in. How are you Dow, Page, sisters, and my only brother?"

August 10: His friend Asa Rowe died.

August 11: Having heard—erroneously—that Emery had also died, he went to check on his friend. Men teetering on the brink of death sometimes became extremely self-centered as their brains focused on preserving their lives, but others, including Melvin, were the opposite. They drew strength from caring for others, which could also be a survival mechanism. "I concluded to try and take care of him," he wrote of Emery. "Cooked him some rice and it tasted good to him. In the afternoon a shower was coming on, & up he came and asked for shelter, which we gave him. He was in good cheer and I felt encouraged. He stayed here all the time, but did not sleep much. The weather was very hot and oppressive."

August 12: "Made some rice soup for Emery, which he ate and liked, but he seemed to be worse after that, and he lay quiet until afternoon, when he was taken worse and was pressed for breath. He ate no supper, and continued to fail. I was very sick all night, vomiting. I asked him towards morning if he felt as though he could stand it long. He said 'No.' I asked him if he had any word to send to his folks. He said 'No,' and I left him. Things go the same as ever, no parole yet, and all our comfort is in Hope." The next day Emery died, leaving behind a wife and four children back home.

August 15: Another friend died. "I never saw men slip off so easy as they do here. They die as easy as, as can be."

August 27: "This is a cool, beautiful morning. As Handy is very sick and probably won't survive long, there is another good man going to die in this horrid place." Handy died two days later.

September 3: Two more friends died. "How I would like to see Dow and my folks."

September 4: "After all the morning, I sold Emery's shoes for $1."

September 5: "When I get to London with Dow I guess we won't starve like this!"

September 7: "Today I met with an accident that I was awful sorry for. I never felt so bad about anything. I lost my pocket book with my gold pen in it, that I prized, for Dow, Page, & I had used it for two years, a lock of John's hair, and some pretty pictures that Dow made. I want Dow to make me a present of one when I see him, which I hope will be in two weeks." By now prisoners had begun to be removed from the camp.

September 10: He wrote of how much he enjoyed hearing the rail cars leave in the night, loaded with prisoners. He noted that his friend Edward Holt had a sore throat, and "I am afraid it may be bad. How I long for the Stars & Stripes! How I long to meet Dow!"

September 11: Holt's throat was worse. The next day he died. "He died about dusk, very hard indeed, choked to death."

September 13: Melvin was finally among those being removed, but the train wrecked only four miles from camp. "My car was badly broken," he wrote, "but the Powers that Be saved me."

September 14: "This morn I could hardly stand." With the help of a friend he made it as far as the depot but had to be taken to the hospital. "It is an awful, nasty, lousy place, and I am disgusted," he wrote. "My diarrhea is very bad and will soon carry me off, if it is not checked, I am afraid. It is too bad, for I should hate to have my anticipations fail now, for they are so near, their termination or beginning."

September 15: He had no appetite, and what he ate went right through him. He had yet to see a doctor. "I am lying in a tent on my rubber blanket, with an old Irishman next to me. Can't make him hear anything. He is most dead with the diarrhea. The next is a Dutchman, most dead with scurvy. And then the tent and blankets are just as full of lice and fleas as ever can be. As things look now, I stand a good chance to lay my bones in old Ga., but I'd hate to as bad as one can, for I want to go home."

September 25: Melvin died and was buried at Andersonville in grave No. 9,735.

Chapter Ten

RELEASE

IN SEPTEMBER THE PRISONERS SAW THE FIRST SIGNS that their long ordeal was coming to an end. The odds of survival increased with every trainload of prisoners that left the Andersonville stockade, though it would be months before all of them were released.

The reason for the initial removals was not the long-sought exchange of prisoners but Sherman's occupation of Atlanta, which increased the threat of a Union raid. In response, the Confederate military began moving most of the prisoners from Andersonville to other camps in South Carolina and coastal Georgia. Among the prisoners, jubilation over their release was muted by uncertainty over where exactly they were going—and by past experience. They had seen their hopes dashed before.

John Ransom was among those who chose to revel in the moment. After hearing that seven detachments were to be removed from the camp, he wrote on September 6, "Hurrah! Hurrah!! Hurrah!!! Can't holler except on paper." The next day, the buzz was wearing off. The prisoners were told that those who were unable to walk had to stay behind.

George Weiser was circumspect about the news. Noting that the longed-for exchange had still not come, he wrote, "It appears that the federal government thinks more of a few hundred niggers than of the thirty thousand white here in bondage." Three days later he was more optimistic. On September 7, he wrote, "Hot. Thank God I have lived to see a day of rejoicing for at least a portion of the miserable wretches whom I call my fellow prisoners. Ten detachments have gone out of the stockade and are being shipped on board the cars." No one was sure where the trains were headed. Some of the guards said the prisoners would be paroled, but the prisoners correctly speculated that they were simply being moved because the Union Army was advancing into Georgia.

On September 10, Weiser's detachment of a thousand men was removed from the stockade and taken north by train. Only then did he allow the gravity of his imprisonment to fully sink in. All of his shebang mates had died, he had endured worse than he could have ever imagined, and he was wary of the future. "Now I was very sad indeed," he wrote. If nothing else, Andersonville was now the known. Weiser had trouble rebuilding trust in the future.

On September 12, William Farrand Keys wrote, "Four Detachments left this morning. We lay in the sun among the fleas till near dark and then left also. My emotions at passing out the gate were not what they would have been if I had been sure of a speedy transit to the federal lines . . . They have given us three days of rations of cornbread & bacon, and we are moving, but our destination is unknown."

Watching the departures was disheartening for those who remained behind. After the exodus began, George Hitchcock wrote,

"It seems lonely and drear to see the thousands of deserted burrows and dens."

Keys, who was still inside the stockade on September 26, wrote that the weather was "splendid" but added, "We seem to be cut off and forgotten both by our friends and enemies left to linger on, to suffer, to die and sink in oblivion under the great ocean of existence. Well, let us endure while we can." He did: Keys would be paroled the following February.

Hitchcock, who was still inside the stockade two months after the first trains left, wrote, "Shepard and his crowd left us. It did me good to see him go, though my heart sank to feel that I must always be left behind." He finally left on November 22 and was taken to Savannah, where, he wrote, "Citizens have been bringing in food and clothes all day, but I am not smart enough to get any." A week later he bought some straw with borrowed $5 Confederate scrip and mended his clothes, which he wrote "are in a miserable condition: The sleeves of my blouse and shirt are almost entirely gone, showing some skeleton arms, the backs of both garments are as thin as gauze, while my pants are worn from the knees down, entirely away, and my cap is two simple pieces of cloth sewed together." He proved to be among the lucky ones. On December 8, after he and a friend found out they were finally to be paroled, he wrote, "Too overjoyed to think of anything else, we clasped each other's hands and cried like babies."

Weiser was first taken to Florence, South Carolina, where, he wrote, "Trading and talking with the guard is freely permitted, and rings, knives, jackets, boots, shoes, and clothing of all kinds is bartered for sweet potatoes, grapes, apples, etc., etc." Still dubious about what the future held, he later managed to escape near Wilmington, North Carolina.

Thomas Newton ended up in a camp on Charleston's horse-racing track. "Our treatment there was a great improvement on Andersonville, we receiving more rations and better," he wrote. "The citizens showed us a good deal of sympathy, furnishing clothing and provisions, all they could, although contrary to orders. The ladies would come near enough to the camp to throw us from one to half a dozen loaves of bread at a time. I trust they had their reward."

By October Newton was in Florence, "which for cruel torture compared to the number there, was not much, if any improvement on Andersonville. The cold was worse to endure for many of us than the heat; we had more space to the man, a little more water, a little more wood, but our rations were more limited than at Andersonville." While in Florence he estimated that three-fifths of the prisoners came down with fevers. "I was carried out by my comrades, as they supposed to die, to what bore the name of hospital," he wrote. "The first thing was to cut my hair short, causing me to get a severe cold. I recovered somewhat, so in about nine days was sent into camp. It seemed as if I would starve quicker in hospital than in camp; but caught another severe cold, which caused a severe pain in my right side which has clung to me in some positions ever since."

On the day after Christmas, Keys wrote, "Rainy. No comfort to be found either in retrospection, anticipation or the contemplation of the present."

In a cruel twist, many of the prisoners were eventually sent back to Andersonville. Chester Berry, who had been sent by train to Savannah in October, marched with a large group of prisoners overland back to Andersonville, where he arrived on Christmas Eve "with scarcely a ray of hope."

J. Walter Elliott remained at the prison in Macon during the forced wanderings as the prisoners were shunted around Georgia and the Carolinas. He offered no explanation why, and there is no indication that he was too sick to be moved, as were the majority who remained, but he stayed in Macon until March 1865. About five thousand other prisoners were still inside the stockade, where he was eventually transferred, and when word came that the prisoners would finally be exchanged, "Oh! the joyous shout that made the castle walls ring out," Elliott proclaimed. "How each of us laughed and cried, shook hands with and hugged his fellows, and joining hands in a circle, in good old Methodist campmeeting-alter style, as we all joined in singing 'Rally Round the Flag, Boys.' The joy of that good hour more than repaid all past tribulations."

As he waited at the depot with about six hundred officers and enlisted men who had been inside the stockade, Elliott continued to gather information, noting that the men "were begrimed and blackened by exposure, without a pretense of protection from summer's sun or winter's rain; all weak and lean from starvation; many, too feeble to take care of themselves, were literally encased in scales, beneath which were myriads of living vermin eating all vitality away. Two I saw doubled up and scarred all over, having been literally torn in pieces by the dogs, because they attempted to escape from the devil's domain." He quoted a prisoner from inside the stockade describing the entrance of Wirz through the gates on a white pony to announce the exchange: "Behold death on a pale horse."

The two armies had reached an agreement in February 1865 to release their prisoners to neutral ground until an official exchange could be worked out. For the captives who were from the Midwest, that meant relocation to Camp Fisk, a neutral holding pen for prisoners of war, four miles east of Vicksburg, Mississippi. Prisoners who originated from the East Coast were to be transported to coastal sites. Newton was officially released in February 1865, near

Wilmington, and wrote, "emaciated as I was, I felt almost as if I could jump clear over the flag that stretched across the street."

Elliott and Berry were among those sent to Camp Fisk. They made the trip partly aboard trains and steamboats and partly on foot. The journey itself was in many ways an inauspicious end, with many prisoners dying en route of disease and injuries, including from several train wrecks. "We left a good many poor fellows dead along our entire route," Elliott wrote. "Thrice derailed, twice we had two cars wrecked, crippling a good number of the boys."

Joseph Taylor Elliott, who was no relation to J. Walter, wrote that at each station the train passed, a few bodies were left behind. "How hard to die on their morning of deliverance, with all the bright hopes of meeting father, mother, wife or children," he observed.

After reaching Montgomery, Alabama, by train, the prisoners were taken by steamboat to Selma, then by train to Demopolis, during which the derailments occurred. Men injured by the wrecks were impeded on the final leg of the journey. Upon reaching Jackson, Mississippi, the Rebels "simply turned us loose, and directed us to the road to Vicksburg," Joseph Elliott wrote. A cold rain began to fall the morning of March 29 and continued all day. The men walked seventeen miles that first day, to near Bolton, Mississippi.

After crossing the Big Black River, the prisoners made their way to the sprawling encampment of tents known as Camp Fisk, which straddled the rail line into Vicksburg. There they exchanged their dirty rags for clean clothes, wrote letters, rested, and gorged themselves on hardtack and boiled cabbage. Soon the rations would be limited because a few prisoners died and many were sickened from overeating. As J. Walter Elliott recalled, the men "ravenously devoured the cabbage and licked the vinegar from our fingers, the sweetest dainty to my bleeding gums that I ever tasted. We feasted on pickles."

Elliott wrote that he cried when he saw the United States flag flying on the opposite bank. "Out from the gates of hell—out of the jaws of death—going home."

"I never experienced a happier day in my life than I did when we marched under the old Stars and Stripes at the Big Black river bridge and drew my first cup of coffee and a single hard tack," Chester Berry wrote, adding, "I have seen many beautiful things in my life, but never anything that looked more beautiful than the flag of my country did upon the 1st day of April, 1865."

Sergeant John Clark Ely, an Ohio infantryman, wrote of his arrival at Camp Fisk, eight miles west of the Big Black, "Oh this is the brightest day of my life long to be remembered."

EVERYTHING CAME TO A HEAD at Cahaba in March, when the Alabama River jumped its banks. The winter of 1864 and 1865 had been particularly rough, and it would have been hard to imagine how the situation could possibly get worse before the water started to rise.

The prisoners could not see what was coming, though they may have heard from the guards. It had been raining hard for weeks, and the compound was already a muddy mire, tracked by the feet of thousands of wet and restless men, when the river began seeping into the low places along the edge of the stockade at about the first of March.

The first pool slowly crept across the yard. As the men moved warily away, more seepages appeared elsewhere along the stockade wall, and within a few hours the flood manifested itself, pouring its turbid excess through the compound. By midnight the water was three or four feet deep. No one knew how high it would get, and there was no place to go.

The men were alert to any sign of new trouble and had learned that mortifying moments had a way of surpassing themselves, but the flood brought many to the breaking point. As the water rose, the ever-present campfires went out. Some prisoners crowded into the higher bunks or climbed into the rafters of the warehouse, but the rest had no choice but to stand in the very water that everyone was urinating and defecating in. To make matters worse, they had to drink it. Fingers and toes shriveled. Their only hope, other than for a retreat of the flood waters, was that the long-rumored exchange of prisoners of war would miraculously come.

Jesse Hawes recalled that the odious Colonel Jones, who had been left in charge while General Henderson, the commandant, was away, visited the flooded prison at the request of a group of prisoners and, when asked if they could be moved to higher ground, replied, "Not so long as there is a God-damned Yankee's head above water can you come out of that stockade." According to Hawes, Jones said they were only looking for an opportunity to escape, which under the circumstances seemed both warranted and implausible. "The whole country was flooded," Hawes wrote. "The whole prison was without shoes to their feet or covering to their backs. If they had been turned loose with permission to walk unmolested to their own armies, there were not twenty men in the whole three thousand who possessed enough endurance to have accomplished the feat."

About sixty sympathetic prison guards signed a petition asking Jones to allow the prisoners to be removed to higher ground, but initially he balked. Three days later he seemed to have a change of heart and allowed a few prisoners out of the compound, under guard, to gather logs and other debris to build platforms above the level of the water. Soon he allowed about seven hundred men to be transferred to Selma, but he left the remaining twenty-three hundred stranded for a week longer. The foul water exacerbated a perennial problem among the prisoners: Diarrhea, which compounded itself again and again. Hawes wrote that every man he knew was suffering from diarrhea, and whenever a weakened man cried out for a drink, the water "was dipped from its filthy pool to moisten a pasty mouth."

At one point a Confederate officer rode into the flooded stockade, and his horse fell into a submerged cistern with a splash. This caused a roar of laughter to sweep through the compound. Hearing it, the townspeople—with the obvious exception of Amanda Gardner and a few others who knew better—concluded that the prisoners were doing well despite the flood.

The water was cold, and although a few prisoners managed to fashion minuscule hearths from skillets and pans balanced precariously on debris, most had no way to build fires to cook on or keep warm by. For ten days they subsisted on crackers or raw cornmeal and bacon washed down with sewage-laden water. Hawes wrote that many men whose constitutions were strong enough to endure the preceding months began to break down physically, emotionally, and mentally, and some never recovered. Many would nurse their tormented bodies for the rest of their lives, however long that might be.

Even before the flood, men had spent countless hours engaged in useless calculation of their chances of survival, devising strategies and considering the factors that came into play: The force of their own will, the power of religious faith, the usefulness of remaining focused, of not giving up. But it was impossible to know which factors would determine the outcome, assuming any of them would.

At the height of the flood, Melville Cox Robertson wrote in his diary that a thousand or more prisoners stood day and night in knee-deep water amid drowned rats, while the men who had taken refuge in the roosts tried to bolster their supports. One of the roosts had collapsed, sending a large crowd into the water, though Robertson's own bunk remained dry. "To-day will be remembered in the history of the nation as the day of the Second inauguration of 'Old Abe,'" he wrote in one entry, "and in my history as one of the days of the great flood in Castle Morgan."

Henderson, the prison's official commandant, was then in Vicksburg trying to negotiate a prisoner exchange, and when word reached him of the flood he asked his Union counterparts to send a steamboat with provisions to Cahaba, as had been done once before. Instead, the decision was made to parole the prisoners and send them home. Before the flood fully receded, steamboats began arriving at the Cahaba landing to take them away.

"Late in the evening a few hundred were taken out and more have gone this morning," Robertson wrote. "The rebs tell us it is for exchange." The next day the water began to fall, and more men were taken away. Release came too late for some; about thirty more died before Cahaba closed, but it seemed to the rest that their troubles were finally coming to an end. By March 6, only about five hundred prisoners remained, and a week later the water had drained from the stockade. Robertson wrote that in preparation for their release the prisoners were required to turn over their skillets and blankets. The next day he boarded a steamboat for Selma, which, he noted upon his arrival, "is a nice place."

As at Andersonville, those whose homes were in the Northeast were to be transported to the Atlantic coast, while the rest, mostly from the border states and the Midwest, would head toward Camp Fisk and the network of inland rivers that would carry them from Vicksburg, on the Mississippi, to the valleys of the Missouri, Tennessee, and Ohio rivers.

The releases were staged over the course of a month, and even as they were taking place, prisoners continued to die—twenty-one in March and eight in April. As they were departing, C.W. Hayes, a prisoner who had served as a steward in the Bell Tavern hospital, took the time to write a letter to Amanda Gardner, thanking her for her generosity. On March 5, 1865, he wrote, "We are all about to bid farewell to Castle Morgan. Some are already on their homeward journey . . . Yet I cannot leave without first expressing my heartfelt thanks to you for the noble & humane kindness you have so generously bestowed upon the prisoners while confined here—aiding them, by the kind dispensation of your books amongst them to while away the tedious hours of captivity, both pleasantly and instructively." He lamented that "there were some among them who were so worthless as to abuse your books in a shameful manner but the majority, appreciating the noble impulses of thy generous heart were careful in the use of your works, knowing full well that you were making a noble sacrifice of your library for their benefit." Addressing her as "our kind benefactress," he added, "Many a one will speak in glowing terms of thy noble generosity and you will ever be remembered as a *friend* of the *unfortunate*. The day is not far distant when peace, the great tranquilizer, will again unite our destructed country in perfect harmony and unity. The end is fast approaching."

From Selma and Demopolis, the journey took the Vicksburg-bound prisoners to Meridian, then Jackson, where they embarked upon the final arduous thirty-five-mile march to Camp Fisk. Hawes wrote that after spending the night in Meridian, his group traveled to Jackson on a train that moved so slowly that at times men walked alongside. The hospitals at Jackson were not equipped to care for the sick and injured, and reports of men collapsing and dying along the roadside prompted the Union Army to dispatch ambulances from Vicksburg under Confederate guard. As at Andersonville, the denouement of the prisoners' incarceration saga was not exactly celebratory, but excitement grew once they reached Jackson and realized that the Union lines were close.

As they plodded westward from Jackson they passed through a ruined countryside. Reaching the Big Black River took two days, and most of the men were soaked by spring rains, but on the evening of March 16, after more than a week of travel, the first group reached the Confederate-held bank of the river, within sight of the Union lines. Other groups soon followed, including prisoners from Andersonville, Meridian, and Macon, Georgia.

Tolbert and Maddox arrived on April 10 at the height of spring. Everything was verdant. The dogwoods, irises, jonquils, and wild roses were in bloom. The creeks were full. They were finally headed home.

Chapter Eleven

SOLD UP
THE RIVER

THEY CAUGHT THEIR BREATH AT CAMP FISK. IT WAS where they would officially put the war and prison behind them. But for the military command, Camp Fisk was also a vast, potentially dangerous holding pen, with unique, pressing demands made not only by the prisoners, who needed everything, but by the representatives of the steamboat companies hired to transport them home, for whom the camp was a warehouse of lucrative, perishable commodities.

Camp Fisk was named for Colonel Archie Fisk, a Union Army assistant adjutant general at Vicksburg. Fisk had proposed the site, which had also been used to hold Confederate prisoners on their way to being paroled, for paroling the Union prisoners. Operated jointly by the Union and Confederate armies, it was little more than a broad sloping field, with no real infrastructure other than the nearby Union Army post and the railroad into Vicksburg. Considering what the men had left behind, it was an improvement, though. There was food. The American flag flew overhead.

Fisk had come up with the parole plan in response to pleas from the Confederate military for supplies for its Union prisoners. He felt that because the war was ending it made more sense to simply send the prisoners home. He chose the site and designated members of the U.S. Colored Troops as guards (until they were paroled the men were technically prisoners, though in Union hands). During the war the timber had been cleared for several miles along the Big Black for army camps, and the river, spanned by a pontoon bridge, represented the dividing line between the Union and Confederate domains. Everything east of the Big Black was officially controlled by the Confederacy, while everything to the west was in Union hands. The Union Army post, with its orderly lines of white tents, overlooked the site.

After crossing the river, the prisoners were loaded onto flatcars for a laboriously slow, hour-long train ride to the camp, which was eight miles from the river and four miles from Vicksburg. The prisoners, most of whom would remain at Camp Fisk for several weeks, immediately set about building crude shelters of branches and cane, organizing themselves into communities, singing by the campfire, and fighting—everything they had done in the army and in prison, though now in a comparatively more convivial atmosphere. On April 14, Union Major General Napoleon J.T. Dana, commander of the Department of Mississippi, reported the population of Camp Fisk at forty-seven hundred. Of those, more than a thousand— mostly men from Andersonville—were sick. "The rest of the prisoners are in excellent health," Dana wrote, "the Cahaba prisoners particularly." Their health, of course, was relative.

The day Dana submitted his report, the steamboat *Sultana* was docked in Cairo, Illinois, where an announcement in the local newspaper read, "The regular and unsurpassed passenger packet

'Sultana,' in command of Capt. J. Cass Mason, departs tomorrow morning at 10 o'clock for New Orleans, Memphis and all way landings. The 'Sultana' is a good boat, as well as a fleet one. Mr. Wm. Gamble has control of the office affairs, while our friends Thomas McGinty and James O'Hara will be found in the saloon, where everything of the 'spirit' order can be had in due time."

River traffic had been picking up since the fall of Vicksburg in July 1863, and much of it involved the transportation of Union troops. Military contracts were a profitable economic niche, coveted by steamboat companies, whose owners knew that the focus would soon shift to transporting former prisoners of war. None of the companies were fully prepared for the task, nor was anyone aware of how profoundly the national dynamic was about to change. On the night of April 14, after Dana sent his report to Washington, John Wilkes Booth shot President Lincoln at Ford's Theater in Washington, D.C. When the *Sultana* embarked from Cairo, it carried the news downriver.

Union Army officials were consumed by deliberations over how to get the prisoners home, which was not to be a simple matter, and repeated delays proved costly for the sick prisoners. Among the casualties was Melville Cox Robertson, the soldier from Jefferson County, Indiana, who had left this plaintive message in his father's Bible when he went off to war: "To-day at 2 o'clock P.M. I leave home perhaps forever. If I should return at the end of three years alive I hope to have the proud satisfaction of saying 'my country is saved and I have done my duty as one of its citizens.' If I fall, let my friends *forget* my *faults* and remember me only as a dead soldier of the republic. I want no brighter immortality." Robertson had reiterated his desire to make it home, dead or alive, in his last diary entry at Cahaba on June 24, 1864. "While writing the preceding the death gasp of a fellow soldier called me away . . . God preserve me from such a burial," he wrote. "Let me die and be buried at home by friends no matter how humble they may be."

Ten days after leaving Cahaba, in a letter to his brother from Camp Fisk, Robertson wrote, "Now there is a great deal I could tell you and a great deal I would of perils by land and water, among thieves, false brethren and confederates if I could do it orally instead of by letter." At that point, he wrote, he was in good health, and weighed perhaps 180 pounds, "but am in rather poor trim for walking having bruised my feet considerably by a march of about twenty five miles day before yesterday, the most of it in a heavy rain." He reported that the men at Camp Fisk were being aided by the Christian Commission and the citizens of Vicksburg, who provided them with combs, spoons, tobacco, and other items. But during the lengthening wait, Camp Fisk became its own breeding ground for disease, and Robertson contracted typhoid fever. He would later board a steamboat named the *Baltic* but would not make it home. While on the *Baltic* he again wrote home to say that he was sick. He died in St. Louis before his father and brother could arrive to escort him home. Robertson apparently knew that his chances of surviving were slim. He had mailed home the earlier pages of his diary after his capture, and at Camp Fisk he entrusted the parts concerning his captivity to a friend who later boarded the *Sultana*.

During the wait at Camp Fisk, J. Walter Elliott steadfastly maintained his ruse as Captain David E. Elliott. As he later explained, "never until I had shaken the dust of the Confederacy from my feet did I disclose my identity to friend or foe—and the sixty autograph albums gotten up by my companions in Castle Reed will attest to it."

After as long as a month in limbo, the men were itching to get under way. Dana was under pressure to move them, not only be-

cause they were anxious but because tensions were developing between them and the guards. On April 4, a near riot broke out over
a confrontation between one of the white officers of the U.S. Colored Troops and an officer representing the prisoners. In response,
Dana replaced the guards with white soldiers, and the tensions
died down. As Gene Eric Salecker wrote in his book *Disaster on
the Mississippi*, the prisoners tried to make the most of their wait
during the first two weeks of April. Some were able to get passes
to visit Vicksburg, a battle-scarred town atop a series of undulating
bluffs overlooking the river, where they inspected the Confederate works and marveled that the seemingly impregnable city had
fallen. Some had money wired to them from home. Private Lewis
McCory used his money to buy a new suit of clothes, a valise to
put them in, and a sturdy pocketbook in which he stashed $100.

Soon, word came that Richmond had fallen, then that Lee
had surrendered at Appomattox Court House. Now the Confederacy was in no position to quibble over the details of a prisoner
exchange. A telegram arrived in Vicksburg on April 13 instructing
that all prisoners be paroled unconditionally, and the next day there
was an official celebration. The prisoners cheered and sang patriotic
songs. The guards fired their guns. They organized military parades.
John Clark Ely wrote in his diary, "Today Major Anderson again
raises the same old flag over Sumter and today the North rejoice
over their victories and today came an order from General Dana for
us to be paroled and sent North. Bully, we may soon see our sweethearts." But jubilation quickly gave way to mourning. News of Lincoln's death reached the camp on April 15, and that prompted the
understandably nervous Confederate officers and guards to withdraw across the Big Black River into more friendly territory. With
no suitable objects for their anger, some of the prisoners sang a song

called "Hang Jeff Davis from a Sour Apple tree" before settling in for the night.

The official exchange of prisoners took place on a sunny spring day, with officers from both sides seated in Windsor chairs at a small outdoor table, signing the papers. It was a milestone event, though little changed at Camp Fisk right away. The prisoners were not aware that the delays were the result of more than typical army bureaucracy. Steamboat owners were paid by the head for each man they carried, and everyone wanted in on the action. Among the central figures in the negotiations over who would carry the paroled prisoners north was Colonel Reuben Hatch, the Union Army's chief quartermaster at Vicksburg, whose name had already been sullied by allegations of government graft. The *Chicago Tribune* had reported allegations that Hatch had skimmed profits from government lumber purchases in Cairo in 1861. Though Hatch reportedly dumped his incriminating ledgers in the Ohio River, they had washed up on the bank and been found, and he had been arrested and court-martialed. During the course of the investigation it came to light that Hatch also sold army supplies for personal gain and chartered steamboats to carry Union troops while taking part of the fee. When he was brought to trial, he turned to his influential brother, the Illinois secretary of state, who used his political clout to pressure President Lincoln, a personal friend, to intercede in the "frivolous" charges. Lincoln did.

As late as February 1865, a government examining board had concluded that Hatch was "totally unfit" to serve as quartermaster, but instead of getting rid of him the army brass had sent him to Vicksburg, where he became involved in loading the boats. Officially, Captain Frederick Speed—assistant adjutant general for the region—was in charge, but Captain Mason of the *Sultana* apparently felt it would be more useful to work through Hatch.

On April 17, Speed hurriedly supervised the boarding of a group of comparatively fortunate Illinois parolees on a steamboat provided by the quartermaster's department, and sent them on their way. But the process soon bogged down in what would later be characterized as a conspiracy of bribery and greed. When the *Sultana* docked at Vicksburg on her way to New Orleans, Hatch paid a visit to Captain Mason. According to Salecker, the meeting left Mason with the impression that Hatch was in charge of loading the parolees, and he wanted to get as large a load as possible when he returned from New Orleans. For good measure, Mason asked a friend, Union General Morgan Smith, to pull some strings. According to later testimony in a government inquiry into the matter, Smith told the *Sultana*'s agent in Vicksburg, "I will give Captain Mason a load as he comes up and if Hatch or Captain Speed don't turn the men out to him, you let me know it."

Meanwhile, Speed began organizing the passage of paroled prisoners on whatever boats were available. Dana had instructed him to send them upriver in groups of about one thousand, but keeping the groups together proved difficult. Although each prisoner's name, company, and regiment had ostensibly been recorded upon his arrival at Camp Fisk, discrepancies and confusion over the continuing arrival of new prisoners complicated the process. Even worse, as Salecker wrote, some boat captains and their agents, in an effort to get their share of the human cargo, "were not above offering a monetary inducement to any officer willing to be a party to their hustling and scheming. It was no coincidence that such an offer was made in the office of Colonel Hatch."

What followed was a frenzy of lobbying, corner-cutting, and perhaps bribery by steamboat captains, their agents, and the Union military in Vicksburg. Even when all the negotiations were above board, it was clear that whichever boat a paroled prisoner ended up on was going to be seriously overloaded. Few steamboats were equipped to carry more than a few hundred passengers; yet, one of the first to embark from Vicksburg, the *Henry James*, was crowded with more than thirteen hundred men. For the men, it was all about getting home. The *Sultana*, the *Henry James*, the *Olive Branch*, the *Pauline Carroll*—the boats were all the same to them.

IN A SENSE, TOLBERT AND MADDOX had been here before. So had every other soldier waiting at the wharf to board the *Sultana* that balmy April day. They had waited in line at the muster office when they enlisted, had waited in line to be issued their uniforms, had waited in line during drill, had waited in line to enter the god-forsaken prisons, and once inside, had waited in line for their daily rations and their turns at the latrines. They had waited in line to get out, had waited in line to board the filthy, rickety trains and the overburdened steamboats that carried them from Georgia and Alabama to Mississippi, had waited in line to cross the pontoon bridge across Big Black River, had waited in line to be issued new clothing and food and medicine at Camp Fisk, and finally had waited in line to board the cars for the short ride into Vicksburg. Now the line stretched from the gangplank of the *Sultana*, along the wharf, and up the hill out of sight. The delays that had kept the men sequestered at Camp Fisk for as long as a month continued until the moment they boarded.

The delays were the result of multiple factors. There was confusion about names. Steamboat captains and Union officers interrupted the flow, jockeying for position and scrambling for favors.

Hasty repairs were being made to the *Sultana*—in secret. Though some of the recently paroled prisoners were bewildered by the delays, others were taciturn and cared only about getting on the boat. Many were seeing the Mississippi River for the first time, which no doubt made the wait more interesting. Tolbert's father had traveled the Ohio and Mississippi rivers between Madison, Indiana, and New Orleans, shipping and selling whiskey and other commodities. Tolbert's own experience with rivers was limited to the Ohio, along which he had grown up, and the Tennessee and smaller waterways that he had crossed and recrossed during the war. The Mississippi was impressive—wide, deep, and forbidding, flowing fast and full with snowmelt from the north. Timbers and rafts of logs bumped against the hulls of the great filigreed boats tied up at the wharf. The waterfront was lined with ravaged storefronts and warehouses, and in the distance, the bluffs were surmounted by mangled trees, damaged mansions, and silent Rebel batteries.

Like the men at Camp Fisk, the *Sultana* had spent the last few days in a kind of limbo. On the return trip from New Orleans, one of the massive coal-fired boilers, which heated water for the boat's steam engines, had sprung a leak, threatening to thwart Captain Mason's plans to haul his share of paroled soldiers. None of the prisoners were yet aware of the trouble, and few concerned themselves with how they were to be loaded, or on which boat. The war was over and they were going home. Traveling north in spring would mean going back in time, not only from the verdant flowering of the deep South to the first buds at the end of the Midwestern winter, but to a place that had remained static in their memories as the world around them unraveled again and again. Samuel Raudebaugh, a paroled prisoner who boarded the *Sultana* that day, wrote, "We were on our way home from those horrid dens of *cruelty* and *starvation.* Yes, we had lived through it all, and hoped, yes expected soon, to see loved ones and home and enjoy some of the peace we had fought to restore. Home!"

But not everyone was ready to rejoice. The men had encountered new perils at every step of the way during the war, and many times they had been mistaken in believing their troubles were behind them. Ohio soldier William Boor was among the wary ones. He heard the sound of hammering on the *Sultana*'s boiler and went to investigate. When he saw what was going on, he advised his friends that they should avoid sleeping atop the boiler room. They did so—but they boarded the boat anyway. They were desperate to get home.

The *Sultana* was licensed to carry three hundred seventy-six passengers and already had about one hundred eighty private passengers and crew on board, all of whom no doubt watched in dismay as more than two thousand additional passengers—the paroled prisoners, their Union Army guards, a few Rebel soldiers headed home, and members of the U.S. Sanitary Commission—snaked from the gangplank along the waterfront.

The *Sultana* had been built two years earlier for Captain Preston Lodwick of Cincinnati, at a cost of $60,000, and outfitted with dual side wheels. Coal-fired furnaces heated four high-pressure boilers, each eighteen feet long, which in turn drove the steam engines. The boilers were of a new design, of lighter construction. The *Sultana* was not a particularly luxurious boat, but it was, under normal circumstances, commodious: Two hundred sixty feet long and forty-two feet at its widest point. A wide stairway led from the bow to the second-floor deck, where a long hallway or saloon led to the staterooms. The saloon was finely appointed with glass chandeliers, elaborate woodwork, and stylish carpets and furniture. There were both a bar and a ladies' lounge. The panels of the stateroom doors were embellished with distinctive oil paintings, but most of the staterooms were small—about eight feet square, furnished with bunk beds and a chair, wash basin, and chamber pot, with a second door leading onto the deck, where Windsor chairs and cuspidors invited passengers to view the passing scenery. At mealtimes a long collapsible table was set up in the main cabin, where food was served on fine china and crystal. Most of the paroled prisoners would not see any of this. The better accommodations were restricted to private passengers and officers, though no one was truly comfortable once the ragged masses came aboard. Cots were set up in the hallways and on the decks, and in between men claimed any spot they could find. They relieved themselves over the rails.

Beneath the cabin floor were quarters allotted for cheaper fares, where the passengers shared space with the crew, the freight, and the boilers; dined on tin plates; and slept on the floor. Above the promenade deck was the hurricane deck, where a yawl hung that the crew sometimes used to test the water's depth ahead of the steamer. Still higher was the Texas deck, which included a small enclosed area where the boat's officers were quartered. Crowning it all was the pilot house, enclosed by glass windows, with a large spoked wheel five feet in diameter, a rope that operated the steam whistle, and a cord leading to a brass signal bell below. There was also a bench where passengers could visit with the pilot and observe the scenery from a lofty perch.

Despite their embellishments, the fine china, and their often pretentious names, steamboats were not built to last. As a result of fires, boiler explosions, and hull-puncturing snags, their average life span was only a few years. By 1860, almost two hundred boats had been destroyed in boiler explosions alone, and more than three hundred fifty people had died. Owners considered such accidents part of the cost of doing business. The *Sultana* had paid for itself twice over during its first year of operation, after which Captain Mason and five associates bought her for $80,000. Mason had begun his steamboating career as a clerk and got a leg up when he married the daughter of a shipping magnate, Captain James Dozier of St. Louis, in 1860. At the time he took over the helm of the *Sultana*, Mason was thirty-four years old and "cut a handsome figure in his black frock coat, the uniform of his calling," according to J. Walter Elliott's grandson, James W. Elliott, author of *Transport to Disaster*. The mates, Elliott the younger wrote, were a different sort. "Typically, the steamboat mate was big and burly, whiskered and tattooed, and he attacked his sundry problems with a raging gusto which was awesome to behold. Even his smallest command was delivered in an angry roar, and his every 'heave' and 'belay' was accompanied by a sulfurous stream of profanity." On the *Sultana*, the first and second mates were William Rowberry and William Butler.

Among the seventy-five or so passengers who had boarded at New Orleans was the Spikes family, emigrating north from Louisiana and reportedly carrying with them their life savings, $17,000 in gold. Seth Hardin, a former Illinois infantryman who was returning with his wife from their honeymoon, also boarded at New Orleans, as did a Kansas businessman named William Long, who deposited $700 in the boat's safe, and Daniel McLeod, a crippled veteran from Illinois whose right knee had been shattered by a bullet at Shiloh. As the *Sultana* embarked from New Orleans, carrying a modest cargo of hogs, mules, and sugar, Lincoln's funeral train was starting its seventeen-hundred-mile course through the North.

When the *Sultana* was about seventy-five miles below Vicksburg, Mason's chief engineer, Nathan Wintringer, informed him that one of the boilers had sprung a leak. According to Elliott's grandson, the boilers had been a source of "frequent, almost constant, annoyance" for months, and on previous trips the boat had been forced to stop at Natchez and Vicksburg for repairs. The *Sultana's* boilers were of a newer tubular design, lighter than the older versions, which were essentially giant kettles over a firebox. Tubular boilers were considered more productive and fuel efficient, but they proved difficult to keep free of sediments and other debris that impeded the flow, particularly on the muddy Mississippi, because the water was drawn directly from the river. A blockage in a boiler was potentially disastrous because it would lead to a concentration of superheated water, which in turn could cause an explosion. Likewise, the accumulation of sediments could lead to corrosion, and any careening of the boat could cause water to drain, opening dangerous air pockets in the superheated tubes. A resulting leak could cause a sudden eruption of pressurized hot water and steam. The *Sultana's* tubes and tanks had been cleaned before the boat left St. Louis, but on the return trip from New Orleans, a trickle of water began dripping from between two warped plates. Wintringer told Mason that the repairs could not be made while the boat was underway and the metal was hot, so Mason agreed to make the repairs at Vicksburg. His plan was to put off doing anything major until he reached St. Louis. Instead, the leak would be patched with a plate, about two feet by one foot wide and a quarter-inch thick—which, significantly, was thinner than the boiler itself.

The *Sultana* arrived back at Vicksburg at 4 p.m. on Sunday, April 23. The embers from the fireboxes were dumped overboard, the boilers were allowed to cool, and "Without waiting for the gangplank, one of the fire men sprang onto the wharf and went racing toward town," James Elliott wrote. The fireman (so named because he stoked the fire that heated the boiler water) headed to a foundry, where he requested the services of a boiler mechanic and a riveting hammer. Meanwhile, the *Sultana's* business agent hurried down the steep bluff to meet the boat. By then the *Henry James* had left with its thirteen hundred parolees, and the *Olive Branch* had left with seventeen hundred. The two boats had been overloaded, but the regulations had been routinely ignored by the military during the war. The standard price paid was $5 per head for enlisted men and $10 for officers, and even at the bulk rate the *Sultana's* owners reportedly received—$3 per head for two thousand men—they could expect $6,000 in extra profits.

The *Sultana* was the fifth boat to carry the name (the word has several meanings, including the wife, sister, or mother of a sultan), and its predecessors had all ended their runs in disaster. One collided with another steamer, resulting in great loss of life. One burned at the St. Louis wharf. Another lost her smokestacks to a gale, and the fourth burned at Hickman, Kentucky. The current *Sultana* had its persistent boiler problems, which, coupled with the wartime interruption of commerce, had caused it to decline in profitability to the point that Mason, a part-owner of the company, was forced to sell part of his share in early 1865. He then joined an association of boats called the Merchant and People's Steamboat Line, which contracted with the federal government to transport troops and supplies. As part of its contract, the *Sultana* was inspected in St. Louis on April 12, 1865, where the inspectors were surprised to find a pet alligator that served as the crew's mascot. The boilers passed the inspection.

Upon his arrival, Mason and his agent went to Hatch's office to try to get a commitment for passengers. According to Salecker, "Hatch was anxious to see Mason get the men and, perhaps at the time, to line his own pockets." Mason reportedly became angry over the length of time he was told it would take to assign passengers, and he told Hatch it would not be worth waiting an extra day for the prisoners' rolls to be completed. Hatch blamed the delay on Speed, so Mason visited him, and Speed told him that he could give him anywhere from three hundred to seven hundred parolees, depending upon how many were on the finished rolls. Mason responded that he was "entitled to those men," according to his agent's testimony during a later inquiry, and said Hatch would take care of the trains to get the men to the waterfront. Speed insisted that he could not come up with any more men on Mason's schedule, but eventually he agreed to hasten the process by checking the names of the parolees as they were being loaded on the boat—a plan Dana approved. Speed told Mason that he had about fourteen hundred men left at Camp Fisk, though he later learned there were more than two thousand, and they agreed that all would go on the *Sultana*. The repairs to the boilers, which continued through the night, were never mentioned, and Captain William Kerns, who was normally in charge of river transport, was not informed of the plan.

The next day, as Speed was dressing, Hatch arrived and said he wanted to divert some of the parolees to the *Pauline Carroll*, which was also tied up at the Vicksburg wharf. While Salecker surmised that Hatch had gotten a better kickback deal with the other boat, it was Hatch who raised the possibility of bribery after Speed insisted on putting all the remaining men on the *Sultana*. At about 11 a.m., another boat, the *Lady Gay*, docked at Vicksburg beside the *Sultana*. There was talk of diverting some of the *Sultana's* passengers to the boat, but the idea never got off the ground. At about noon, the first trainload of remaining parolees left Camp Fisk, and an hour later they began filing from the depot on their way to the waterfront. Among them were twenty-three patients confined to cots and two hundred seventy-seven men who were unable to walk unassisted, all of whom had been in area hospitals. The cots were to be placed on the forward end of the cabin deck, above the boilers, where the patients would be warmer. The train continued to shuttle between the city and Camp Fisk for the rest of the day. Seeing that the *Sultana* was getting overcrowded, the Union surgeon in charge at Vicksburg requested permission to remove the seriously ill men and to prevent the nonambulatory patients from boarding, because he felt they would be in jeopardy. Dana granted him permission to do so—a decision that no doubt saved many lives.

The last trainload arrived just before dark, and the officials in charge of the loading were still jockeying for position, attempting to undermine one another's efforts. It was obvious that the men would be more comfortable, and the passage safer, if some were shunted to the *Pauline Carroll*, but that never happened. One officer later testified that he stopped Speed at the wharf and warned him that the *Sultana* was becoming dangerously overloaded, but that Speed simply walked away. The loading continued. When the men from the last train saw the overcrowding aboard the *Sultana*, and the empty decks of the *Pauline Carroll* beside it, about a third of them resisted boarding. An officer then told them that the *Pauline Carroll* was infected with smallpox, and the men reluctantly shuffled aboard the *Sultana*. With so many aboard, the men had to be redistributed to prevent structural damage to the boat, despite hastily installed auxiliary supports to the decks. According to later testimony, even Captain Mason protested the overloading. "Mason by this time was thoroughly alarmed," James Elliott wrote. "He had been anxious to make a profit—and still was, for that matter—but he had no desire to see his boat crushed under foot. Throughout the afternoon he had managed to maintain an uneasy silence. But now, as the shadows lengthened with evening's approach, he could keep quiet no longer. Stepping in front of the gangway he held up his hand and halted the marching line. One of the prisoners heard him say that he had enough men on board and could take no more." But he had lost control and was overruled.

After the last man boarded, the initial head count was thirteen hundred, which was absurdly low. The first and third trainloads alone had carried sixteen hundred men combined. Told that an additional six hundred fifty men had come on a second train, Captain George Augustus Williams, who was charged with keeping records of the loading, simply added them in and came up with just under two thousand. In fact, there were many more; Gambrel's tally was about twenty-four hundred, not counting a hundred civilian passengers and a crew of eighty, for a total of almost twenty-six hundred.

At 8 p.m., Kerns left the boat and headed toward the *Pauline Carroll*. He had earlier convinced the boat's captain to delay his departure until the *Sultana* left, hoping it would become obvious that some of the men should be transferred. The captain had agreed to stand by, but now Kerns told him he might as well go. Soon the *Pauline Carroll* backed away from the wharf, bearing a total of seventeen paying passengers.

Attempts to keep the parolees in orderly groups, putting most of the Ohioans on the hurricane deck and the Indianans on the boiler deck, proved futile. The men went where they wanted to go. In the end there was not even a reliable accounting of the passengers' names. Nearly all the men were young—on average, twenty to twenty-one years old—but most were also weak and weary, and crowded uncomfortably together. As they milled around on the decks the floors creaked ominously underfoot.

At about 1 a.m., the *Sultana* cast off. Soon after, Gambrel, the boat's clerk, stopped by Ohio soldier Alexander Brown's stateroom, where they talked about Andersonville and the war. Brown asked Gambrel how many passengers were aboard the boat. Gambrel gave him a figure of twenty-four hundred and said that if the *Sultana* reached Cairo, it would set the record for the greatest number of passengers on a boat on western waters.

Among the civilians who had boarded at Vicksburg was Anna Annis, the wife of Lieutenant Harvey Annis, who was ill. She had come to Memphis with their young daughter to escort him home. Also boarding was the Chicago Opera Troupe, en route to a performance in Memphis. The troupe would later put on a free show for the *Sultana* passengers, including blackface routines and the singing of familiar soldiers' songs, on the bow of the boat. Meanwhile, twelve women of a group sometimes referred to as the Sisters of Charity—officially, the Ladies Christian Commission, a volunteer organization—wandered through the throngs, handing out hymnals and crackers.

James W. Elliott wrote that neither Mason nor his engineer felt good about the situation. Wintringer "nursed his fractious boilers with more than usual suspicion and watched apprehensively for the next sign of trouble." Meanwhile, Rowberry and his crew continued adding supports to the sagging decks. The boat was so top-heavy that she rolled slightly with every turn and strained under the weight against the flooded river. The pilots attempted to hug the banks, avoiding the strongest currents, but periodically had to cross to the other side when the boat shuddered against the grain. Occasionally, floating logs struck the sides.

The *Sultana* reached Helena, Arkansas, at about 7 a.m. on Wednesday, April 26, thirty hours after leaving Vicksburg. The first night and day had gone uneventfully, J. Walter Elliott recalled, though there was a brief scare at Helena when the passengers crowded to one side to pose for a photographer. Curious townspeople had also gathered at the waterfront, and when the passengers saw the photographer they rushed to the port side, wanting to be in the photo, the boat listed and nearly capsized.

The *Sultana* remained at Helena only about an hour. The Chicago troupe performed another show, the crew put a stop to the alligator-gawking by moving the reptile to a locked closet beneath a stairway, and the passengers went back to their chosen spots. The one stove on the deck was used solely for making coffee, and even that was difficult to get to, so most of the men had to eat hardtack and dried meat and wash it down with river water. The water closets were largely inaccessible, too, which mattered because many of the men suffered from chronic diarrhea. Their only option was to hang over the rails or to use holes some of the men had cut in the wheel housings. The men entertained themselves by watching the passing scenery—mostly plantation houses, slave cabins, and other boats. As the sun set, painting the sky vivid orange, Chester Berry, who had spent most of the day leafing through one of the hymnals given out by the Sisters of Charity, sat against a wall and sang "Sweet Hour of Prayer," a song that had been popular when he left home. When the *Sultana* finally reached Memphis, an Illinois cavalry regiment stationed on the bluffs cheered, and the men on the boat responded in kind.

The *Sultana*'s main reason for stopping in Memphis was to discharge one hundred twenty tons of sugar, ninety-seven crates of wine, and the herd of hogs. With the cargo went most of the boat's ballast, and Mason, still anxious about the overloading, was reportedly a frequent visitor to the *Sultana*'s bar. No doubt the Irish bartenders, McGinty and O'Hara, were nervous, too. But as Chester Berry later wrote of the paroled soldiers aboard the boat, "A happier lot of men I think I never saw than those poor fellows were. The most of them had been a long time in prison, some even for about two years, and the prospect of soon reaching home made them content to endure any amount of crowding."

MEMPHIS WAS THE FIRST sizeable city most of the men had seen in months—in some cases years—and though they were told to remain on board, the flickering gas lights leading up the bluff from the waterfront beckoned. Half an hour after the boat docked, hundreds of men disembarked into the city. They made their way to the Soldiers' Home, one of several way stations operated in major cities by the U.S. Sanitary Commission, where soldiers could find a bed or a meal, or nosed their way around the riverfront saloons. As roustabouts unloaded the *Sultana*'s cargo of sugar beneath oil lamps, George Robinson pitched in to help, and afterward he and a friend headed into town for supper. Two boy-soldiers, William Block and Stephen Gaston, the latter of whom had served in the 8th Indiana with Tolbert and Maddox, took advantage of several broken sugar casks, loading their pockets, haversacks, and hats.

Memphis was the final destination for some of the passengers, including the Chicago troupe, and a few new ones boarded, no doubt with some trepidation, including U.S. Representative-elect W.D. Snow of Arkansas, (whose election Congress had not yet agreed to recognize). According to Elliott's grandson, when Snow visited the clerk's office to pay his fare and receive his stateroom assignment, he "expressed curiosity" over the number of people aboard. Among the other private passengers boarding at Memphis were two women, one of whom Elliott's grandson described as "a great beauty"—she no doubt drew much attention from the passengers—and a man he described as "the finely-groomed J.D. Fontaine of Dallas City, Illinois." Elliott also wrote that his grandfather, "on an impulse" the night before, had given his cot to a sergeant he had met at Camp Fisk, and so slept in a chair. Now, as J. Walter Elliott sat reading beneath one of the cabin chandeliers, the sergeant approached and asked where he was going to sleep. Elliott pointed to a cot on which his hat lay, but the sergeant said it was in a hot and dangerous location above the boilers and suggested another cot (which presumably had already been claimed by someone else—it is doubtful there were any empty ones) near the end of the ladies' cabin. According to J. Walter Elliott's own account, he initially demurred. '"Give it to some poor fellow who had none last night,' I said; but a moment afterwards he came and told me he had removed my hat to the cot selected by him, and that I would have to take that or none." For the record, then, Elliott was coerced into sleeping outside the ladies' cabin, where he would read in his cot until he fell asleep, "dreaming of the loved ones at home—a motherless daughter, a noble christian mother, two devoted sisters, and my brothers."

At about 10:30 p.m., the crew rang the bell on the hurricane deck to announce the *Sultana*'s impending departure, and guards began roaming the waterfront streets rounding up soldiers. Gaston and Block sat on the Texas deck gorging on sugar until, remarkably, they drifted off to sleep. William McFarland of the 42nd Indiana remembered seeing an unusually tall man from Tennessee who got drunk onshore and had to be escorted onto the boat by guards. "He was a thin seven-footer, and he came down to the boat shouting and cursing, at the point of bayonets, so drunk he could hardly walk. He was brought up to the hurricane deck, where he caused considerable disturbance." Having been at Andersonville, McFarland did not know that the man went by the name Big Tennessee and had been a friend to the downtrodden at Cahaba. In fact, Big Tennessee's identity is still subject to debate, but according to Elliott, he cursed the guards as he was forced onto the gangplank and onto the Texas deck. McFarland "poked fun at the Tennessean and, infuriated, the intoxicated trooper lunged toward his tormentor," Elliott wrote. "But he succeeded only in stepping on a number of innocent men, and was soundly cuffed on all sides."

Private Epenetus McIntosh had arrived in Memphis on the *Henry James* but had tarried too long in town and missed the boat. He considered himself in great good luck when he was able to get on the *Sultana*. Several other *Sultana* passengers failed to make it back in time. Michigan soldier W.C. Porter found on his return to the boat that his space in an empty coal bin had been taken, so he moved to a spot between the smokestacks but was rousted from there and eventually settled down to sleep on the stair landing. The men in the empty coal bin pulled the hatch shut to stay warm, which would prove a fateful decision. Elliott recalled awakening as the *Sultana* backed away from the wharf, then falling back asleep.

The *Sultana* crossed the river to a coal yard on the Arkansas side and loaded a thousand burlap bags of coal to fuel the furnaces. In a case where seeming bad luck would have actually been good, and where seeming good luck was actually bad, one of the men who had missed the boat in Memphis. George Downey of the 9th Indiana Cavalry (who had telegraphed home for money from Camp Fisk) paid a boatman $2 to row him to the coal yard, where he again boarded the *Sultana*. He was no doubt proud of this maneuver, which would cost him his life.

At 1 a.m. on April 27, the *Sultana* left the coal yard and headed upriver. The guards posted at the Memphis waterfront watched the brightly lit boat steam around the bend, and would later recall that it presented a beautiful sight. The night was dark, the moon and stars shrouded by clouds that soon began drizzling rain. Pilot George Kayton was behind the wheel. At midstream he began to steer through the cluster of flooded islands known as Paddy's Hen and Chickens, with Rowberry, the first mate, alongside him in the pilot house. Down below, Wes Clemens, the assistant engineer, was at his post by the boilers. The boat was traveling at about ten miles per hour. At fifteen minutes before 2 a.m., with most of the passengers asleep, Kayton began steering past submerged Island 41 in a broad reach of river that because of the flood was roiling along, close to five miles wide.

Chapter Twelve

THE DISASTER

G EORGE ROBINSON WENT TO SLEEP THAT NIGHT ON the *Sultana*'s promenade deck, between the twin smokestacks that towered above the filigreed pilot house. He bedded down beside his companion, one of his previous partners in escape, John Corliss. During his many escape attempts Robinson had learned how to size things up and choose his moment. The moment was about to present itself again.

At about 2 a.m. Robinson awoke with a start, in agonizing pain. Inexplicably, he lay in the *Sultana*'s coal bin, and Corliss was sprawled dead across his legs. His own chest and wrist were injured. His arms were scalded. He had trouble breathing. Someone nearby was screaming that he was being burned alive.

Robinson had not heard the explosion. He had no idea what had happened. All he knew was that the world had come unglued while he slept, and his gut told him that this time he had reached the end. It hit him in high decibels, with blistering heat: There would be no way out. Then he heard a voice say to someone else, "Jack, you can get out this way," and the drive to survive suddenly kicked in again.

He climbed from the coal bin onto the wrecked deck. As he stood there, trying to figure out what was going on, someone placed a hand on his shoulder and said, "What will I do? I cannot swim." It was soon to be a common refrain.

Robinson, who may have been too stunned to answer, drifted off toward the bow of the boat, where he saw people being trampled in a rush for the rails. Hundreds of men, a few women and children, and horses and mules were racing back and forth on the decks and streaming into the cold, dark river, where people flailed about for anything to keep their heads above water and drowned each other in waves. Robinson quietly sat down and wrapped one arm around the *Sultana*'s jackstaff. He had to think. He would not have long.

Ben Davis was on the hurricane deck near the rear of the boat when the boilers exploded. A Kentucky cavalryman originally from Wales, he was one of the few passengers still awake at that hour and, feeling restless, had decided to have a smoke. Picking his way through the soldiers spooning wall-to-wall across the deck, he descended the stairs to the main level in search of a light, found a splinter of wood, stuck it into one of the fireboxes, lit his pipe, then retraced his steps. He was about to take a swig from his canteen when it whirled from his hands into the darkness. Pieces of metal, wood, and body parts began raining down through a cloud of superheated steam, and flames erupted from the heart of the boat. Davis had been sharing blankets with three fellow Kentuckians who had been with him at Cahaba, but he lost sight of them in the pandemonium. As he scoured the boat for something buoyant he came upon one of his friends, Joe Moss, who told him ruefully that he could not swim. Davis gave him a window shutter he had found, and Moss jumped into the river with it and drowned. Davis dove in and swam toward the invisible Arkansas shore. The river was darker than the starless night and bitterly cold with snowmelt from the north, swirling upon itself with implacable velocity and force, but Davis was confident he could make it. He was a strong swimmer.

Perry Summerville awoke to find himself flying through the air. His first thought was that the *Sultana* had been running close to shore and he had been swept off the deck by an overhanging limb. When he hit the water he plummeted into the depths, came up about a hundred feet from the boat, and began swimming back toward it, calling for help, only to see that it was on fire. He instinctively turned downstream and swam away, which was not easy on his bum leg, with his shoulders and chest severely bruised by the blast and fall, and his back scalded by the steam. He found a section of the boat's railing to hold on to, and he glanced back in wonder at the terrible scene, at the silhouettes of people clamoring on the decks, some being consumed by flames, while hundreds dove into the water, in most cases to drown.

Joseph Stevens, the English sharpshooter, was sleeping near the stern with his brother-in-law, William Finch, and awoke to see a crowd surging toward the metal yawl suspended above the *Sultana*'s stern. Stevens tried to calm Finch, telling him they would survive if they kept their wits about them, though neither could swim. He watched men piling into the still-unlaunched yawl and trying to fend off anyone else who attempted to get in. Finch scrambled among them. After the lines were severed, the yawl hurtled into the water upside down, and most of the men hanging onto or inside of it, including Finch, drowned. Stevens dove in, tried his best to dog-paddle away, and was saved by a friend floating nearby on a bale of hay, who grabbed him by the hair. As they drifted into the darkness he saw the *Sultana*'s captain, Cass Mason, hurling shutters into the water.

W.A. Fast had also been sleeping near the yawl when he felt "a jerk and jar" and hot water on his face and hands. Within moments, perhaps a hundred men were tugging at the yawl. Observing the panic, he moved toward the bow. He noticed that one of the *Sultana*'s side paddlewheels was wrecked and the other was hanging perilously overhead. Flames were racing through the remains of the pilot house, which was acting as a flue. He jumped onto the middle deck and entered the staterooms, searching for one of the boat's cork life preservers, but found none. "The men were rushing out from the lower floor or deck, and pouring over the prow into the dark water like a flock of sheep through a gap in a fence," he later wrote.

J.W. Rush, who had grown up on the shores of Lake Erie, had seen his share of boat disasters and knew he had to get off the *Sultana* "before the crowd realized the peril they were in," but it was already too late. As he watched the mob attempting to launch the yawl he saw a woman begging to be allowed on. Though she appeared to be the wife of one of the men already in the boat, she was left behind. With the help of a friend, Rush launched a smaller boat from the upper deck, but it was quickly overwhelmed. "These boats were turned over and over," he wrote, "and many were drowned in trying to get into them, as every time they would turn bottom side up they would bury from fifty to seventy-five, who were trying to climb in from the opposite side. This was kept up until the crowd had thinned out and the boats drifted off."

Rush and his mate began throwing anything that would float overboard. They then tried to force a mule into the water, hoping to ride it as it swam, but it would not budge. He saw Mason exhorting people to remain calm. He saw a group of women on their knees, bowed in prayer, their heads resting against the rail.

M.C. White's first thought was that a Rebel battery had fired on the boat. He heard officers shouting orders for everyone to remain calm, saying the *Sultana* would head to shore, but it was obvious that with the pilot house gone the boat was out of control. It was every man for himself. The flames were spreading rapidly, illuminating hundreds of faces gasping for breath in the roiling water, horses breaking through the rails, a woman fastening a life preserver on a little girl, mangled men crawling among the frenzied crowds, soldiers stripping their clothes and diving in. The acrid smoke and steam carried the scent of burning flesh. It was a hallucinatory scene. Everyone's brain and body chemistry was going wild.

Unable to find a life preserver in the staterooms, Fast pulled a door from its hinges and in a moment of brilliant restraint decided to wait for the drowning masses to subside before diving in. He had observed the terrible ebb and flow: Hundreds of people grasping for anything afloat, drowning each other en masse, after which there would be a brief intermission before the next group dove in. He gathered fifteen or twenty feet of rope and tied it to his door, leaving several loops to use as handholds. All around him, men were "struggling, swimming, sinking. My plan was to stick to the boat as long as I could and until the swimmers were well out of my way." He observed people cursing Lincoln and Jeff Davis and Grant, "any and everybody prominently connected with the war. Some were crying like children." Others prayed loudly and beseechingly, or formally and gracefully, "all in dead earnest." Now and then his gaze landed on a strangely calm face. A few retreated from the crowds and absently sang old familiar songs. As Fast waited for his moment, a group of dockhands tried to wrest his door from him. He backed into a stairway, wedged the door between some timbers, took out his small jackknife, and drove them away. As the crowd in the water thinned he undressed; checked his pocket watch, which was tied to his underwear, and saw that it was 2:30 a.m.; tossed his door; and jumped in after it. He was immediately set upon by drowning men, and he struggled to pry their hands from the door one after another until he was exhausted. Within minutes he lost his hold. At that point his memory of the disaster ended. "From the time I lost that door until daylight there is in my life an entire blank, I do not know where I was or what I was doing," he wrote.

Chester Berry was sleeping forward of the boilers, near where he had sung his hymn at sunset. When the boilers exploded he was struck in the head by a piece of flying wood, which fractured his skull. Dazed, he lay on the deck until a shower of boiling water soaked his blanket and scalded his uncovered bunkmate to death. He found a piece of a board and started forward but changed his mind about jumping when he saw that the water was filled with drowning people. Trying to maintain his presence of mind, he roamed the deck in search of friends and came upon a man who said he could not swim. Berry told him to pull a board from the debris to hang on to. The man found a board, but someone promptly took it from him. Berry told him to get another. He did, and it was taken from him, too. Berry lost patience, shoved the man away, and said, "Drown then, you fool"—words he would regret the rest of his life. Then he moved on.

Albert King was sleeping with a group of friends about thirty feet from the stern, beside the engine room partition. After the explosion he and his companions tried to pry loose part of the partition but were driven away by a frantic rearing horse. His friend Adgate Fleming shouted that he could not swim, and King told him to stay close and away from the crowd at the rail. It was good advice, but Fleming was carried overboard anyway and drowned. King leaped from the starboard rail, bobbed up near the rudder, and was dunked by several men. Seeing an opening in the foundering crowd, he tried to swim away but was submerged by another man. He resurfaced, and a woman grabbed him by the shirt, but King fought her off and swam away. When he came upon a floating board he returned for the woman, and the two paddled away "out of the circle of firelight into the night." The woman was Anna Annis, and as with most of the others on board, her life's travails seemed to have been building to that harrowing moment.

Annis, her husband, and their young daughter had occupied a stateroom. Lieutenant Annis had been stationed with the U.S. Colored Troops at Vicksburg after being captured at Shiloh and paroled. He was Anna's third husband; incredibly, the first two had drowned in shipwrecks, one of which she had survived. Harvey Annis was too ill to make it home to Wisconsin alone, so Anna had traveled to Vicksburg to escort him. After the explosion they put on their life belts, and Harvey led his family to the stern, where he placed his daughter on his back, descended a rope to the water, and told Anna to follow. As she descended the rope a man jumped from above and knocked her off and into the hold of the boat. She climbed out and again descended the rope. Once she was in the water, her life belt began to slip off, and she grabbed the boat's rudder, remaining fixed to it as she watched her husband and daughter drown. She held on to the rudder with several others until the flames forced them to let go. Her arms were burned from the backs of both hands to her shoulders. She drifted off, struggling to remain afloat. As King passed she tried to cling to him, but he fended her off. Then he came back for her.

Nathaniel Foglesong hung over the rudder post, brushing coals and cinders off his shoulders, until the flames burned his boot and he slid down onto the shoulders of a man below. "Get off from me!" the man shouted, to which Foglesong replied, "In a minute." Nine men were hanging on to the rudder post. Finally Foglesong let go, calling out, "Here goes for ninety days!"—the prescribed time for militia enlistment. As he surfaced he grabbed someone's ankle, was kicked away, grabbed it again, and with the other hand caught a cable dangling from the blazing stern. Looking over the fire-lit river, he saw the burned bodies of a man and two women on a section of floating wreckage. An Irishman named Patrick Larky, who had fought with a Michigan regiment, cried, "Come help poor Pat, he is a-drowning!" just before Foglesong saw him go under. Clutching a piece of flotsam, Foglesong dog-paddled to a section of broken floating deck, where a familiar soldier reached out a helping hand. "My God, Thaniel, is that you?" the man asked. "Yes, all that's left of me," Foglesong replied.

Inside his stateroom, William Snow, the newly elected congressman from Arkansas, had not heard the explosion and was initially unaware of how dire the situation was. He took the time to dress and to tie his tie. When he emerged, the wind was carrying the fire rapidly over the center of the boat, the decks of which had been sundered by the explosion. Snow took off his coat, returned it to his stateroom, and trotted toward the stern, stepping over trampled bodies. The water was so crowded he decided it would be impossible to jump without landing on someone. Finally he found an open spot near one of the paddlewheels and dove in.

Truman Smith was treading water when he came upon Henry

Norton, another member of his Michigan cavalry, who was furious because someone had stolen his bundle of clothes. Smith told him to forget about it, but Norton was confident he could swim to the bank, and he wanted to find the thief. Norton had entered the water with an empty barrel but had a hard time holding on to it. When someone grabbed hold of his shirt, he slipped out of it. "I swam but a few feet when I found myself with four or five others," he later recalled. "It seemed as though we all wanted to get hold of each other. I succeeded in getting the rest of my clothes off and got rid of my company." Smith and Norton then swam away.

Like most of the former prisoners, Joseph Bringman was in no condition for a major survival challenge. Thin, weak and sick, he had been sleeping fitfully when the boilers exploded, dreaming that he was on a leisurely walk up a long hill, at the top of which a rocky ledge jutted out over a river. Suddenly the dream merged with reality: When he stepped on the rock to look down at the river, it burst beneath his feet with a sound like the report of a cannon. "I felt pieces of the rock striking my face and head and I seemed to be hurled into the river," he wrote. When he surfaced he was not yet fully conscious, but he shed his clothes and grabbed a few pieces of wood to keep himself afloat. The first piece was no bigger than his hand, but he quickly scooped up other bits of detritus and clutched them to his chest. A horse swam close by and nearly pushed him under. By the light of the fire he could see perhaps two hundred yards across the river, which was full of people, some swimming boldly, others splashing for a few moments before going under.

William Peacock, who had lost a hundred pounds during his imprisonment, awoke buried in wreckage, bleeding and bruised, with one hip badly scalded. He had been thrown from the boiler deck wearing only his underwear, his hat, and a handkerchief tied around his neck—the parting gift of a friend who had died at Camp Fisk. He crawled off the side of the boat and into the water. A large section of the boiler deck had been thrown into the river intact, along with the men who had been sleeping on it, including Ohio soldier Jotham Maes. Everyone was ejected from the wreckage when it struck the water, but Maes managed to climb back on, along with nine others. Looking back at the boat, he saw the smokestacks collapse in opposite directions, crushing everyone in their way.

William Boor, who had noted the repairs being made to the *Sultana's* boilers at Vicksburg and opted not to bed down on the deck above them, was pinned beneath a section of the upper deck that collapsed under the falling smokestacks, but he managed to free himself and his friend Thomas Brink. As they made their way down a wrecked stair Boor asked Brink if he could swim. Brink could. Boor could not. Brink disappeared after diving in, and Boor never saw him again. Boor was afraid of both the water and the crowd. He tied his spare shirt inside a rubber blanket, picked up a piece of wood, tucked the bundle under his arms, and waited.

A large group of Indiana soldiers had been bedded down on the Texas deck, while Romulus Tolbert's 8th cavalry had chosen a spot directly in front of one of the wheel housings. All were dispersed after the explosion. Tolbert would never offer many details about what happened except to say that he found something to hold on to.

J. Walter Elliott was awakened from his dreams by a sound he compared to the discharge of artillery or a train wreck. His recollections would have a theatrical ring. He was standing on the collapsed deck, wondering what to do, "when the scene lights up from below, disclosing a picture that beggars all description—mangled, scalded human forms heaped and piled amid the burning debris on the lower deck." He heard shrieks and moans and the hiss of escaping steam. His face, throat, and lungs burned. He hastily dressed, groped his way over the debris, and through the gaping hole in the deck saw red-hot coals below and flames running up the splintered superstructure. He realized that his former cot had disappeared into the conflagration. Huge sections of iron and wood had been driven upward through the cabin, the hurricane deck, the Texas deck, and the pilot house.

When W.S. Freisner heard shouting outside his cabin door, he stepped into the main saloon and peered into the maw, where he saw a man pinned beneath a heavy timber, being burned alive. The man saw him too and cried out, "Help, help, for God's sake!" but as Freisner lamented, "There was an impossible gulf between us and I turned from the horrid sight."

William Crisp, a Michigan infantryman, was pinned to the floor beneath red-hot metal and could not move until it cooled. By then the cavern of the explosion was a hellish scene of hundreds of screaming people being burned alive. Crisp went over the side.

George Young's first thought was that lightning had struck the boat. He was pinned beneath wooden wreckage along with several other men, some of whom had been killed. He managed to extricate himself and struggled to free another man who was still alive, but he could not budge the heavy timbers. Soon the flames drove him away. "We could not escape from his hoarse cries," he recalled, "and, cruel as it seems, we were relieved when death ended his horrible agony."

Commodore Smith, whose weight had dropped to less than a hundred pounds during his imprisonment at Cahaba, was buried in "dead and wounded comrades, legs, arms, heads, and all parts of human bodies, and fragments of the wrecked upper decks." He remained on the boat for perhaps half an hour, during which he helped throw overboard dying men who would otherwise have been burned alive.

Elliott would later claim that he had done the same. As the fire spread he watched stairways and portions of the decks collapse, then the smokestacks groan and topple. He pushed his way back into the smoke-filled cabin, entered an empty stateroom, and found a life preserver. On his way out he came upon a frightened young woman in a nightgown, followed her outside, grabbed her arm, and called a chambermaid to adjust the life preserver on her. Though it seems ludicrous that the chambermaid would still be at his beck and call, Elliott seems to have thought nothing of enlisting her service. Then, as he stood on the burning deck, he reported hearing a polite voice entreating him, and turned to see a calm yet gravely injured Daniel McLeod sitting on a cot at the edge of the burning cavern. McLeod had been reading at a table near the center of the cabin when he was blown across the room by the explosion. He was bruised, cut, and scalded, with both ankles broken so badly that the bones protruded. With his suspenders he had improvised tourniquets for both legs to keep from bleeding to death. Elliott recalled telling McLeod that he could not help him because he could not swim, to which McLeod responded that he wanted only to be thrown overboard so he would not burn alive. In Elliott's telling, he and another man hoisted McLeod to the rail, from which he descended on a hog chain to the water. McLeod's account would differ from Elliott's in one important detail: He would not mention Elliott at all.

On all three decks, injured people were begging to be thrown overboard, believing that burning to death was worse than drowning. The brief choking of those who went under no doubt appeared less horrible than the extended, screaming agony of those being burned alive. M.H. Sprinkle and Billy Lockhart claimed to have thrown at least fifty helpless soldiers over the rail. Commodore Smith threw his share, too, and said it was "the hardest task of my life . . . the most heartrending task that human beings could be called upon to perform." Some were so badly scalded that their skin slipped off as Smith struggled to pick them up. He watched them briefly writhe in the water before they went under.

After watching two Kentuckians lament to each other that they could not swim, then jump overboard to drown together, Elliott felt compelled to find something that would float, "but everything available seemed to have been appropriated." He tried to make a life preserver out of a stool, but that did not work. He threw a mattress overboard, but it was immediately submerged by drowning men. He found another mattress and slipped off to a quieter spot, "but it no sooner touched the water than four men seized it, turned it over, and it went under as I jumped. Down, down I went into the chilly waters. Some poor drowning wretch was clutching at my legs, but putting my hands down to release myself and vigorously treading water, I rose strangling to the surface, my scalded throat and lungs burning with pain. The mattress was within easy reach, with only one claimant. God only knows what had become of the three others." Like many others that night, Elliott had for the first time caused another man to drown.

As he floated near the boat Elliott narrowly missed being crushed when one of the boat's wheelhouses collapsed, and he nearly went under the resulting waves. "There seemed to be acres of struggling humanity on the waters, some on debris of the wreck, some on the dead carcasses of horses, some holding to swimming live horses, some on boxes, bales of hay, drift logs, etc. Soon we parted company with the wreck and the crowd and drifted out into the darkness almost alone."

A.C. Brown had awakened on the opposite side of the cabin from where he had fallen asleep, and had seen the chandeliers of the ladies' cabin swinging crazily as smoke and steam billowed through the rooms. Once on the deck, he helped a woman push her trunk into the river, watched as she jumped in after it, and then followed her. He would later recall his moment of joy when the *Sultana* departed Vicksburg, and conclude, "It is well, my friends, that we cannot see into the future."

Stephen Gaston, at fifteen one of the youngest soldiers on board, had spent the evening gorging on pilfered sugar and now searched in vain for his partner in crime, William Block. Failing to find him, he swung down to the boiler deck on the smokestack supports, then onto the starboard deck, where he found a flour barrel, undressed, and jumped into the river with it. Two or three men tried to overtake his barrel but drowned before reaching it.

George Safford, who was traveling with his father, a member of the Sanitary Commission, fastened life belts to both of them before they dove in together. Once in the water they climbed upon a door. but as they paddled away a horse leaped from the main deck and landed on it, separating them.

William McFarland saw a woman rush out of a stateroom with a small child in her arms, put a life preserver on it, and throw it into the river. When the child hit, only its bottom bobbed above the surface. The woman ran back into the stateroom, came back out, jumped into the water, and grabbed the child. McFarland did not see what happened next. By then he had noticed the seven-foot-tall Tennessean who, back in Memphis, had returned drunk to the boat at the point of bayonets, and he was concerned because he had teased the man.

Ogilvie Hamblin was still on the deck when he heard men shouting that they were trapped inside the cargo hold. One of Hamblin's arms had been amputated by Rebel surgeons soon after his capture, but with another man's help he managed to pry open the hatch. The men "came rushing out of the hold like bees out of a hive, followed by dense clouds of steam and smoke." Hamblin stripped and stood naked on the deck for a few long moments, deliberating until he had no choice but to escape the flames. "Screwing my courage up to the sticking point," he later wrote—borrowing a phrase from Lady Macbeth—he watched for an opening amid the drowning crowds, then dove in and quickly swam away as best he could with one arm. Helpless against the strong currents, he resorted to floating—a wise move, and a remarkable feat in a moment of extreme agitation.

Most of those who survived, as Elliott's grandson later observed, did so "by thinking and acting independently." Ohio soldier William Lugenbeal thought of the alligator in its crate, went to the closet where it was kept, broke in, dragged the box out, and ran his bayonet through the hissing reptile three times. He undressed, threw the box overboard, and climbed in. As he later wrote, "When a man would get close enough I would kick him off, then turn quick as I could and kick someone else to keep them from getting hold of me." Occasionally someone pleaded that he was drowning, but Lugenbeal knew that if he helped, both would probably die. To those who later expressed shock upon hearing the story, he posed this question: "What do you think you would do?"

By now the disaster was becoming evident from miles away. About seven miles downstream at Memphis, where the waterfront sentinels had admired the brightly lit *Sultana* steaming around the bend at midnight, the U.S. military packet *Pocahontas* lay moored at the foot of Beale Street. Shortly after 2 a.m., its watchman noticed a glow upriver and reported it to the pilot. The watchman thought that perhaps a house was on fire. As the glow brightened the pilot surmised that it was a boat, but he did nothing.

In Mound City, Arkansas, two miles below the disaster scene, farmer John Fogleman was awakened by the sound of the explosion and from his veranda saw the burning steamboat in the distance. He aroused three neighbors, but none had a boat. The *Pocahontas* had been plying the river around Memphis for days, destroying all boats in private hands to prevent Confederate guerillas from using them.

William Woodridge was asleep in his mother's house on their flooded farm about a mile upriver when he was awakened by the noise of the explosion, which he said "rolled and re-echoed for minutes in the woodlands." His room was soon lit by a strange light, and he raced to the porch. "It was so light, I could have picked up a pin," he said of the fire's glow. Standing with his mother and the farm's overseer, he heard the cries and saw people jumping into the water. He had secreted a boat away, so he and the overseer hurried to it to begin helping with the rescue. A short distance upriver was a wood yard operated by William Boardman and R.K. Hill, who also set off in a hidden skiff when they heard the screams.

No one, even those on shore, was prepared for what was now unfolding—for the number of lives at stake or the difficulty of coming to their rescue. The Mississippi, even at a normal stage, is not a languorous river. From a distance it appears to move slowly because it is so large, but its velocity is stunning. It is one of the greatest forces on earth, pushing and pulling relentlessly toward the Gulf even though its bottom at Vicksburg is below sea level. The bottom itself is a river of flowing sand, and the channel is riddled with whirlpools strong enough to suck full-grown trees beneath the surface, then propel them violently upward to break with a splash, seemingly from nowhere, miles downstream. As they drifted downstream some of the swimmers were sucked under by whirlpools. Joseph Taylor Elliott and three other men were holding tightly to a section of floating stairs, moving tantalizingly close to the Tennessee bank, when suddenly they struck a cross-current that began to whirl. "Into this we went, and such a twisting and turning round, upside down and every other way, was never seen," he later recalled. He held on for the ride until the stairs "shot out into the current and on down the river, less one man who was left in the whirlpool and drowned."

The currents were particularly risky during a flood, more so for weakened men who suddenly found themselves subject to the strange, terrifying, inescapable pull of gravity in a cold, deep, surging river. The sick and injured were also more vulnerable to the water's bitter chill. The river at that time of year would have been less than sixty degrees, which sounds relatively warm but in fact is extremely cold to a human body. Water draws heat from the body more than twenty times as fast as air, and a body begins to fail when its core temperature drops below about ninety degrees. In water as cold as the Mississippi was that night, even a strong swimmer would have only about ninety minutes before serious trouble started, and swimming—expending energy—would simply hasten the process. Even the shock of entering water that cold can cause an involuntary gasping reflex, sending an able swimmer straight to the bottom. As body temperature drops, heart rate and blood pressure increase dramatically. Blood vessels near the surface constrict as blood is shunted to vital organs. Muscles tense, generating more body heat, which is then lost. Blood pressure then begins to go down. Mental processes become impaired. People become irrational, lose dexterity, and make bad calls, such as swimming away from shore or from rescuers. Often they lose consciousness. Those in the water, even if they could swim, were in a race against time.

At this point, perhaps five hundred people remained on board, including Boor, George Robinson, and the newlywed Hardins. Most had been driven toward the bow by the flames. As long as the remnants of the *Sultana*'s wheel housings remained upright, the hull had drifted downstream stern first, perhaps because the housings funneled the brisk north wind and kept the bow pointed upstream. But the currents were pushing the boat slowly downriver. Once the wheel housings collapsed, the boat's wind and water resistance changed, and the resulting pivot sent the flames racing in the opposite direction. Soon thick clouds of smoke, laden with burning cinders, were rolling toward the refuge of the bow. As the flames approached, two Kentucky cavalrymen hurriedly looped a cable and heavy chain to a mooring ring for use as a handhold, thinking that they might be able to lower themselves into the river and escape the fire while holding on to prevent drowning. Boor finally decided it was time to dive in, and when he did, he heard a sizzling sound and realized his bundle of clothes had caught fire. Seth Hardin, who was separated from his bride in the confusion, was also driven into the water, where he swam through the crowd calling her name. On the forecastle stood one of the Sisters of Charity, entreating those in the water to avoid drowning one another. Some survivors later said her words did have a calming effect. She would survive in their memories as a totem figure who eventually went up in flames.

When George Robinson at last dove in, he felt his confidence and stamina flagging almost immediately. Fear normally causes a surge of adrenaline, but it can also sap energy incredibly fast. Fortunately, Robinson caught sight of a dead mule, which was to be the vehicle of his final—and only successful—escape. He climbed on the floating carcass, which was still warm, and drifted away down the river, which must have been both unnerving and, under the circumstances, sublime. As he floated Robinson was apparently calm enough to notice that "some amusing things transpired." He came across a man going over and over on a floating barrel; the man would crawl upon the barrel, pause briefly to pray, then go over like a clown in a bizarre circus sideshow. Robinson also heard someone calling out, "Morgan, here is your mule," which had new meaning for him now.

Hiram Allison was drifting in the dark river when he came upon two men holding the ends of a horse trough and praying with their eyes clenched shut. Neither stopped praying when he grabbed the middle of the trough and spoke to them. For a few moments Allison lost track of where he was, and when he looked back both men were gone. He was now alone in the darkness of the open channel.

William Marshall had managed to grab the tail of a swimming horse. His friend Samuel Pickens also grabbed hold of one but let go after the animal panicked and headed back toward the *Sultana*. Pickens then climbed atop a dead horse and drifted away.

George Young managed to float on his rubber blanket until someone grabbed his shirt sleeve: "To break that hold required a great effort, but, drawing myself up, I put my fist into his side, gave a strong, sudden push and broke from him, and a moment after freed myself from another drowning person who was dragging me beneath the water." As he floated away Young snagged a pair of pants floating in the water, which he decided he would need when he got out. Determined to survive, he fashioned a better raft from half a cork life belt, his rubber blanket, and a cracker box. He later gave the cracker box to a drowning man to ward him off. "I was very watchful for drowning men," he recalled, "and the least movement made me cautious." He eventually came upon a man floating on a log, who warned him not to come closer. Young suggested that they work together to reach the flooded trees. "This met with his approval enough for him to come nearer, but not close enough for me to become a partner with him in the possession of the log." Together they made their way to the trees, where a voice instructed them to come closer, saying it was possible to touch bottom. The voice belonged to an Arkansas man in a dugout canoe, who had heard the explosion and ferried the two men ashore.

Unable to break free of the currents, Summerville watched the dim outline of the islands and the flooded timber on the banks moving past. He found a large plank about two miles above Memphis and positioned it across his rail. He held the rail with his feet and the plank with his hands. At one point a gunboat passed but did not stop. He also saw a snorting horse swimming downstream with six or eight men hanging on. "When I heard him coming I tried to get to him, but when I saw his load I kept clear for fear some of the boys would get all I had at the time in the world—my rail and plank," he recalled.

Later, a Michigan cavalry man named Jerry Perker floated close to Summerville on a barrel. Several other men were clinging to debris nearby, and Perker "would cheer the boys by telling them to hold out and we would get out." Summerville recalled that he was still wearing his socks, which "bothered me more than anything else. They worked partly off my feet and would catch on my rail which caused me to almost sink." In fact, some men drowned because they could not get their fitted long johns past their feet and became entangled in them. Summerville floated in his annoying socks alongside a man named Kibbs, who he said "was cheerful except when talking of his little girl. There were three of us from Brazil, Ind., two were lost, I being the only one of them saved."

J.W. Rush was also drifting down the river, driven by the currents so hard against a floating stump that he would bear the scars of puncture wounds for the rest of his life. "Those who have any knowledge of trying to handle a round piece of timber in the water can realize how difficult it is to support one's self," he wrote, "especially in the current of the river, upon a piece of wood of such ill shape as a stump with roots protruding in all directions." Unable to balance himself on the stump, and fearing that the effort would wear him out, he eventually let go.

Ohio soldier L.W. McCrory held on to his valise, with the new civilian clothes he had bought at Vicksburg, and his pocketbook containing $100. With his wallet between his teeth, gripping his valise with one hand, he had jumped eighteen feet from the boiler deck into the river. He proved to be a strong enough swimmer to swim three miles with baggage. But when the man he was swimming alongside said he could go no farther and disappeared beneath the water, McCrory lost his nerve and let go of his valise. He held on to his wallet and swam about two miles farther before reaching land.

While he was still on the boat, Ben Davis, whose canteen had flown from his hands, had fretted about where the *Sultana*'s alligator might be, and now, in the darkness, men were likewise fearful of encountering it. At one point a group scattered when a horse threw its head over the log they were floating on and they mistook it for the alligator. Everyone was at wit's end, wary of everything. Truman Smith was floating alone in the darkness when he heard someone cough. "As I came near he kept swimming away," he recalled. "I called him and asked what regiment he belonged to. He asked what I wanted to know for." Smith told him he would write to his parents if he drowned, but the man told him not to come any closer.

They swam at a distance from each other until someone called out, "Halt!" It was the voice of a guard on the Tennessee shore.

Simeon Chelf managed to hold on to his diary and pictures of his wife and children, though he was otherwise naked in the water. He had been sleeping on the bow of the boat when the boilers exploded, and a friend beside him had been instantly killed. As he watched others jumping into the water he searched for a bucket to fight the fire. Unable to find one, he changed his focus and began looking for something that would float. He found a board, then traded it for a pole to a friend who could not swim. He and his friend then said a prayer and jumped in. When Chelf was halfway between the *Sultana* and the Arkansas shore, a boat—probably the *Bostonia II*, which was the first to arrive on the scene—mysteriously appeared, and its crew began dumping hay bales in the river. The boat's wake nearly drowned him.

The *Bostonia II* had been about two miles upstream from the *Sultana,* headed toward Memphis, when its crew noticed the vivid glow on the horizon. The captain thought it was a forest fire until the *Sultana* came into view. The *Bostonia II* slowed as it plowed into a mile-long string of victims, and the crew began scattering the hay bales and anything else that would float. But the boat did not immediately stop.

As he drifted Chelf shared his pole with another naked man until they reached a cluster of flooded saplings. Finding that he could not touch bottom, Chelf swam back out into the river, thinking he might be picked up by one of the rescue boats that were starting to arrive.

At half past three the alarm had still not been sounded at the Memphis waterfront, where a dozen boats—packets, gunboats, and other vessels—were moored along the long wooden wharf. Inside the wharf boat, with the door ajar, two men sat in straight chairs beside a pot-bellied stove. Hearing a noise outside, they looked at each other quizzically and stepped onto the deck. It was a cry for help from the river. The first survivor had reached Memphis—at least, the first one to drift close enough to be heard at the wharf. One of the men jumped into a skiff and rowed out into the river. In the dim light of his lantern he saw a partially clothed boy, Wesley Lee of the 102nd Ohio, clinging to a pair of boards. Lee had wasted no time getting off the *Sultana*. As he explained after he was pulled from the water, he jumped in with two planks he had pried from a stair. Hearing his story, one of the men immediately tapped out the news on a telegraph. Afterward it would be said that the first report of the disaster came from the *General Boynton*, a military courier boat that had started upstream from Memphis a short time earlier and turned back when its crew discovered the river was full of people. Elliott, in fact, watched, floating on his mattress, as the *General Boynton* approached, then turned, blew its whistle, and headed back toward the city. According to Lee, the *Boynton* arrived at the waterfront several minutes after him, carrying a few survivors, and with his permission claimed the bounty that was routinely paid for the first report of a boat disaster.

Lee said that as he drifted alone in the river he had been buoyed by thoughts of home and the desire to simply live as long as he could. As he was warming himself by the wharf boat's stove, the city's master of river transport ordered three steamers—the *Jenny Lind*, the *Pocahontas*, and a ferry named *Rosadella*—to fire up immediately and head upstream.

By 4 a.m. the riverfront was clogged with swimmers, many badly scalded or otherwise injured, all numbed by exposure and exhausted. Lifeboats; small craft from the U.S. ironclad *Essex*, the

U.S.S. *Grosbeak*, and the U.S.S. *Tyler*, and a dozen or more steamboat yawls and skiffs soon left to aid in the rescue.

As the boats were leaving Memphis a skiff and a dugout canoe from Arkansas were picking up survivors on the opposite shore. In the skiff were William Boardman and R.K. Hill, who operated the wood yard in Mound City. In the canoe was Frank Barton, a Confederate lieutenant who had been camping close by. Still wearing his Confederate Army jacket, Barton rescued Ben Davis and several others, but watched as one man relaxed his hold on a willow tree and slipped beneath the water when the skiff was only a few feet away. As Elliott's grandson later observed, "The difference between life and death could be measured. It was a matter of yards, feet, inches. It was the length of a reaching arm that was long enough, or a little too short." Barton paddled his survivors to the wood yard, then went back for more. A shanty at the wood yard was soon crowded with shivering men.

After dropping anchor downstream, the crew of the *Bostonia II* lowered her yawl and by the light of torches began plucking survivors from the water, among them young Gaston and, according to Elliott's grandson, "the lady in the hoopskirt." The boat gathered about a hundred survivors, then headed for Memphis.

Robert Hamilton, who had been struggling to overcome the currents on a floating board, watched crestfallen as the *Bostonia II* departed at about 4:30 a.m. To make matters worse, the boat's wake swamped many of the survivors still floating in the river. But Hamilton noticed in the gathering light that a few men, including those who had affixed the cable and chain to the mooring ring of the *Sultana*'s bow, were climbing back aboard. Most of the boat had burned down to the waterline, and the men had survived by lowering themselves into the water, holding on to the cable and chain, and submersing themselves when the fire got too hot, then coming up for air. It had been a stroke of genius. Two or three shivering, naked soldiers were now pulling others onto the bow, and Hamilton paddled in their direction.

Rush, meanwhile, had joined a demented man floating on a door. "A yawl came near us when I called for help," he recalled, "but as I reached with my right hand for the rope, my companion reached for me and got hold of my hair, which at the time was very long. He seized my hair with a grasp firm enough to pull me on my back and get me under water, but his hold soon relaxed, and as I came up the yawl passed out of sight, and I was again left in darkness and drifted along with the current of the river. I was a good swimmer, but realized the fact that I could do nothing but keep above water, so I made no effort only to float, in hopes the current would carry me to shore."

As the *Essex* drifted downriver from Memphis, picking up survivors, sentries at Fort Pickering twice fired on her. The *Essex*'s ensign, James Berry, would later lodge a complaint against the officers of Fort Pickering for not only refusing to aid but actually hindering the rescue. Sentries at a post about a mile upstream from Memphis also fired on survivors calling for help in the river.

In his official report, Berry later wrote that he had been awakened with the news that the *Sultana* had blown up and was burning a few miles upriver, and that the river was full of drowning people. He ordered all the boats under his command to be manned, then boarded a cutter. "The morning was very dark, it being about one hour before daylight, and the weather overcast, and the shrieks of the wounded and drowning men was the only guide we had," he wrote. "The first man we picked up was chilled and so benumbed that he couldn't help himself, and the second one died a short time after he was taken on board. We soon drifted down to Fort Pickering, when the sentry on the shore fired at us, and we were obliged to 'come to' while the poor fellows near us were crying out and imploring us for God's sake to save them; that they couldn't hold out much longer." Pulling close to the bank, Berry hailed the sentry, who ordered him to come ashore. Berry refused. As the *Essex* backed out into the river and its crew began picking up more drowning men, the sentries fired on the boat again. "It was not daylight, and though our two boats and a steam-boat's yawl, which came out to lend us a hand, made a large mark to shoot at, I would not leave the poor fellows in the water to attend the sentry on shore," Berry wrote. "When the day began to dawn the cries of the sufferers ceased, and all who had not been rescued had gone down." Berry went ashore, where a sentry pointed his musket at him. Berry asked for the officer in charge, who told him that he was under order to fire on any skiffs in the river. "I told him that these boats were not skiffs; that they were a man-of-war's gig and cutter, and again reminded him of what had happened, and of the drowning men whose cries he could not help hearing, and for the sake of humanity why could he not execute his orders with some discretion in a time like this. He said that he had as much humanity as any one, and in firing at me he had only obeyed orders. I saw a number of skiffs and other boats laying hauled up out of the water, and from appearances no one had made any attempt to launch them, and I reminded him that that did not look much like humanity."

Though his charges were later contested, Berry claimed that no one at the fort offered to do anything for the survivors in his boats except the watchman of the coal barges, "who, with the assistance of some of my men, built a fire on the shore, and I left a few of the rescued men by it, who wished to remain, and the others I had put on board vessels near by, where they were well cared for. I then crossed the river, and after looking carefully around I returned on board, having taken out of the water sixty men and one lady."

After the scalded swimmers were pulled from the water, they were sprinkled with flour to relieve their pain and given water and whiskey. Among them was George Robinson, who was plucked from his mule. He had drifted fourteen miles to near Fort Pickering. By then he was "nonsensical," and he awoke to find himself in the care of an elderly woman.

Like Robinson, many survivors floated past the city before being rescued. Joseph Bringman saw the gas street lights ascending the bluff, heard the shouts of rescuers and the ringing of wharf bells, and saw dozens of boats departing to participate in the rescue, but he could not make his presence known, though he "hallooed for help." He soon lost consciousness and drifted by. "I was so chilled that I was powerless, and a kind of drowsiness came over me," he later recalled. "I felt that I was going to sleep, and I seemed as comfortable as if in a downy bed. I soon dropped to sleep, or unconsciousness, with the music of the bells of the steamers ringing in my ears." He would never know how he survived.

Eventually Joseph Taylor Elliott and the other men on the floating stairs drifted up to a man on a log, and the four floated together until Elliott, in a semiconscious state, was somehow separated from the others. He remembered passing Memphis and seeing the same gas lights climbing the bluff, but after that his memory was blank until he heard the splash of an oar. He tried to call out, but his voice failed. "It was some such feeling as when one tries to call out in a nightmare," he recalled. But one of the crew members from an *Essex* cutter saw him, dragged him into the boat, and gave him a shot of whiskey.

After trying to swim ashore and being continually defeated by the currents, Chester Berry was ready to give up—"to shorten my misery"—when he thought of home and in his mind was transported there. He imagined himself walking up the path from the road through the gate to the house, "but, strange to me, when I reached the door, instead of entering at once, I sat upon the step." His mother was very religious, as his father had been, but because his father was deaf and dumb his mother always read the family devotionals, and he imagined her at that moment praying for him. "As I sat upon the step I thought it was nine o'clock in the evening, and as plainly as I ever heard my mother's voice I heard it that evening. I cared but little for the prayer until she reached that portion that referred to the absent one, when all the mother-soul seemed to go up in earnest petition—'God save my boy.' For ten long weary months she had received no tidings from her soldier boy, now she had just learned that he was on his way home and her thoughts were almost constantly upon him; and for him her earnest prayer was made." Bolstered by his vision, Berry renewed his efforts, almost immediately heard "a glad cry," and turned to see the bow light of the *Essex*. His struggles were not over—the *Essex* continued past—but he managed to make his way to a snag, where he was eventually rescued by the *Pocahontas*.

At daybreak, Fast, who had passed out, regained consciousness in the top of a small tree surrounded by deep water. About a quarter-mile downstream he saw the hull of the still-burning *Sultana* slowly turning round in an eddy, with a small group of men clinging to its bow. He decided to try to swim toward it, a seemingly foolish idea that probably saved his life. He made his way from flooded treetop to flooded treetop until he was close enough, then swam to the hull and caught a line from its bow. He was so tired that it took him an hour of slipping and scuffling to heave himself onto the deck. The hull was about three-quarters of a mile from the flooded Arkansas shore, and when Fast reached it, a few dozen men were still there, some of whom were badly scalded or otherwise maimed. The debris on the hull was still burning—everywhere except the twenty feet or so where the men were marooned—and the able-bodied men were beating back the flames with waterlogged clothes.

After he pulled himself from the water, Fast spotted another swimmer, whom he recognized as a man who had escaped Cahaba and been recaptured. He threw him a length of rope. With another length of rope the two tied the hull to a flooded tree to hold it in place. Then they began throwing water from the river onto the still-advancing flames. As they did so a young man was clinging to a brass mooring ring on the side of the hull, away from the bow, hemmed in by fire. "We could easily hear all he said indeed, could not help hearing it," Fast recalled. "Sometimes he would pray, then shout for help, then would cry and beg and coax, in the most heart-rending manner. He said that he had a mother in Indiana, and that she was well off, and if we would save him she would give us all that she was worth." This went on, he recalled, "for an hour or two," but the men could not save him because a wall of fire surrounded him. They attempted to float ropes to him, but each one caught fire before he could grasp it, and he was unable to swim. "Finally, as the fire crept closer and closer to him, and he breathed the hot air and smoke, his voice grew hoarse and more feeble." The young man soon released his grasp and sank into the river.

Fogleman, the Arkansas farmer, watched the remains of the *Sultana* drift into the flooded trees and realized that the men on the bow were fighting a losing battle. No one on the rescue boats seemed to have noticed them, so Fogleman and his neighbors began hastily building a raft of twelve-foot-long logs. They set out at about 8 a.m., according to Fast, who saw them coming. By then there were perhaps three dozen men on the bow. About a hundred feet from the hull, Fogleman stopped to negotiate. He called out that he could take six at a time but would not come nearer unless they agreed to go in an orderly fashion. He was afraid, and rightfully so, of being swamped. Fast recalled, "Finally, a comrade, whom I called all the morning 'Indiana,' and myself stepped to the edge of the burning hull, and declared in the most solemn manner that if he would approach we would not get on his logs, and would not permit over six persons to get on." So began the ferrying of the last passengers from the burning boat to the shore. In the interest of time, Fogleman discharged each group among the flooded trees, where they could await the final trip to dry land. Each time the passengers paddled with as much strength as they could muster. Meanwhile, the floor beneath the waiting men began to smolder and burn, and they covered themselves with wet blankets and poured water over their heads. Finally, with thirteen men left, the consensus was that they did not have time for everyone to be ferried to the trees before the remainder of the deck was consumed by fire. As Fast recalled, "'Indiana' and I, and others, hurriedly discussed the situation. Should we strong ones take to the raft and leave the helpless? Human instinct struggling for self-preservation seemed to argue yes. But the maimed ones took in the situation at once, and begged for the strong ones not to abandon them." When the raft returned, Fast and his Indiana friend loaded the injured men aboard. Because seven would have to go on this load or the next, Fast said, "Seven goes this load," and slid onto the log. "We landed, the raft went back, got the other six off almost overcome with heat and smoke. The raft had got only about six rods from the burning hull when it sank, leaving nothing but the jack-staff sticking above the water to mark where she went down." Hugh Kinser, who was resting in a treetop nearby, watched the *Sultana*'s hull go under, sending hissing water and steam high into the air.

Fast heard men in the distance calling out from their perches in trees or aboard debris in the river. Some sang army or minstrel songs. Others mocked the singing of the birds or the croaking of frogs.

Fogleman took the survivors to his plantation house, where they warmed themselves by the fire, and lay the seriously injured out to tend to their wounds. Among the men were Nathaniel Foglesong, William Boor, and Dewitt Clinton Spikes, who had lost his family. Spikes reportedly became crazed with grief when the bodies of his mother and sister arrived, but eventually he calmed himself and went on to help rescue survivors.

Daniel McLeod, with his broken ankles, bleeding wounds, and scalded skin, floated downriver about two miles before he managed to lodge himself in flooded brush at a place called Cheek's Island, where he was rescued, along with Ogilvie Hamblin, and taken to the wood yard. As they were headed back to the yard they saw a young girl fighting to keep her head above water. She was about seven years old and wore a life belt, but it had slipped too low on her waist. McLeod, despite his injuries, dragged himself half over the gunwale to try to reach her, and the one-armed Hamblin struggled to assist, but she went under before they could save her. The last they saw was her tiny feet in "miniature high-heeled gaiters."

When they reached a cabin in the Arkansas woodyard, McLeod was carried inside, as was Young, who dipped his burned hand in a barrel of flour to relieve the pain. Looking out the window, Young saw "a one-armed comrade who was entirely naked, poor from a long prison life, and shivering in the wind." It was Hamblin, who hesitated to come inside because he was naked and there were women present. He lingered, shivering, outside until Young gave him the extra pants he had snagged soon after leaving the boat.

Albert King floated for hours on his raft of debris with Anna Annis, who continually called for help. Early on she had seemed to verge on hysteria, but she grew quieter over time, only asking now and then if he thought they would be saved. King said little because he was unsure himself. Then he touched something underwater, perhaps a submerged sapling, and found a foothold. They climbed atop a log, which partially sank, but kept their heads above water. By the time they were rescued, they were so cold they could barely speak. Fogleman ferried them to the cabin, where they were wrapped in blankets to warm by the fire. Meanwhile, young William Woodridge and the overseer of his family farm rescued a dozen victims with the help of a long pole and their skiff. Carefully avoiding large crowds of swimmers, they saved about forty-five men and built a bonfire on a spot of dry land.

Still floating in the river, Rush heard men calling out support to one another in army and prison camp slang: "Lie down and keep cool," "Fresh fish," "Mister, here's your mule." But not everyone was feeling sociable. Lugenbeal, in his alligator box, kept quiet when others were nearby. Some survivors were so terrified, and so alert to the threat of others in the water, that they would not even allow their rescuers to approach.

As the survivors drifted into the flooded cottonwoods and willow trees on the Arkansas side, a new problem presented itself. "As it got lighter," White wrote, "I could see comrades all around me, some in trees and some on drift-wood, and nearly all naked. To make it worse, the buffalo gnats were so thick that they nearly ate us up."

Otto Bardon, clinging with a group of survivors to flooded saplings and shivering in the cold, broke open a floating trunk but found that "it contained only ladies' dresses so it was no help to us." It was an odd time to be concerned about being caught in a dress, particularly because, as Bardon added, "One of these men that had clung to the trunk was so cold that he drowned with his arms around a tree." Instead, they remained exposed and were tormented by gnats and mosquitoes until their rescue at about 9 a.m.

J. Walter Elliott and his companion floated three miles before reaching a stationary raft of driftwood near the Arkansas shore, where he crawled onto a cypress log and found he had difficulty using his legs. He took three packets of quinine that one of the Sisters of Charity had given him and rubbed his legs until he could stand and walk. His companion remained listless, and that prompted Elliott to begin hitting him with a switch. The man groaned each time and begged him to stop, but eventually he came around and climbed onto the log. Together they pulled a young woman and two men from the water, though the three died of exposure within minutes. Elliott watched the sunrise from his spot atop the drift. Up and down the river he could see men on debris, on rafts of driftwood, perched on snags, clinging to flooded trees. About a hundred yards upriver he saw a group atop a flooded barn.

James Brody, who had floated with fifteen or so men on a large board, and who had lost one sock to a drowning man, had by now made it to what was actually a flooded log stable, where twenty-three men awaited rescue. After the sun came up, "as far as the eye could see, upon every old snag and every little piece of drift big enough, you would see a man. That sight I never will forget. I see it now as I pen these lines." He also saw a man swim to a drift a short distance away who had been "scalded almost to pieces" and who hollered "boys, it is going to kill me" before he died. "Then, there was a nice mule swam out to us just after daylight. He had a piece of railing twelve or fourteen feet long tied to his halter strap. One of the boys got down and unfastened it. What became of the mule I do not know, as he was there in the water the last I saw of him with just his back, neck and head out of water." Soon they saw the smoke of the approaching *Jenny Lind*, which sent smaller boats to rescue them. A doctor on board "gave us something to make us throw up the water," though Brody did not vomit until later, in a Memphis hospital.

In the early light, J. Walter Elliott watched the young man repeatedly trying to climb a tree trunk, each time losing his grip and falling. The man was clearly about to go under when Barton poled into view, retrieved him, and took him to the barn roof. Soon the *Jenny Lind* dropped anchor nearby, and Barton began transferring survivors to the steamer. Elliott and his companion were the last to go. He later wrote that he was helped aboard by an Ohio lieutenant whom he had known in prison, whose name was McCord but who was affectionately known, oddly enough, as "Susan." Elliott recalled that Susan "had the autograph fever" toward the close of his prison stay, "but I reckon he lost his Andersonville collection," because when he saw him he was dressed only in "a bob-tailed shirt. I stripped & gave him a pair of red flannel drawers." Stunned to see a dugout canoe pull up to the boat with Daniel McLeod inside, "I helped lift him on board and lay him on deck and gave him a tumbler of whisky."

As the *Pocahontas*, the *Rosadella*, the *Bostonia II*, and the *Jenny Lind* nosed in and out of the flooded trees, two more steamers arrived: The *Rose Hambleton* and the *Silver Spray*. The latter picked up Congressman Snow, Commodore Smith, Perry Summerville,

William McFarland, and the woman he had seen dropping the infant into the water—all of whom survived. Summerville had been picked up a few miles from Memphis by a man in a canoe who ferried him to the *Silver Spray*. He was freezing, could not stand, and was spitting blood. "After I had been there a few minutes a young man was brought in who was so badly scalded that his skin slipped off from the shoulders to the hands," he later wrote. "They wrapped him up in oil and he walked the floor until a few minutes before his death. There was a lady brought in also who had a husband and some children on board. She was almost crazy. I don't think she ever heard of them after that terrible morning."

Aboard the *Pocahontas*, McCrory ate breakfast, then sidled up to the bar and asked for a brandy. The bartender set out a bottle and a glass, and when McCrory held up his treasured wallet and said proudly that he could pay, the bartender said it was on the house. McCrory recalled that the survivors congregated on the starboard side, while the dead were placed on the larboard, and that a few who initially survived made the crossing from one side to the other before the boat landed at Memphis.

McFarland—who either was obsessed with Big Tennessee or was making things up, recalled that he again saw the big man near Memphis, where he refused to come aboard a rescue boat and swam the rest of the way. Big Tennessee—or, at least, his legend—also was said to have later refused a ride from a hack at the waterfront, and a detail of guards had to march him to a hospital.

At the Memphis waterfront, which was now teeming with people, women of the Sanitary Commission met the survivors; washed the soot, mud, and blood from them; and gave them blankets and red long johns. As the day wore on, large crowds remained at the waterfront, handing out coffee, food, clothes, and blankets, or simply gawking. The survivors were carried to several hospitals—Adams, Overton, Washington, Gayoso, Officers—and to the Soldiers' Home. At Adams, McLeod was told that one of his legs—the right one, which had been shattered at Shiloh, and which he had convinced the field surgeon to save—would have to be amputated. At Gayoso, Anna Annis was heavily sedated and treated for shock and burns; she fell asleep while begging for news about her family.

J. Walter Elliott went with "Susan" to the telegraph office, where he gave his correct name, rank, and infantry division. It was the first time he had given his true identity since his capture, and, as he noted, "a Cincinnati paper published it so next day." As a result he was listed as a survivor, while his assumed name was listed among the lost.

By early afternoon, the search for survivors was called off, though bodies continued to turn up for weeks, some as far downriver as Vicksburg. Among them was a dark-skinned soldier wearing a horsehair bracelet, and a red-haired man with an eagle tattooed on his arm, neither of whom was ever identified. Most of the bodies were never retrieved.

In the confusion of the aftermath, Romulus Tolbert's hometown newspaper reported that he and his friend John Maddox had been killed. In fact, Tolbert was sent to Adams Hospital, where he was treated for chills. Maddox ended up at the Memphis Soldiers Home.

Chapter Thirteen

IN A DEAD MAN'S POCKET

A MONG THE SOLDIERS' JOURNALS THAT SURVIVED THE disaster, John Clark Ely's is one of the few that encompass the entire spectrum of events—the war, camp life, imprisonment, and finally the doomed voyage upriver from Memphis. Most diaries were lost during the disaster. John Clark Ely's survived, waterlogged. Ely did not.

Before the war, Ely taught writing in school in Cuyahoga Falls, Ohio, where he lived with his wife, Julia, and their four children. He was handsome, with a full dark beard, and, judging from a surviving photo, liked to wear his kepi cocked jauntily to one side.

After the disaster, all that survived of his life were the moments he had recorded—the prelude. He was an orderly sergeant in the 115th Ohio infantry before being captured near Murfreesboro, Tennessee, in December 1864 and sent to Andersonville, after which he was promoted to lieutenant *in absentia*. What is most remarkable about his journal, aside from the fact of its survival, is the similarity of many of his accounts, whether he was a soldier or a prisoner.

They illustrate the maxim: "Wherever you go, there you are." As he inched toward his doom he wrote most often of performing "usual duties" in army camp—distributing rations, building and repairing shelters, writing and reading letters, cutting firewood, and participating in drills. Now and then Ely's musings turned lyrical. Of the war he wrote, "Oh, how deep and dark is the human mind, how black are many of its pages, how edge'd with red and splattered, too." He wrote of "the dark bitter flood" that flowed through his veins, then added, "Band went downtown for a general serenade this evening. Large drove of horses passed today."

He wrote of picking blackberries and attending church services. After one service he noted that the sermons seemed dull and failed to evoke the realities of his life. He wrote of two women, Lizzie and Angeline, who visited a sick soldier for a "gay smutty time." As the first menace crept his way, on August 31, 1864, he wrote, "Excitement continues, rebels coming closer, will probably see them today . . ." He rode into a town in an ambulance to buy a bottle of whiskey. Eight days later he wrote, "One year ago today I was home with those most dear, will another year find me there to enjoy their love and happiness, I hope and trust I may." On September 23 he wrote of receiving a care package from his wife, Julia, which included a bottle of wine, "a lump of maple," a can of tomatoes, and a letter. From September 30 to October 16: All were beautiful or very fine mornings.

Ely wrote of heavy and brisk cannonades during the night and on the morning of his birthday, when he turned thirty-nine, "for better or worse." It would be his last. He was captured the next day and marched with about one hundred other prisoners, including twelve musicians, to a camp near Nashville, where he lay about the next day and wrote a letter to Julia. From there the men marched in sleet and snow along muddy roads, through abandoned towns and forests of oak and chestnut trees. He was soon "very lame." He spent his last Christmas on a train loaded with prisoners, passing through West Point, Mississippi. "Hungry, dirty, sleepy and lousy," he wrote. "Will another Christmas find us again among friends and loved ones?"

In late January he had arrived at Andersonville, where adhering to routines kept him going. His description of arriving at the stockade was remarkably brief and opaque: The ground was sandy, the weather was cold, and there were four thousand prisoners inside. "Commenced fixing a place to stay, worked all day," he wrote.

He wrote frequently, even in the purgatory of prison, of "fine days," but by February 12, it was evident that a fine day could only count for so much. He wrote, "Again a fine day ... Feel much depressed in feeling today, anxiety of home weighs heavy." On February 22, someone stole from his shanty a shirt, a pair of pants, a haversack, and four days' worth of rations. Five days later, he was sick again. Just as he seemed to be reaching his lowest ebb, after hearing unfounded rumors of a parole for months, Ely and the other Andersonville prisoners were removed from the stockade. He departed on March 24, traveling by train and boat to Jackson and from there to the Big Black River bridge on foot. In an odd coincidence, the Confederate troops who released his group to the Union Army were the same who had captured him near Murfreesboro. He immediately began building a shelter—something he had gotten pretty good at by now—and fashioned a bower of cane above it for added shade. He then wrote a letter to Julia. He kept his mind on the future.

In early April, Ely was sick again, and he wrote Julia another letter. He was feeling better by April 13, when the prisoners heard a heavy cannonade in nearby Vicksburg, signaling the fall of Richmond and the surrender of Robert E. Lee. He was jubilant. On April 14, he wrote of his joy at the war's end and the news that they would be exchanged: "Bully, may we soon see our sweethearts." On April 15, the prisoners from Andersonville drafted a resolution thanking the Sanitary and Christian commissions for their aid. On April 16, he wrote, "Beautiful morning and day, wrote to Julia." On April 18, they heard of Lincoln's assassination. April 19 was another fine day.

On April 24 he wrote, "Beautiful day but very warm sun, about 10 a.m. we were ordered to take train to Vicksburg and then up the river, went from cars to boat Sultana, a large but not very fine boat. Vicksburg is truly a city set on not only a hill but hills. Left sometime in night for Cairo, Ill." The next day: "Fine day, still going up river very high over country every where, no places along the river where white people live but very many monuments of where people had been." April 26: "Very fine day, still upward we go"

There was no punctuation at the end.

Chapter Fourteen

THE BEGINNING
OF THE END

A s J. WALTER ELLIOTT ROAMED THE MEMPHIS WATER-
front he ran into George Safford, whom he had known back
in Indiana, and who was searching for his father's body. "Together
he and I opened more than a hundred coffins on the wharf," Elliott
wrote, "hoping to have the satisfaction of giving him a burial, that his
body should not be lodged on some bar to become food for fishes."

It is hard to imagine a more daunting task than peering into a
hundred coffins containing the remains of people who had died in
every conceivable horrible way, and Safford was no doubt equivo-
cal about finding his father there. Though he desperately wanted
to know what had happened to him, and finding his father's body
would have been better than not, it would have eliminated the
chance that he had somehow survived. As it turned out, he was not
there, so Safford and Elliott decided to visit a local newspaper office
to see if there had been any word. There they met a U.S. Army scout
who had been aboard the *Sultana*, who produced the elder Safford's
watch and said that he had, in Elliott's words, been rescued "in an

unconscious state by some Negroes on President's Island." George Safford took a boat to the island, where he found his father alive. It was likely the high point of the younger Safford's life.

Accounts of the number of survivors vary, as do those of the total number of passengers aboard the boat when it went down. Many people boarded without being counted, and the counting itself was questionable. By the most reliable accounts, more than twenty-four hundred people were aboard—about six times the boat's legal carrying capacity. Of the more than seven hundred who initially survived the disaster, between two hundred and three hundred died in Memphis hospitals in the days after. Even allowing for a fairly wide margin of error, the accepted toll of about seventeen hundred made it the worst known maritime disaster in American history and it would remain so even after the sinking of the *Titanic,* in which about fifteen hundred died.

The Washington, Adams, and Gayoso hospitals each took in about one hundred fifty survivors, while Overton took in just under one hundred. About two hundred fifty of the less seriously injured, including John Maddox, Oglevie Hamblin, William Peacock, and Commodore Smith, went to the Soldiers' Home. The *Memphis Daily Bulletin* reported that an additional twenty-four people did not require or declined treatment. For many it would be years before their injuries took their toll. But in some cases those injuries and debilitations would be the primary or contributory cause of death up to sixty years later.

Erastus Winters was taken to the Adams Hospital, which, like all the facilities, was overwhelmed by the disaster. He reported that his burns went unattended until almost nightfall. In the following days, Winters roamed the hospital searching for old friends and meeting new ones, including the indomitable Daniel McLeod. Among the other patients at Adams were Romulus Tolbert, Truman Smith, George Robinson, Stephen Gaston, and Nathaniel Foglesong. Robinson was treated for chills, scalded arms, and injuries to his wrist and chest; Gaston, for scalds and a thigh wound; Foglesong, for diarrhea. Only nine men of Tolbert's and Maddox's 8th Indiana Cavalry survived, and one of those later died of exhaustion at Gayoso.

In *Disaster on the Mississippi*, Gene Eric Salecker noted that Indiana, the only state that attempted to compile a cumulative tally of its soldiers lost on the *Sultana*, settled on a figure of two hundred forty-seven lost of the four hundred thirteen Indianans on board.

Survivor John Lowery Walker, who was taken to the Soldiers' Home, was less concerned with his own recuperation than with learning the fate of his best friend, William Morrow. The next day, after hearing that Morrow might be at Overton, Walker borrowed a pair of pants and set out for the hospital, barefoot. He later remembered that "people would stop and look, and I could hear such expressions as, 'There goes one of them,' or 'There's a Sultana victim.'" He arrived at Overton before it opened at 9 a.m. and sat down outside, where he could see the clock. As he entered the door he encountered Morrow leaving, in search of him. They embraced. Walker recalled that it was "indeed a happy meeting; we had been together for so long, had endured the same hardships, and had shared the same joys, that only those whose lives have been so closely attached to each other can fully comprehend just what this reunion meant to us." It may have been similar for Tolbert and Maddox, but there is no record of their reunion, and in fact they lost sight of each other until reaching home.

Simeon Chelf, who survived after another man allowed him to share his floating log, also ended up at the Soldiers' Home, where he remained for more than a week. The April 28, 1865, Memphis *Daily Bulletin* listed a Private Richard Pearce—whom some identified as Big Tennessee—among the survivors being treated at the Gayoso Hospital for six days.

The disaster was obviously big news in Memphis, as it was in the passengers' hometowns, though its importance was muted elsewhere by coverage of the Lincoln assassination and the end of the war. On April 29, the *New York Times* ran a brief article titled "Dreadful Disaster," and four days later the newspaper noted, "No troops belonging to States east of Ohio were lost." Then the *Times* apparently lost interest and ceased mentioning the disaster altogether. *Harper's Weekly* ran an illustration of the boat in flames. The Memphis *Argus* interviewed first mate William Rowberry, who reported that he "saw a flash, and the next thing he knew he was falling into the water with a portion of the pilot house." Slightly injured, he had grabbed on to a plank with five soldiers. In addition to Rowberry, the *Sultana*'s chief engineer, Nathan Wintringer, and pilot George Kayton survived, the latter of whom was found uninjured on Island 42. As Elliott pointed out, Kayton knew better than anyone else the nature of the currents and the lay of the land along that reach of the river, even if most of that land was inundated by the flood. Twenty-three other crew members survived, including deck and cabin hands, which would later become a source of controversy because they had allegedly forced other passengers from the eventually righted yawl. Five crew members escaped aboard the yawl, and all five of the crew members' wives aboard died. Wintringer left Memphis for Pittsburgh shortly after the disaster; a subsequent investigation concluded that the boilers had been inadequately repaired and that he was ultimately responsible, though one crew member claimed the cause was the frequent careening of the boat as the crowds moved from one side to the other—an argument that seems implausible because most of the passengers were asleep at the time.

On May 3, the *Jenny Lind* returned to the site of the wreck, and its crew retrieved several bodies. The next day, the boat retrieved twenty-eight more, and the *Rosadella* found six. Fogleman and his sons tied twelve decomposing bodies to the shore for recovery. Scores of others were recovered at various points along the river, but some were buried where they were found as the water fell, because they were in such advanced states of decay. One boat pilot saw bodies being devoured by feral hogs. The Memphis *Argus* reported on May 7 that a total of one hundred thirty-three more bodies had been found. Eventually about two hundred were buried in city cemeteries. The majority were never accounted for.

When the steamer *Arkansas* traveled upriver soon after the disaster, its crew reported that the water was "full of bodies floating like cordwood, and all of them were dressed in the uniforms of Union soldiers." The engineer of the *Vindicator* reported that his crew had to frequently dislodge bodies from the boat's paddlewheels.

Among the survivors, Anna Annis remained at the Gayoso for at least a month, possibly as long as six weeks, during which time she searched numerous morgues in vain for the bodies of her husband and daughter. Newspaper articles reported that the Sisters of Charity collected clothes for her, and the crew of the *Essex* raised $1,000 to help. Annis eventually departed for her home in Oshkosh, Wisconsin. The Chicago Opera Troupe, which had disembarked in Memphis before the disaster, also held a benefit for the survivors; their performance and other fundraisers distributed money to beneficiaries, including $200 to Dewitt Clinton Spikes and $100 to Daniel McLeod.

A few days afterward, Truman Smith was walking downtown in his red underwear. When asked if he had been on the boat and he said he was, he received a new suit of clothes and $13. Such scenes were repeated all over town. After the hospitals overflowed, private residents took in survivors, and one woman even took in the bodies of the Spikes women, fearing they would not be properly cared for otherwise (they were buried in Elmwood Cemetery the next day). Seth Hardin ran an ad in the local papers offering a $100 reward for anyone who recovered his wife's body, but there is no evidence that she was ever found.

Young remained a bundle of nerves after his rescue. He could not sleep for several nights, and even when he was able to sleep, "Night after night I would jump up on hearing any noise, and I had to change my sleeping-place from a bunk to a cot, for I had bumped my head till it was sore." After two weeks in Memphis, he was put on a steamer home.

Fast recalled that he also wore only his red long johns after being released from the hospital. "We promenaded the streets of Memphis three days in that picturesque garb, hatless and shoeless. Then Uncle Sam came to our relief, hunted us out a full new suit of army blue, and soon we were on our way to Cairo and Camp Chase."

By then, most of the surviving paroled prisoners were once again setting off for home, where for many of them a different, and longer, survival challenge awaited.

Two days after the disaster, approximately three hundred surviving soldiers boarded the *Belle of St. Louis*, headed upriver. They were bound for Cairo, Illinois, a rowdy steamboat and railroad town at the confluence of the Ohio and Mississippi rivers. From there they would travel by train to Camp Chase, near Columbus, Ohio, and be discharged.

Senator-elect Snow had managed to get out of town the day before, also headed for Cairo. Kayton, the *Sultana*'s pilot, chose—perhaps wisely—to head in the opposite direction, to New Orleans.

Within a few days, about a hundred of the survivors in Memphis hospitals had died, which left nearly four hundred men who were ready to travel but had no clear plan for getting home. A group of them, impatient to leave and weary of the military's delays, approached J. Walter Elliott and asked him to help organize their transportation. Elliott, who said he was selected because he was the senior able-bodied officer among those still in Memphis, clearly relished the opportunity to assume a leadership role. He managed to book passage for about two hundred fifty men, including Tolbert and Maddox, on the *Belle of Memphis*, also bound for Cairo. That Saturday he toured the Memphis hospitals and invited those who were well enough to travel to come to supper at the Soldiers' Home, where he unveiled the itinerary.

A few of the more industrious survivors had already departed on their own, including Rush and a friend who smuggled themselves aboard an earlier steamer and, "being out of money, begged our way home, telling our story as we went." From the steamboat, Rush made his way overland to Lake Erie, where he managed to find a boat and row the remaining twelve miles alone, in the middle of the night, to his home in Sandusky, Ohio.

Some of the survivors were so afraid of setting foot on a boat again that they booked travel by train, which delayed their departure by several weeks. Those who were in the worst shape—about a hundred and thirty men—remained behind in Memphis hospitals. "Almost forgotten among the departure of the paroled prisoners," Salecker noted, "were the *Sultana's* surviving crew members," though they would not be forgotten for long. The five crewmen who fled in the yawl were later arrested in St. Louis, allegedly for contributing to the deaths of other passengers.

About a dozen injured men who were still able to travel were placed on the *Belle of Memphis's* cabin floor. Most had to be carried aboard and nursed by their friends along the way. The remainder bedded down in whatever space was available, much as they had on the *Sultana*, though conditions now were obviously much improved. The atmosphere was one of trepidation as the *Belle of Memphis* departed the city shortly after nightfall. The men on the deck, who included Tolbert and Maddox, were notably quiet. The river was dark but for the rippling water reflected in the lights of the boat. It was the second time they had left Memphis on an upriver steamer in the darkness, and nerves were on edge. If anyone felt a tinge of joy about being headed home, it was doubtless undercut by memories of similar feelings only a week before. During the night, Elliott wrote, some of the passengers sprang up at each unexpected sound, and John Lowery Walker recalled that the men became "greatly alarmed" when the boat ran aground as the pilot took a shortcut between bends in the channel.

William McFarland, among those who had taken matters into his own hands and caught a ride on the *St. Patrick*, reported similar misgivings. He was so frightened about being on the boat that he climbed into the yawl and did not get out until he reached Evansville, Indiana. He later said he jumped every time the crew blew off steam or sounded the whistle.

When the *Belle of Memphis* reached Cairo, the injured were taken to area hospitals, and the rest were put up in army barracks. A few slipped away to the city's Soldiers' Home in search of food. The next morning they departed Cairo by train and reached Mattoon, Illinois at about 11 a.m. Along the way, some again felt a wave of panic each time the train lurched across rough spots in the rails. It was becoming clear that surviving the aftermath of the disaster was going to be a long and disturbing haul. Most of the men had had nothing to eat for twenty-four hours and were grateful to see that the people of Mattoon had turned out at the station to greet them with baskets of food—roasted chicken, boiled ham, cake, pies, eggs, and hot coffee. That night they were treated to welcome speeches at a local hotel. Many of the men no doubt wanted only to get home, though William Boor, for one, was up for the celebration. His favorite part was when a group of forty women dressed in red, white, and blue sang patriotic songs. It was at the Mattoon event that the public evolution of the *Sultana* story began—a process that would continue, for many, for the rest of their lives. As survivor William Hulit observed, "some comrade would give his experience while a prisoner, or relate the frightful scenes and marvelous escape from the burning boat." Though it seems strange that such terrible memories would be trotted out so soon for entertainment, Hulit was there, and the outpouring of memoirs and public speeches in the coming months and years confirm a pressing need among some of the survivors to lay claim to the tragedy. Others, including Tolbert and Maddox, had the opposite reaction and rarely spoke of it again.

Because the survivors' passage had not been booked beyond Mattoon, Elliott had to bargain with the station master to allow the train cars to continue to Indianapolis, pledging that they would be returned. He then telegraphed the Indiana governor and the mayor of Terre Haute to announce their impending arrival, and the train departed at 1 a.m. From Terre Haute the train continued to Indianapolis, where the governor met the survivors and intervened on their behalf, saying it was unnecessary for them to continue on to Camp Chase to be discharged. He ordered the sick to be admitted to area hospitals and the rest to be sent home. The soldiers who were not from Indiana continued on to Columbus.

Tolbert and Maddox, who were separated during the disaster and afterward treated at different hospitals, did not keep up with each other on the trains either. Maddox's chronic diarrhea, which he had contracted in camp, and which had gotten worse at Cahaba, hit him hard again on the way home, when he was further weakened from his *Sultana* ordeal. As he later wrote, "I was taken with Chronic Diarrhea as I was coming home on the cars between Cairo, Ill. and Indianapolis, Ind. It was between the first and forth of May 1865 I was not with eney one that I noad the name of All the comred that had bin with me in the prison had bin seprated by the expotion of the Sultana I did not report to eney dockter as I thought get a furlow home."

He and Tolbert both arrived in Madison, Indiana, by train on May 6.

Tolbert would later write his own brief account in support of Maddox's application for a military pension, in which he claimed physical disability as a result of his service: "I am ackuainted with John C. Maddox," he said, in obvious understatement. "I have been ackuainted with him every since he was a boy. I believe him to be truthfull and onest. I was with him in prison and on the Boat Sultana when it exploded and then we were seperated I did not see him until after I got home and not living in the same neighborhood did not see him verry ofton. He told me he had diarea bad. I took diarea under the same circumstances. But few left after the explosion and being seperated makes the required evidence hard to find. Will he haft to go unpensioned because his eye witnesses died in prison or was blowed away or drowned."

The answer would be a long time in coming.

Chapter Fifteen

HOME

After months, even years, of resting their heads on the hard ground of army camps, spooning on cold winter nights with other men, and in some cases sleeping in upright fetal positions in holes in the ground, the *Sultana* survivors finally made it home, where they could retire at night to their own beds. For Tolbert it was the familiar wooden four-poster in his mother's home. But many of them slept fitfully, whether as a result of injuries or diseases or because they had developed a bad case of nerves. It was not as if they left it all behind.

For the most part, the general public did leave it behind. After four years of massive bloodletting, and with everyone's attention focused on the fallout from the Lincoln assassination and the end of the war, the magnitude of the disaster could penetrate only so far into the national psyche. Stories of Southern depravity were favorite chew-toys in the postwar North, and for a while there was an eager audience for prison tales. Henry Wirz, the commandant of Andersonville, was tried and hanged for war crimes, partly as a result of a groundswell of popular support for revenge against the Rebels. (Champ Ferguson was also hanged.) But the *Sultana* story was not so satisfying to contemplate. The disaster was overwhelming and the enemy unclear. The Union Army had won the war, and the number of casualties had far exceeded the losses aboard one steamboat. The story quickly faded from the headlines, even as the federal government undertook a perfunctory investigation into the events that brought it about.

Many saw what happened on the *Sultana* as a terrible accident. A few, particularly among the survivors, claimed that it was a case of Rebel sabotage. In May 1888, a St. Louis newspaper published an article about a veterans' reunion in which a local resident, William Streeter, claimed that a Confederate blockade-runner had sabotaged the *Sultana* by placing a bomb—specifically, a disguised torpedo—in the coal bin, knowing that it would later be loaded into the furnace. The story was incredible for many reasons, not the least of which was the difficulty of secreting a bomb aboard the boat and the unlikelihood that the crew would have failed to recognize that something was amiss. Added to that, the problems with the *Sultana*'s boilers were by then well known. Testimony during a congressional inquiry left no doubt of that.

Though testimony at the tribunals and inquiries revealed that the great loss of life was the responsibility of the army's chain of command and the greed of private contractors, the prosecutors showed a lack of verve for punishing anyone. They pointed an accusing finger at Wintringer, the engineer, but he suffered no significant repercussions. His engineer's license was revoked, but in no time the governing agency, the St. Louis Board of Inspectors, reinstated it. In June 1866, a military tribunal found Captain Frederick Speed guilty of negligence and ordered him dismissed from the army, but the verdict was reversed by the judge advocate general, and Speed was honorably discharged. Speed chose to remain in Vicksburg, where he became a criminal court judge and a powerful Mississippi politician. A street in the city still bears his name.

The commissary general over Union prisoners concluded, following the inquiry, that Speed and Captain Rueben Hatch were "the most censurable" but that Captain Kerns (who supervised the loading) and Captain Williams had also contributed to the disaster. Hatch claimed in a rather petulant letter to a fellow officer on September 29, 1865, that he "had no control over the loading the steamer Sultana" and predicted that Speed's dispatches would provide supporting evidence, though in the end he never had to prove anything. The prosecutors in one inquiry were unable to compel Hatch to testify, likely because of his political connections. A request to the secretary of war to have him arrested and transported to Vicksburg was ignored. Hatch's career did end on an ignoble note, however. On a later trip aboard the steamer *Atlantic*, he deposited almost $15,000 in government funds in the boat's safe, which was subsequently, curiously, robbed. The thief was caught, but the recovered funds did not include $8,500 in government money that Hatch claimed to have put there, and he was forced to pay it back.

Ultimately the *Sultana* inquiries were mostly for show. Even the death toll was never fully reckoned. Officially, it was listed at just more than twelve hundred, which failed to include an entire trainload of passengers from Camp Fisk. Chester Berry, who later became a preacher, lamented in his book *Loss of the Sultana and Reminiscences of Survivors*, first published in 1892, that because of the public's limited interest the tragedy found "no place in American history." He found that "strange."

The investigations did reach one meaningful conclusion: That the boilers were the cause of the explosion. After the last survivors departed Memphis and the river level began to fall, much of the *Sultana*'s surviving machinery was recovered from the wreck, piled on barges, carried to Hen Island, and sold for salvage. The *Sultana*'s safe, containing at least $32,000, more than half of it in gold, was never recovered. Two weeks after the disaster, pieces of the boilers were inspected, and one was intact, indicating that three of the four had blown. Salecker concludes that the explosion was caused by too much pressure and too little water in the boilers, the latter condition being exacerbated by the frequent careening of the top-heavy, over-loaded boat, which left water gaps that caused the tubing to overheat. There is no proof that the patch was a factor, but it seems logical.

For the survivors, there was no real closure, and even returning soldiers who had not endured the *Sultana* disaster often found their homecomings anticlimactic. As survivor Benjamin Magee wrote years later, "With many of us there was a very noticeable difference between 1862 and 1865—between the going and the coming vol-unteer. No fluttering handkerchiefs greeted the return of our regi-ment. No committees of invitation or reception met us at the depot; no loud sounding cannon belched forth thunders of welcome. More than half of the 208,000 Indiana soldiers were already discharged, and the land was full of soldiers then; nearly every other man you met was a soldier." The returning veterans, he wrote, "had been coming home, and kept coming, till their coming had become monotonous, and ceased to cause remark or ripple in the busy circles of life." The war had been their shared world, and it was over. After they were mustered out in July, the *Sultana* survivors faced the next phase of what was to be their long-running challenge, largely on their own.

They were in some ways primed by past travails, but in others they were dangerously ill equipped for the new and different set of stresses that came to bear during the remainder of their lives. A person in any survival situation goes through predictable phases. There are the stages of facing death—denial, anger, bargaining, depression, and acceptance—and, as Laurence Gonzales has pointed out, a person who does not linger too long in any of the stages has a better chance of survival. Denial can cause a person to ignore important cues. Anger can be self-defeating. Bargaining is largely ineffective, and depression sets in motion physical changes that both harm the body and contaminate the chemistry of the brain. Acceptance is probably the most conducive to survival but can itself lead to passivity toward death.

To hold death at bay for as long as possible, a person must strike a balance, at each stage, between thoughtfulness and blind resolve—not an easy task. And just as the descent of a perilous mountain is technically more difficult than the ascent—a fact that is remarkably easy to forget—the *Sultana* survivors had to come to terms with the cumulative losses, with the injuries and scars, both physical and mental, that they would carry with them the rest of their lives.

THERE WAS A BLINDING RAINSTORM, with vivid lightning, the day Tolbert finally made it home. It was early May, a time when the fields of Saluda were rank with yellow wildflowers, awaiting the plow, and ferns and may-apples were pushing through the mulch of the wooded ravines. The familiar landmarks of his former life were still there: The stone bridge spanning a rushing freshet along the pike between Madison and Saluda; his family's red-brick farmhouse,

with its wooden gingerbread framing the front porch, midway between the Tryus Church and the cemetery where his father lay; the
little hamlet of Paynesville, where Maddox's family farmed.

But otherwise the world had changed in profound ways, and it
must have felt strange to finally be home. His brother Tyrus was
dead. His younger brother Sammie was basically a broken old man
at fifteen. Daniel had lost three fingers and the use of his left hand
and would never work again. Mathew, who had endured scurvy and
pneumonia as a prisoner of war, would soon marry and move away.
Only Silas had come through four years of war largely unscathed.
Romulus himself had passed through his own nine circles of hell
and was now back where he started from.

The *Courier*, which had reported him dead only a few weeks
before, announced on May 6, 1865: "Romulus Talbot and John
Maddux, both of company H, 8th Indiana Cavalry, arrived in Madison yesterday, en route to their homes in Saluda township. They
are among the survivors of the ill-fated Sultana, on which they had
taken passage as paroled Union prisoners."

During the previous week, both had taken on entirely new identities. They were now *Sultana* survivors. Tolbert's momentous capture was reduced to a footnote. "Talbot was with Messrs. Knowles,
Taylor and Sherman, at the time those unfortunate soldiers fell into
the hands of the rebel fiends and were so cruelly butchered," the
newspaper reported. "He was taken prisoner, but escaped death.
Maddux was taken at another time."

Among the first things Tolbert's friends and family would have
noticed, aside from the fact that he was gaunt and tired, was that he
had trouble talking, not only because he was naturally reserved or
because the memories were so raw, but because his tongue had been
pierced by one of the bullets that struck him during his capture. He

had also lost a tooth and was pained by the gunshot wound to his shoulder. He could not reach his arms very high.

Inside his mother's house was a photograph of him with his friend James Taylor, taken before their enlistment. Now in the hands of his great-grandson, the photo reveals two boys who clearly thought of themselves as men. Their cheeks, tinted by a photographic artist's hand, are rosy, but their expressions are resolute. Tolbert's arms are crossed as if he were spoiling for a fight. It is probably the last photo of Taylor, who was killed in the ambush in which Tolbert was captured.

In another family photo, taken a few years later, Tolbert looks more wary. He is handsome in a slightly pouty way that brings to mind a nineteenth-century Edward Norton. Then, in the next photo, taken after his return, the real change comes. As in every other photographic portrait of him, his hair is carefully coiffed and he is dressed to the nines. But he looks much older, more rugged and worn. His expression is defiant.

Though Tolbert moved back into his mother's house and began trying to reconstruct his life, the war was clearly still on his mind. The *Courier* reported that he and Maddox attended the first Jefferson County soldiers' reunion in Madison in July 1866, along with his brothers Samuel and Mathew, Maddox's brother William, and their former commanding officer, Thomas Graham, who had survived the ambush in which Tolbert was captured. Tolbert was also among a group of veterans who ran a notice in the paper urging others to attend, to help keep the memory of their service alive.

The reunions were bittersweet affairs, typically held on the anniversaries of major battles, and would continue for decades until all the veterans were gone. Tolbert and Maddox attended an 8th Indiana Cavalry reunion at a campground in nearby Chelsea, where the veterans perhaps felt more comfortable—away from their houses, outside by the firelight, with other men who had experienced similar trials and were trying to assimilate them into their lives. Tolbert and his brother Samuel were again present at the two-day reunion in Madison of Rousseau's raiders, at which, the *Courier* noted, the men "assembled in the City Hall to grasp hands once more and rehearse the story of the days that tried men's souls." The reunion, on August 19 through 21, 1879, began with a 5:30 a.m. reveille, followed by an artillery salute and a march through the city, complete with "crippled veterans in omnibuses" and a band. The day's activities included addresses by dignitaries, singing by a choir, the reading of the poem "Relics and Recollections" by Captain W.G. Lawder, and military reenactments that were no doubt somewhat awkward to watch.

If Tolbert sought to preserve some of the camaraderie that had been born of dramatic, shared trials, his postwar life was characterized by a striving for normalcy. After his mother died in 1868, he decided to strike out on his own and moved to Olney, Illinois, where he opened a grocery store. In the spring of 1873, he married Sophronia Eldridge, a strong-boned and strong-willed woman thirteen years younger than he. From his pension application it is evident he was still recovering from his experiences: In March 1875, an examining surgeon reported that he weighed only one hundred thirty-five pounds (at five feet seven inches tall), could not raise his arm above his shoulder, and had lost bits of muscle and bone that limited the use of his tongue "and slightly interferes with distinct articulation in speech." According to Tolbert's own testimony, his wounds had largely healed at the time of his release from Cahaba, and further medical treatment was "impracticable & could do no good whatever."

He and Sophronia had their first child in 1874, and a few years later they moved back to Jefferson County, where he bought his own farm. It was a small parcel of swampy land on a plateau in Chelsea, not far from his family's old home place. There he built a simple frame house with a picket fence—perhaps the kind of place he had dreamed of during his ordeal—and planted maple trees in the yard. Sophronia convinced him to quit drinking and to move their membership to the New Bethel Methodist Church. She had a template for an orderly life together, and Tolbert followed it. They raised five children: Stella, Edmund, Rolland, Laura, and Ambrose, and they eventually took in Sophronia's elderly mother, Asenath Eldridge. To judge from a photo of the family lined up along the picket fence, it appears that Tolbert managed to find something like normalcy—something as close to peace and plenty as was possible under the circumstances.

Amid the outpouring of often grandiose and melodramatic published reminiscences in the postwar years, Tolbert and Maddox remained notably mum. They were not overly literate—Maddox signed his enlistment papers with an X, though he later wrote his account for the pension board in longhand—and neither seems to have felt a compulsion to participate. Tolbert's pivotal moment near Campbellton, when he turned in excitement and fear toward his assailants and was shot through the jaw and shoulder, would be preserved only in his memory and, briefly, in official records. The same would be true of the week he spent lying at death's door in a stranger's house in Georgia, drifting in and out of consciousness; of the six weeks in the military hospital in Montgomery; of his imprisonment at Cahaba; and of all the withering episodes that came after—the unnerving train ride to Jackson, when the cars shimmied and threatened to go off the rails and sick and injured men bounced off the walls; the long walk to Vicksburg, with his feet blistered and bleeding as he struggled through the mud; and finally the interminable hours in the river after the explosion of the *Sultana*. Each episode had brought him one step closer to home, yet seemingly farther away. Now he was finally back. For whatever reasons, he was not inclined to record any of it. When his son Rolland asked how he had managed to survive, he said, "I could swim."

But if anyone understood what Tolbert had been through, it was Maddox, whose life, like those of so many of their peers, was profoundly changed by his war experiences. The survivors were like a flock of birds that takes flight from a spreading tree and for a moment maintains and approximates the shape of the tree as it wings away across a field. Some maintained the formation longer than others, but eventually they all broke off on their own. If anyone chanced to meet Tolbert on the street, he would have seemed only a quiet, unassuming farmer. There would have been no obvious sign.

It was different for Maddox. Undercutting whatever joy he may have felt upon returning home, he found that his sister Margaret had died at age twenty-three on the same day the *Sultana* went down. And he and Tolbert, after having spent so many tumultuous days and nights in each other's company, slowly drifted apart. Perhaps their closeness had to do with their having been stuck together so many times, but back within the small confines of Saluda, their lives carried them in different directions. Maddox never worked much again, though he tried. He suffered numerous maladies, including chronic diarrhea, attacks of vertigo, "nervous debility," and "smothering spells."

While Tolbert stayed with Sophronia for the rest of his life, Maddox married five times, and his life had an uneven cast. He often changed the spelling of his name. Born John Christian Maddox, he sometimes spelled his surname Maddux or Maddex, and he went variously by Chris, Christian, John, and, for some reason, C.J. He first married in 1868, but his wife, Elvira, died within two years, after which he moved back in with his parents. Later that same year he married Elvira's sister Margaret, and he stayed with her until 1880, when he moved in with his mother again (his father had by then died) and sued for divorce. Margaret did not bother to show up for court. He next married Mary, but she died in 1884. The following year he married Sarah, who appears to have been the love of his life—he would be buried beside her—and after she died in 1901 he married Martha, who outlived him (and was later buried alongside him and Sarah).

Despite his disabilities, Maddox had trouble getting a $2-per-month pension, in part because of mix-ups over the spelling of his name and because he had lied about his age when he enlisted. He first applied in 1887, saying he had been disabled by diarrhea, which he attributed to bouts of malaria, improper food, impure water, and exposure during the *Sultana* disaster. In various documents he said he had first contracted diarrhea in Nashville, or in camp at Cahaba, or after the disaster. Perhaps it was hard to pinpoint exactly when everything went wrong.

Robert C. Lawson, who served alongside Tolbert and Maddox in the 8th Indiana, filed an affidavit on Maddox's behalf, in which he wrote, "we were separated a while toward the close of the war I know he came sick from the war complaining with Cronic Diarrhea. I have lived a neighbor to him ever since I now of him doctoring with several doctors for two or three years I know of him suffering from said disease to the present time." He added, "I know this by waiting on him while he was sic."

Maddox's decline was unquestionably precipitated by his wartime experience, but there was a cumulative impact, too. As Indiana soldier Benjamin Magee observed after encountering one of his former comrades years later, "something in the sunken lines of his face, in his hair, in the stoop of his shoulders, tells us that the years of peace have broken him more than all the marches and vigils of war."

Tolbert and his brothers struggled with their health, too. The determined, hapless Samuel, who joined a Saluda band as a violinist, two years later disregarded his disabilities and at the still tender age of seventeen reenlisted as a drummer and fifer in the 4th U.S. Infantry, in October 1867. No doubt he wished that he had been a drummer and fifer during the war, instead of a soldier. He was subsequently stationed at Fort Laramie, Wyoming, and served for three years. Afterward he bounced around. When he applied for his pension in 1887, he was thirty-seven years old and unable to do anything that involved taking deep breaths, and he often awoke at night feeling as if he were suffocating. Twenty years after the war, he was still complaining about his side, and his only treatment was the application of liniment. His brothers were as powerless to help him then as they had been during the war. His brother-in-law wrote on behalf of Samuel's pension application to say that he had paid him to do work now and then, but he could do little, and "If he had not been my Brother in law, and poor & needy, I would not have hired him."

Samuel's former captain, A.C. Graves, who saw him again about a decade after the war, said he "looked considerably stouter, but he had not grown much in height." Ten years later, Samuel visited Graves at his home and spent the night. "We talked over our army life, and how we, both, had been broken in health, etc.," Graves recalled. "He asked me if I remembered the trouble he had with his side in the army, and on my replying that I did, we were then out in the stable—and unbuttoning his pants, and pulling up his shirt, he showed me a lump in his side, and asked me to feel of it. I felt of it and it felt almost as large as a hen's egg . . . He also told me that he was very poor, and that he did not know what he was going to do to better himself as he could not labor. He was so poor that he could not pay for the county clerk's seal that attested the affidavit I gave him, so I paid for it."

Samuel's pension application was initially rejected, so he applied again. In addition to the hernia and respiratory problems, he claimed to suffer eye disease as a result of his service. The night Samuel spent with Graves at his home, the two slept in the same bed, "and when we were lying there just before going to sleep, he said, 'Capt., I have smothering spells, so if you hear any disturbance tonight, don't be alarmed,'" Graves wrote. "But, it takes a good deal of racket to wake me, so I did not hear him breathe extraordinarily hard that night. But he is a magnificent snorer, as I learned near morning." Samuel also suffered heart disease and nervous disorders. A special examiner for the pension board later concluded that Samuel's "whole system has been permanently injured by the hardships endured in service, and in line of duty." His pension was finally granted. By then he was also suffering from "premature senility." He died in 1917.

Mathew Tolbert, who had spent eighteen months in prison, reportedly in Andersonville, though his records do not say exactly where, settled in Plow-Handle Point, a steamboat landing in Saluda, where he, his wife, and her mother died of an unnamed fever within two days in October 1878. He was thirty-seven and left behind a three-year-old son named for his late brother Tyrus.

Silas Tolbert, who married late, also died comparatively young of heart disease at forty-seven, at his home in Saluda in 1893. He had enlisted at fifteen, had served four years in the army without being wounded, and was an artist and musician of local note. Oddly enough, the *Courier* repeated an earlier error in his obituary, reporting that among the six Tolbert brothers who served in the Union Army, Romulus had been killed aboard the *Sultana*. Perhaps the error provided for a little levity at the funeral. At the time, their brother Daniel, who had been twice wounded during the war, was living in nearby Paynesville.

Romulus Tolbert's picture ran in *The Rear Guard of Company H.: Officers and Privates surviving January 1st, 1910*, a reunion scrapbook. His expression in the photo is not as tentative and apprehensive as in the images of him as a younger man. He is resplendent in his dark suit, starched white high-collared shirt, and tie. His hair is neatly parted, his white mustache carefully trimmed. He looks stolid and respectable. The photos typically were accompanied by a brief biography, and under Tolbert's is the notation "Gave no particulars about himself but 'Rom' is all right. Just the same as he was as a soldier boy." Maddox is also pictured in a striped three-piece suit, with a long gray beard, close-cropped hair, and a slightly provoked look in his eyes, as if he were expecting a challenge and was not particularly happy about it. The editor wrote, "John did not send any history about himself since the war. So I am unable to say anything, except he says he is always glad to please a comrade. He lives near Hanover, Jefferson County, Indiana and seems to be able to enjoy three meals a day." In the picture Maddox does appear to have put on a few pounds, though the editor would probably not have mentioned his gastronomic habits had he known what Maddox was going through.

After having survived so much, Tolbert and Maddox may have

felt they had proved themselves, or they may have lived in fear of what would happen next. Either way, each moment opened to another, the on-off switches forever flickering but somehow staying on. By the turn of the twentieth century, they had miraculously grown old.

They no doubt occasionally ran into each other and spoke of their experiences together, and may have attended a *Sultana* survivors' reunion in Toledo, Ohio, on April 27, 1914, though the only evidence is a newspaper photo caption that today floats, unattached, on an Internet Web site. If so, it would have been an arduous trip for both of them. Tolbert, who was then seventy-one and one of only two surviving Tolbert sons, suffered from pain in the neck and neuralgia of the face and head, and he was two years away from a debilitating stroke that would leave him bedridden. Maddox was sixty-eight, two years away from his own series of strokes, and suffered from chronic diarrhea, hemorrhoids, liver disease, jaundice, a heart murmur, and slight enlargement of the spleen and prostate. The train ride would have been a long and uncomfortable journey into the past.

The *Sultana* reunion was one of the last chances the survivors had to commiserate about what they had been through together and to see the old familiar faces again. As it turned out, only fourteen made it—fourteen among the thousands who had fought in the war, been imprisoned at Cahaba and Andersonville, and boarded the *Sultana*, and who were now enduring the final challenge of growing old.

As THE SURVIVORS OF THE *Sultana* saga aged and their memories dimmed, the physical reminders of the past began to disappear.

Like the town of Cahaba, Andersonville fell into ruin and slowly rotted away. Immediately after the war, Clara Barton, along with a detachment of laborers and soldiers and a former prisoner, visited the abandoned site to identify and mark the thousands of graves of the Union dead. What had been a stinking burial ground was eventually transformed into a serene memorial, but there was no interest in preserving the stockade itself. A.S. McCormick, a soldier with the 86th Indiana Infantry who was captured at Chickamauga, wrote a brief account about his return trip to Andersonville in April 1888, during which he found little left standing. He cut a piece of wood from the north gate post which contained a minié ball as a souvenir. McCormick, one of a party of five who traveled to the site for a picnic, later wrote, "Just think of sitting down to such a feast as this inside of the old stockade at Andersonville! Fellow survivors of Southern prison-pens, I could not keep back the tears as I ate that meal under the shade of persimmon and black-jack oaks, about one hundred feet east of the spring, and remembered how many, many thousands of brave men had starved to death at that very spot!"

There was a groundswell of support for preserving the battlefields, including Chickamauga, Lookout Mountain, and Missionary Ridge, which became the nation's first Civil War park. Chickamauga eventually hosted veterans' reunions which drew participants from both sides—men who no doubt had more in common in old age, including having tried for two days to kill each other when they were young. The reunions were fertile ground for honing stories of what the men went through, and the results were sometimes at odds with what was recorded in diaries, official army dispatches, military and pension files, newspaper archives, personal letters, and other memoirs and historical accounts. In many cases the carefully crafted accounts suffered from the taint of hindsight, from the desire of their authors to both nail down and sanctify the story.

By the time J. Walter Elliott finished polishing his account of the *Sultana* saga, it looked as if he had carried his thesaurus with him along the way. Elliott's vivid prose tended toward the purple end of the spectrum. In his submission to Berry's book, he wrote of the *Sultana*'s sinking, "I have seen death's carnival in the yellow fever and the cholera-stricken city, on the ensanguined field, in hospital and prison, and on the rail; I have, with wife and children clinging in terror to my knees, wrestled with the midnight cyclone; but the most horrible of all were the sights and sounds of that hour. The prayers, shrieks and groans of strong men and helpless women and children are still ringing in my ears, and the remembrance makes me shudder. The sight of 2,000 ghostly, pallid faces upturned in the chilling waters of the Mississippi, as I looked down on them from the boat, is a picture that haunts me in my dreams."

No doubt the latter was true. Elliott endured epic travails, and it is clear that he was haunted by them for the rest of his life. He had the cast of characters, the drama, the theme, and the scars to prove it. He honed the story for all it was worth, crafting a series of dramatic tableaux that were both stylized and illuminating—the literary equivalent of a series of stained glass windows. Elliott was voluble and occasionally disingenuous, and he seemed always to be working both the story and the room, but it was probably no coincidence that he did so even as his experiences were slowly destroying him. The same dynamic that characterized each of his previous survival trials was still at work in the aftermath of the *Sultana*. The risks did not go away. They were transformed.

In stylizing and amplifying his tale, Elliott had an agenda: To convey to others the full impact of what he experienced and to justify what he was still going through. In that regard he was not alone. Countless others spent the rest of their lives in lamentation. Many of the survivors suffered from what is today known as post-traumatic stress disorder, and the process of drafting a serviceable narrative was a kind of immersion therapy aimed at controlling, containing, and capitalizing upon a terrible past, even as they slowly succumbed to the physical and mental wreckage that resulted from it.

The shaping of memories inevitably led to disagreements. Memory itself is malleable, and a person in the middle of a violent cataclysm often sees events unfolding in slow motion, with almost no peripheral vision, and so may miss important details that are clearly evident from another person's vantage point. George Robinson told the pension board that he had floated on his dead mule alongside Ogilvie Hamblin; in response, Hamblin informed the pension board that Robinson had asked him to sign an affidavit to that effect, "but as I could not recollect any such thing I would not sign." Thomas Newton felt compelled to write a letter to a veterans' magazine to correct what he claimed was an unthinkably palliated account by a fellow former prisoner concerning the pens in Florence, South Carolina, and Andersonville. "I have written as I have because I feel it a duty to my old comrades who endured the sad, sad torments of that terrible prison pen," Newton wrote. "It is strange that Comrade Herman Brown's experience should so nearly coincide with mine at Florence prison and be so different at Andersonville."

Faced with the inevitable disparities, the survivors tended to dig in their heels. To create a workable self-image required a certain confidence in their memory of the pivotal events of their lives, and the reunions, in particular, were fertile ground for swapping stories about the war, prison, and the *Sultana* disaster. Over time the men gave their tales more attractive rhythm, cadence, and purpose; emphasized favorite details; omitted others; superimposed later observations; and borrowed from one another. As Laurence Gonzales notes, the stories a person hears beforehand are part of the preparation for any survival challenge. Likewise, the urge to craft a narrative afterward is part of coming to terms with it. Given time to think—something most were deprived of in the heat of the moment—the survivors naturally sought to incorporate their experiences into a new model of the world.

Countless survivors wrote magazine and newspaper articles, spoke at reunions and other events, and published memoirs. George Robinson contributed an account to Chester Berry's book, as did J. Walter Elliott and Perry Summerville, whose action-packed little piece was a summary of his own full-blown autobiography. In their accounts for Berry's book, most of the survivors devoted only a few lines to the war and captivity but page after page to the disaster. The exercise was aimed not merely at recording what had happened but in explaining what was happening to them now. Among the two hundred thousand troops Indiana sent off to war, twenty-seven thousand died. In addition to those lost on the battlefield or to disease, twenty-one were reported murdered; eight were killed after being captured, one of whom was executed by the Rebels; eleven committed suicide; eight were executed by the Union Army; twenty died of sunstroke; and nearly eight hundred died of causes that were unclassified or unknown. Hundreds died aboard the *Sultana*. For most of the surviving veterans, the war trumped all their previous travails. For those who were also former prisoners, captivity trumped the war. And for those who survived the *Sultana*, the disaster trumped everything.

THE PREDICTABLE FLURRY OF POSTWAR memoirs was both prompted by, and contributed to, the debate over the various cantos of the war. In building his own narrative, Melvin Grigsby decided to fill in the blanks of his memories with living, breathing details. He returned to Cahaba, Alabama, in April 1884, hoping to find out more about Amanda Gardner, who had lent her books to him and other inmates during the war.

There was a clear break in the ranks of survivors over just how bad things had been in the prison camps. Many whose emotional wounds had healed were inclined to accentuate the positive, such as the arrival of the Providence Spring at Andersonville, even to the point of glossing over horrendous details. Others just as determinedly nurtured memories of injustices and hardships, and they sought to lay blame. Grigsby, a nineteen-year-old soldier with the 7th Wisconsin Infantry when he was captured near Vicksburg and imprisoned at Cahaba, was about forty when he returned, and his recollections had softened. In his telling, the Cahaba prisoners were adequately fed and even the enemies were occasionally kind, including two Confederate guards. "We did not know enough then about life in rebel prisons to fully appreciate their kindness," he wrote in his book, *Smoked Yank*, published in 1888. "Every day on the arrival of the mail, one of them would bring in a late paper, stand up on a box and read the news." Even more inspiring was Gardner, who not only had supplied the prisoners with books and blankets but had nursed sick men in her home and given them much-needed fresh potatoes, peas, green beans, and corn. Grigsby traveled to Cahaba from his home in Wisconsin, hoping to find Gardner and her daughter Belle, with whom he had exchanged notes without actually meeting. By then, little was left of the prison itself except for a few broken bricks. The Gardners' former home was occupied by an erstwhile guard, who said they had moved to Selma, along with most of the rest of the town. By then, continued flooding had taken its toll on Cahaba, resulting in a mass out-migration, mostly to Selma, where Belle worked as a dressmaker to support herself and her aging mother.

During his captivity, while corresponding with her about books, Grigsby had found Belle engaging. In his memoir he wrote, "is it any wonder that my correspondence with this young lady began to seem to me romantic and that I began to entertain for her feelings stronger than gratitude?" Grigsby had often volunteered to cook for other prisoners in the stockade yard, and he slowly enlarged a crack in the fence, hoping to catch a glimpse of the girl (how he did this without crossing the deadline he does not say). Upon his return he found not only that he had been watching the wrong house but that the object of his affections had been, at the time, perhaps fourteen years old.

In 1884, Amanda Gardner was sixty-seven and Belle was thirty-three. Grigsby found the elder Gardner much as he remembered her: A woman of culture and refinement, and an elegant conversationalist who still believed the South had been right to secede. She told him she had received numerous letters and presents from former prisoners after the war, and he copied some of the notes, which he later quoted in his book. He also wrote to his own congressional delegation later, seeking, without success, a federal grant to provide her with some financial relief. During his days of watching what he thought was Gardner's house, Grigsby had developed an elaborate image of Belle, and under the circumstances their meeting was a bit awkward. Belle, he wrote, was gracious but reserved. Grigsby did

not say whether Gardner suffered any repercussions for her support of the prisoners, but tellingly, there is no mention of her in
the exhaustive, highly romanticized local history, *Memories of Old
Cahaba*, published in 1908, even though her family was prominent
and she lost a son in the war. Soon after Grigsby's visit, Gardner
moved from Selma to New York City, where she lived out her life.

The rest of the town slowly faded away. A year after the war
ended, the county seat was moved from Cahaba to Selma, and with
it went many residents and even several buildings that were disman-
tled or moved. During Reconstruction, the abandoned courthouse
became a meeting place for freedmen, and a community of seventy
former slave families took root. By 1900, even that community had
largely disappeared, and most of the remaining buildings had fallen
in, burned, or been torn down for their bricks. Gardner's house was
torn down, leaving only a mossy crape myrtle that had stood in her
front yard.

TOLBERT AND MADDOX DID NOT respond to Chester Berry's
request for their recollections for his book, though the appendix includes their names (both misspelled) in small type on the list of
passengers. Berry, who did more than anyone to keep the stories
alive, decried the public's passing interest in the disaster, and himself
ended up being buried in an unmarked grave. The lack of interest
was galling to many survivors, not only because they remembered
what had happened but because for them the disaster was continuing to unfold. Among those who built entire identities around the
Sultana saga, a great many continued to suffer from its physical and
psychological effects.

George Safford, who crossed paths with J. Walter Elliott in the immediate aftermath of the disaster, slowly went crazy over the next forty years. After surviving the sinking of the boat, Safford had peered into more than a hundred coffins at the Memphis waterfront while looking for his father. He had never recovered from either his manifold illnesses or the horrors of what he saw that day. For him the challenges continued to mount. In February 1885, as he was leaving a hotel in Chicago, Safford slipped on ice and dislocated his shoulder, which seems to have hastened his physical decline. In March 1899, when he was working as a railroad conductor, he wrote the pension board to say that he had been rendered temporarily insane for about three months, during which he had to be confined at home. He had tried taking treatments at various spas, but to no avail, and had been briefly jailed for an unrecorded transgression. He later entered the Government Hospital for the Insane in Washington, D.C. Though he was soon discharged into his wife's care, he noted ruefully that after having enlisted in the army at eighteen, spent four months as a prisoner of war, and survived the *Sultana* disaster, he was penniless and mentally ill. In May 1899, a surgeon for the pension office concluded that Safford, who was then fifty-four years old, suffered from "acute, real atrophy of the brain showing dementia with homicidal tendencies. We think there is no recovery." He died at the National Home for Disabled Volunteer Soldiers in Marion, Indiana, in 1902, after which his torment-ridden pension file was stamped "DROPPED" and "DEAD."

Untold numbers of survivors suffered similar fates. Some committed suicide. Others were destroyed by depression, fits of rage, and alcoholism. Many were unable to work again. The more fortunate struggled on as best they could, even as the diseases and injuries they suffered during the war took a cumulative toll. George

Young moved to Colorado, where the air was better for the asthma and bronchitis that resulted from breathing steam and smoke during the disaster, though he noted in Berry's book that "strive as I may, I cannot repress an involuntary fright on hearing in the stillness of the night any unusual noise." Anna Annis, whose husband and daughter died in the disaster, applied for a widow's pension but was rejected repeatedly before finally being allotted $17 per month. She wore long sleeves year round to cover her burns. After surviving a shipwreck at sea and the *Sultana* disaster, she died of a stroke at eighty, in Oshkosh.

J. Walter Elliott also had trouble with the pension board as a result of the confusion over his identity. In correspondence with the board he noted that his family had feared for his life when he was listed as missing in action, again upon hearing that he had been captured and sent to Andersonville, and finally after the *Sultana* disaster. One sister received the erroneous *Sultana* report of his death aboard the boat, then traveled to her mother's house, where a "donation party" was being held for the victorious troops. As Elliott described it, "the war was over, our country was saved, & at least one mother was there who was very happy at thought of letters from her eldest, whom she had mourned as dead, & he was on his way home, would be there soon, when up dashes a buggy and paralyzes the whole party. 'Walter is certainly dead this time. You know he can't swim.'" Elliott recreated the scene with what seems like slightly perverse pleasure: "Eagerly they all gather around the paper to learn the horrible details of the disaster that had snatched the chalice from the lip. Brother John, whose education on the field of Chickamauga & others got close enough to glance over the inverted page & cried out, 'Walter is *not* lost. His name & command is correctly given among the reserve, and none but he could have given it.'" In fact, Elliott was at that moment at the home of an aunt of his late wife's in Memphis, undoubtedly coughing up a storm.

Proving all that to the pension board was not easy. His brother David, who was present when he got home, wrote on behalf of his pension application to say that Elliott had been "reduced by hardships of prison life" and had "a peculiar rasping cough which he said and which I believe was caused by inhaling steam and by exposure at time of explosion of boilers and sinking of Steamboat Sultana." During ten days at his mother's house, he added, "his cough continued and he complained daily of the raw and inflamed feeling of throat and lungs."

Despite his.disability, Elliott rejoined his army command at Chattanooga and was stationed in Guntersville, Alabama, as commandant of the Union post and agent for the local Freedmen's Bureau. He remained in Alabama after being discharged in April 1866, saying the climate was better for his still-congested lungs, though it certainly did not help that he was, as one acquaintance noted, "an inveterate smoker." Elliott told the pension board that he "could not survive the rigor of a northern clime, and, like a leper, I became a voluntary exile—a citizen here during all the long dark days of reconstruction, kukluxism . . ." In 1866 he married again, but his second wife, like his first, soon died. He married for the third time on Christmas Eve 1870, and afterward he homesteaded a hardscrabble farm of a hundred sixty acres in the mountains near Guntersville, where he fathered six children and worked at various low-impact odd jobs, including teaching, bookkeeping, transcribing legal documents, and supervising manual laborers. His brother

David, who visited him in Alabama three times during the 1870s, recalled, "He was still troubled with cough and sore lungs, this being especially the case during my visit there in October 1875."

Elliott worked for a while in the office of Probate Judge Thomas Street, who later allowed that while he was an efficient clerk, sometimes "any little worry would run him down. He had at times a very lank worn out expression on his face and then at other times he would seem to be all right. I remember at times he had a shortness of breath and at times he had a considerable cough." Later, Street wrote, "His mind became affected by loss of memory, and in recording for instance, he did bad work and I had to quit him entirely." He was forty-seven years old.

Elliott eventually got a small pension and over several years sought increases because of his worsening health. He suffered primarily from respiratory problems, but he was also frail, wobbly, and beset by rheumatism and consumption when he visited Indiana for the last time in 1882, at age forty-nine. A surgeon's report the following year noted that he had no use of his right ring finger because of his wound at Chickamauga and that he had chronic respiratory problems as a result of his trauma during and after the sinking of the *Sultana*. A few years later, Elliott ran for circuit clerk but lost to a Confederate veteran named Willis Currey, who also wrote to support his pension application, confirming Elliott's respiratory problems, adding, "I noticed in his speech that he would get his words mixed, he would use the proper words, but he would get them transposed, and he got so bad at our house that we sent him home, and stopped him from work, and he recovered from that condition temporarily, and then he grew gradually worse until he got perfectly helpless."

Elliott, who appears to have suffered a stroke, soon required the use of a walking stick to "shuffle along." A former student wrote, "I have seen him fall down lots of times just walking along in a plain road, and he would get up laughing . . . He also said he had no sense of taste or smell, the he could not smell or taste anything." By 1891, when he was fifty-eight, Elliott was receiving a pension of $20 per month. The next year he suffered another stroke that partially paralyzed his left side. His daughter said in a deposition that the second attack came during the night when he got up to get a drink "and fell before he got to the water bucket, and laughed so that we would know that he was not hurt, and he went a few steps farther then and fell again, and I called him and he did not answer me, and we got up to see what was the matter with him." The family at first thought he was dead, but he eventually came around. The next morning he had trouble using one hand. She added that his health rapidly deteriorated: "He was not in his right mind part of the time" and at others he paused so long between breaths "that it would scare me sometimes, and when he did get his breath he would breathe hard for a minute or two." Toward the end, she said, she could hear his rattled breathing all through the house.

As his wife wrote, "He never had any more attacks, but he just kept getting worse and finally got to be almost helpless about six months before he died, and the last two or three days he was plumb helpless." She told the pension board that "especially along toward the last, he got in a powerful bad fix, and would rattle in his lungs." Elliott also lost the ability to speak. About six hours before his death, his wife wrote, "he groaned awful, I could not tell where his pain was because he could not tell me only from his groaning and rattling in his breast, it seemed to be in his throat and breast." He died on June 3, 1895, at age sixty-two. His doctor stated that the cause of death was asphyxiation resulting from paralysis, which was brought on by "a general nervous condition of the system resulting from the diseased lung and highly inflammatory condition of the larynx and pharynx." It had taken thirty years, but his injuries aboard the *Sultana* had finally killed him.

After the war, George Robinson settled into the quiet life of a cobbler in Owosso, Michigan, with a woman he married while on a wartime furlough. He worked alongside a veteran who had survived Andersonville, which perhaps lent a rarified atmosphere to the store ("You don't like your shoes? You should be glad you even *have* shoes!"). By the time he was twenty-three, Robinson had experienced enough drama for a hundred lives, and he was plagued by insomnia and "general nervousness," according to his doctor, who wrote on his behalf to the pension board. Over time, the injuries he sustained during the *Sultana* disaster made it impossible for him to make shoes, and he became a shoe salesman. In 1888, when he was forty-four, Robinson told the pension board he suffered from chronic diarrhea, hemorrhoids, stomach and liver trouble, vomiting spells, rheumatism, persistent bronchitis, and pain in his chest and wrist, the latter of which were injured in the explosion that killed his friend John Corliss. He added, as a postscript, "I would not pass through that terrible time I did at the destruction of Sultana for worlds again."

By 1921, when Robinson was seventy-eight, he was suffering both from old age and from the injuries and diseases of his youth, and the two were inextricably linked. He was sometimes bedridden for weeks at a time and needed constant care. By then, his son-in-law wrote, "Most of his trouble comes from his heart."

Perry Summerville had nerve problems, and he never regained full use of the leg he broke during his attempt to escape the Rebels. By 1920 he also required round-the-clock nursing, and in October

1927 his wife told the pension board she was "his constant attendant and nurse. He is a complete physical WRECK on account of his disability. I can't exactly explain everything but I am at his side constantly and attend his every wants—he has bladder trouble—can't sleep of nights—can't wait on himself—he is an awful sufferer. Some one must be with him all of the time and I am the one." Summerville died a year later.

The Madison *Courier* of March 17, 1916, reported that Tolbert suffered a paralytic stroke, and noted that he was "a civil war veteran and is one of the few living survivors of the Sultana disaster." When his brother Samuel died the following year, Tolbert became the last of the family's sons alive. By January 1920 he was "entirely helpless requiring two people to handle him. Has spasms every few nights," according to his pension record. Death finally came on April 24, 1920, on his son Edmund's birthday, three days before the anniversary of the *Sultana* disaster. The headline of his obituary announced: "Prominent Farmer Dies." The same description later ran over John Maddox's obituary on January 5, 1925, which noted of Maddox that "his entire life was spent in the neighborhood of his birth"—essentially ignoring the most momentous period, when he was "away."

During all their life-threatening episodes, Tolbert and Maddox would no doubt have been both comforted and shocked to know that they would die of old age and be remembered only as Saluda farmers, which was apparently all they ever wanted to be. They had been through a spectacular onslaught, which changed forms and never fully abated; they had managed to make it home in the face of impossible odds; and they had kept going until there was nothing left to survive.

AFTERWORD

IN THE SPRING OF 2008, THE MISSISSIPPI RIVER spilled from its banks, much as it did in April 1865. Pushing past the Memphis waterfront at about the speed an average person runs, it presented an awesome spectacle of velocity and force. Towboats strained against the flexing back of what was essentially a thousand-mile muscle of water. A lone canoe embarked from the city front, carrying a group of adventure seekers who wanted to experience the river at full force. At first the canoe had trouble gaining the main current, which was laden with logs and other debris, and so strong that it repelled whatever was outside its grasp.

The overflow spread through thousands of acres of adjacent forests and fields, and at some points the actual flow was three miles wide and perhaps a hundred feet deep, riddled with dangerous digressions—riptides, rogue currents that turned back upon themselves and bullied their way upstream, and standing waves that broke upon the surface of the river itself, creating the illusion of shoals. There were whirlpools of all sizes, interrupting and venting the flow, spinning wider and deeper until they broke in final upsurges, as if from muted explosions below. A quick dip of the hand revealed that the water was achingly cold.

People swim in the Mississippi in summer, usually in the slack water along sandbars, or perhaps all the way across on a dare, but not, by choice, in its open channel during a flood. Standing safely on the bank, it was easy to imagine the terror the *Sultana* passengers felt when they found themselves in the pull of bottomless water, fighting off others in the same predicament, in the middle of the night. Far more than the carefully preserved battlefields, interspersed with monuments and parades of insistent signs, the flooded river evoked its part of the *Sultana* saga with disturbing immediacy. The only comparable chance of observing the full power of the other trials—the violence of war and the implosive claustrophobia of imprisonment—would be to travel to Afghanistan or Iraq, or to the holding pens of Guantanamo.

In fact, most of the physical evidence of the *Sultana* saga is gone. The former town of Cahaba was unincorporated in 1989, after it had been reduced to a few hunting and fishing camps. All that is left of most of the nearby houses and stores, as well as the Bell Tavern Hotel, are overgrown piles of broken bricks. The gravel streets are empty, punctuated by a scattering of historical markers and picnic tables. A few derelict houses remain, sagging under the weight of flowering vines. Near the confluence of the Cahaba and Alabama rivers stand the columned ruins of the former riverfront mansion where Confederate Gen. Nathan Bedford Forrest and his Union counterpart sat on a balcony sharing cigars and cordials while discussing a planned prisoner exchange. The site of the stockade is today a pleasant glen of moss-draped trees, part of a state park described in brochures as "Alabama's most famous ghost town." A casual visitor might conclude that aside from the scenic river views there is nothing much to see, and nothing to learn other than that something was here that went away. But after reading the survivors' accounts, even the hint of Cahaba opens a portal into a terrible known, making it possible to telescope history, to resurrect a succession of thousands of flickering, pivotal moments—many of them someone's last—that have otherwise retreated into the past. What appears to be an insignificant depression in the ground turns out to be the site of the stockade privy, where Jesse Hawes and his friends crawled through a bog of human waste a few feet from unsuspecting, armed guards in their attempted escape. The actual prison compound, delineated by unobtrusive wooden markers, reveals how small it was. It is hard to imagine three thousand men crowded into that space, even for an afternoon.

There are obvious limits to our ability to recreate the past from such scattered remnants, even with the help of dead men's words. As Tolbert's great granddaughter, Anne Woodbury, observed, sometimes you have to accept that certain details can never be fully known. But even incomplete survival stories shed light on how people react to mortal threats, and on the factors that influence our own survival, which is what interests us most in the end. While we may feel the weight of the *Sultana* survivors' experiences as we stand by a flooded river or in an abandoned town, what we really want to know is what we would do. Survival challenges are today most often viewed from the opposite ends of a disturbingly wide range: In the context of an unexpected disaster like the September 11 attacks, or as a form of recreation—anything labeled "extreme." In reality, life is a long series of survival challenges, and always has been. How someone reacted to a survival threat in 1863 is no less telling than how people react to very different, yet equally lethal threats today. It is all about luck, physiology, and a circuitous, sometimes obscure process of preparation. If there were a clear template to follow, it would certainly have made its appearance during the long-running, multifaceted experiment in human survival that climaxed with the sinking of the *Sultana*. The fact that some people survived the entire sequence of events, sometimes as a direct result of their own actions, means that in one way or another they were both lucky and prepared, even if they did not know it at the time. Before the war, Tolbert had never ventured far from his family's farm, and as far as is known had never pitted himself against armed men, had never been denied crucial medical treatment or food, had never languished in a rank and crowded pen with festering fly traps of wounds, or been forced to flee a burning boat on a flooded river while most of those around him died. Yet he managed to survive. He may have been lucky, but he was also able to make the most of his good luck.

Many of his survival decisions went unrecorded, and even in cases where other survivors left detailed accounts, it is necessary to separate conjecture from fact, to fill in the blanks from other sources and pit those accounts against their peers'. Sometimes the gaps and discrepancies in the record are significant, even when they concern minor details. The *Sultana* story is riddled with multiple choice and true-or-false questions. Reassembling the truth requires making judgment calls, which carries its own risks. Most, but not all of the discrepancies can be resolved by comparison, but if Tolbert, Maddox or any of the other survivors could read this book, they would no doubt recognize mistakes, and some might be meaningful. Imagine if someone set out to recreate the interior of your home a century and a half from now, based on a few surviving photos and letters and furniture catalogs from the period; what are the chances that everything would be there and in the right place? The best way to check the facts of a book is against facts in other books, which means, in a sense, that you are sleeping with everyone your sources have slept with, which has obvious disadvantages, but where else are you to turn? I hope I have not unwittingly or presumptively relied upon erroneous details, made stupid mistakes, or taken license. My aim has been to use historical events to summon the power of a process that anyone, at any time, may go through, and to breathe life into those dead men's words. When I have been dubious about the veracity of a particular account, such as John Ransom's occasionally incredible memoir, I have noted as much in the text, or used only those passages that reflect personal feelings or can be corroborated through other sources. The line of demarcation between a fact and a fabrication (or a simple error) can be both thin and profound, which is one reason I chose to follow characters from disparate groups, including survivors who left behind exhaustive accounts and others, such as Tolbert, who offered only the barest of outlines. Belaboring the story sometimes muddies it, but coming at it from every possible angle—through diaries, histories, army dispatches and memoirs—increases the chances of reaching, at least, verisimilitude. I chose Tolbert, Maddox, and Elliott as my primary subjects because they were from the same general area and because their records encompass both what is unknown and what is studiously, purportedly known. I was attracted to Tolbert and Maddox because they went through so much together, and because they chose not to sell their stories. I liked that in many ways they seemed determined to become outwardly normal again, despite everything. Elliott illustrates an opposing tendency, to incorporate utterly uncontrollable experiences into a highly controlled narrative, which is part of the story, too. Elliott would have been the first to go on Larry King Live. Fleshing out the story in ways that Tolbert, Maddox and Elliott could not alone were countless other supporting actors, bit players, extras, and even a few celebrity cameos, who represent the full range of narrative responses.

As part of my research I followed the routes that they and other *Sultana* survivors followed from Indiana through Tennessee, Georgia, Alabama, and Mississippi, searching for clues. In some cases there was nothing; in others, what existed seemed artificial and overwrought. Occasionally the physical evidence was satisfying in its plain details. Andersonville fell into both the latter categories. The site is today a national park, and includes a section of reconstructed stockade, a few earthworks and a fountain channeling the Providence Spring, complete with a sign warning visitors that it is not safe to drink. The cemetery is a sobering yet serene place—far from the stinking burial ground it once was. Groomed to within an inch of its life, like Elliott's stories, it still manages to resonate. The visitors' center contains a theater whose video illustrates life and death in the stockade, and dioramas concerning the experiences of prisoners not only there but in POW camps during other conflicts—a nice touch, considering that Andersonville was an extreme episode in a drama that unfortunately has no end.

The site of Tolbert's capture is more or less physically frozen in time, though the sense of emergency today stems only from encroaching development. A few sections of the old roads tramped by the prisoners on their way to Vicksburg survive, including a half-mile of the Old Bridgeport Road, which coincidentally runs past my house. Most of the other routes have long since been bulldozed, and there is nothing to even indicate the location of Camp Fisk other than an empty field near a community college a few miles east of Vicksburg. There is a historical marker about the *Sultana* in Mound

City, Arkansas, but the actual site of the disaster is unmarked. Memphis lawyer Jerry Potter believes he located the wreckage in a soybean field in the 1980s, after which he concluded the cost of exhuming it would be prohibitive, considering the likelihood that few artifacts survived. Instead he wrote a book, *The Sultana Tragedy*, one of the sources I slept with on my way here. There are historical markers summoning the *Sultana* in Knoxville, where a group of area survivors held their own reunions; in Memphis, where the Elmwood Cemetery contains the remains of many of the victims; and in Vicksburg, which also has a beautiful mural on the floodwall depicting the loading of the boat. The markers are useful reminders, though they have a way of pushing the episodes into the murky past. In fact, the point of the stories they evoke remains salient today: To survive a little longer. In that sense, not much has changed.

As I retraced the steps of the *Sultana* survivors I found myself searching for stand-ins—the soldiers in the Atlanta airport, the two guys in the Broadway Inn—who might help bring the story closer to home. There are obvious limitations in recreating stories in which all the key players are dead, because there can be no follow-up questions, and there is no way to observe the expressions on their faces or hear the timbre of their voices. But the more I read about them the more familiar and immediate their experiences seemed.

A lot was going on in my own life at that moment, and it sometimes seemed like I was traveling back and forth between two particularly dark corners in time. On my end, it started with an unusual weather pattern that spawned tornadoes near my home every few days for several weeks, to the point that it seemed our area had been targeted by some malign meteorological force. While that was going on, my father was entering a precipitous, hopeless, downward spiral into dementia. There was more, but it is enough to say that when I became discouraged I reminded myself that nothing could compare with what the *Sultana* survivors went through, which was true. Still, the moment that is unfolding is the one that matters most, and as I vacillated between the troubling present and a disastrous past, I began having strange, composite nightmares in which the dark corners overlapped. At one point I dreamed I was caught in a hurricane, and when I took shelter in a barn, I chanced upon a dying Union mule, in all his army trappings—one of the thousands that populate the *Sultana* story. I live in Mississippi, where what was formerly the worst hurricane to strike the United States—Camille, in 1969—left many people with the feeling that they had survived the worst, that no subsequent storm could compare. Then, in August 2005, Katrina hit, far surpassing Camille by every measure. The same point was being driven home: You never know when you are experiencing the worst. In my dream, as the wind and waves mounted and buildings collapsed all around, and as I heard people dying with a sound that resembled the noise water makes as it is gulped down a drain, I told myself, "Katrina was the worst. This can't be as bad." That is the way the mind works, even in our dreams. We persist in believing the world is manageable, even when faced with evidence to the contrary. Sometimes that belief is fatally flawed, but sometimes it is all that keeps you going, and actually helps you survive.

Life is a process of gathering together different forms of energy, different experiences, different pieces of the truth, after which everything that has been collected is summarily exploded. It is a law of nature. Hurricanes dispel heat from the equator, destroying cities and old-growth forests with equal abandon, and afterward new combinations are formed from the debris. There is no steady state, aside from those that we create in our own minds. The mule in my dream was a refugee from a different onslaught, a misplaced character, down in his traces, dying from injuries received in the storm. I hunkered beside him and tried to ask questions, but the wind was howling and I could not hear his answers. That is the sort of state you can work yourself into when trying to reconstruct the momentous lives of dead people.

But as I struggled to make sense of it all, help came from a familiar yet now, sadly, unlikely source: My father, who had endured his own series of survival episodes while serving in the U.S. infantry during World War II, and who, even then, recalled the difficulty of assembling a reliable narrative of a frenetic event. "Your thoughts are quick and short," he said of his war experiences. "There's too much going on to get beyond a certain level." In fact, he said, much of what passes for memory is reconstructed from bits and pieces, often from other sources, after the fact. At the moment all you hope for is to survive. You create the narrative later. Learning takes place in between. Though my father was never captured or wounded, he endured long marches, beachheads under enemy fire, combat, sniper attacks, sickness, and the misery of cold, remote winter camps. But on those occasions when he faced the possibility of his own demise, he did not recall feeling much of anything other than an urgent need to act, and the importance of keeping a level head. Like Tolbert and Maddox, he had never heard of the amygdala or the neocortex, but he understood the process. For him the worst moment came when he was holed up in a building in a small, abandoned town in northern Italy. He was the radio man for his company, and he and about forty of his men were cut off. The Germans were close. It was night, and as he listened to the low rumble of an approaching German tank, the clatter of its tracks reverberating between the stone walls of the narrow streets, he sent out coded distress signals, calling for reinforcements, alternately by voice transmissions and by telegraph.

Soon the noise grew louder and he saw the tank enter the darkened square, stop, and pivot its gun upward, toward his window. There was a moment of quiet, apparently as the crew prepared to fire. Then, the moment was transformed. Two U.S. tanks entered from the opposite side of the square, in response to my father's calls, and the German tank fled. The next day my father snapped a photo which graphically illustrated what his imminent death or capture had been reduced to: Track marks in the dirt.

He told me this story for the umpteenth time as he sat in a wheelchair in a nursing home, sixty-four years after the fact. He could still talk about the war in great detail, reel off the names and engagements and how he felt at different junctures, but the brain that governed his survival then, and governed it now, was failing. A lot of what passed for thought was just sparks shooting around the dying tissue inside his skull. He was aware of this, and at times became agitated. At one point he asked, "Why is this happening to me?" My answer was not entirely satisfying, but it was true: Because he had survived. He had lived to be an old man. He had overcome a childhood of intermittent loneliness and poverty, had made it through the invasions of North Africa and Italy, had endured the deaths, in separate tragedies, of three of his five grandchildren, had survived a series of minor strokes that rendered him unable to drive a car or make many important decisions on his own, and was now struggling with the worst assault he could imagine—the death of his own brain, the guiding force and the repository of everything he had experienced. His nervous system was going the way of the streets of old Cahaba. But the portal was still open. The story was still unfolding.

It is tempting to believe that part of what sustained Tolbert, Maddox, and Elliott during their trials was the dream of getting there, to the natural end of a long life. In Tolbert's case, the dream of life's peace and plenty might easily have been encapsulated in that scene in the photo of him and his family lined up along the picket fence. It was at home, in old age, that the results of the experiment were known. All the trials of the *Sultana* survivors' lives were explored and assimilated there. But it was not as if the struggle was over.

Based on what I observed in my father, dreams are the last to go. Even after entering his last survival challenge, he dreamed of better days ahead. As the *Sultana* story illustrates, until the end you never really know. Every moment that came before carried the promise of more, and for better or worse, was part of the preparation for the one that is unfolding now.

ACKNOWLEDGMENTS

MEMPHIS ATTORNEY JERRY POTTER INTRODUCED ME TO the story of the *Sultana* in the late 1980s after he and a local farmer found what they believed to be the remains of the boat. The story stuck with me, and I always wondered about the survivors—how they had overcome the series of trials leading up to the disaster, as well as the disaster itself. A few years ago, during a conversation with my agent, Patty Moosbrugger, we discussed the possibilities of following a group of survivors through those trials, and I decided to see what I could find about their lives before, during, and after the disaster. This book is the result.

I am primarily indebted to Potter for introducing me to the story and to Patty for helping me formulate—and for successfully marketing—the concept for this book. I am also indebted to my editor, Elisabeth Dyssegaard, for her confidence in it and her structural suggestions; to fact checker Logan Orlando; and to a host of authors, researchers, and historians who helped fill in the blanks: Robert Gray, who introduced me to Romulus Tolbert and John C.

Maddox, and opened his personal archives to me; Gene Eric Sal-ecker, who wrote a definitive history of the disaster and helped me track down bits of crucial information; Potter, again, who also steered me to John Clark Ely's diary; a succession of librarians and researchers who offered brief but significant guidance (including a woman who identified herself only as Yvonne, who I found on a Web site devoted to "random acts of genealogical kindness"), as well as Jack Lundquist, George Willick, Janice Stanley, and many others who helped me find what I was looking for.

Many of my friends offered meaningful encouragement as I researched the story, but three, in particular, provided crucial advice and support: Danny Burnham, Chris Elias, and Les Hegwood. My family, likewise, aided and abetted me, none more than my mother, Inez Huffman, and my father, A.D. Huffman. Two of Tolbert's descendants, Anne Woodbury and Homer Elliott, helped me piece together the riddle by opening their own family archives, providing important documents, photographs, and observations about his life story. This book could not have been written without Anne Woodbury's involvement, and I am grateful for it. Woodbury's husband David, an expert on the Civil War, also provided a careful review of the book's factual content relating to the war.

Finally, no one had a greater hand in making this a better book than my primary fact-checker, David Georgi, who went far beyond the call of duty to help me organize and refine the narrative, bring the characters to life and ensuring that there are as few errors as possible.

BIBLIOGRAPHY

BOOKS

Berry, Chester D., ed. *Loss of the Sultana and Reminiscences of Survivors*. 1892. Reprint, Knoxville, TN: University of Tennessee Press, 2005.

Billings, John D. *Hardtack and Coffee: The Unwritten Story of Army Life*. 1887. Reprint, Lincoln, NE: University of Nebraska Press, 1993.

Bryant, William O. *Cahaba Prison and the Sultana Disaster*. Tuscaloosa, AL: University of Alabama Press, 1990.

Crane, Stephen. *The Red Badge of Courage*. 1895; Reprint, New York: Penguin, 1994.

Elliott, James W. *Transport to Disaster*. New York: Holt, Rinehart and Winston, 1962.

Evans, David. *Sherman's Horsemen: Union Calvary Operations in the Atlanta Campaign*. Bloomington, IN: Indiana University Press, 1996.

Foote, Shelby. *The Civil War: A Narrative*. New York: Random House, 1963.

Gonzales, Laurence. *Deep Survival: Who Lives, Who Dies, and Why*. New York: W.W. Norton, 2003.

Grossman, Dave, *On Killing: The Psychological Cost of Learning to Kill in War and Society*. Boston: Back Bay Books/Little, Brown & Co., 1995.

Kamler, Kenneth, M.D. *Surviving the Extremes: What Happens to the Body and Mind at the Limits of Human Endurance*. New York: Penguin, 2004.

Marvel, William. *Andersonville: The Last Depot*. Chapel Hill, NC: University of North Carolina Press, 1994.

McPherson, James M. *For Cause and Comrades: Why Men Fought in the Civil War*. New York: Oxford University Press, 1997.

Potter, Jerry O. *The Sultana Tragedy: America's Greatest Maritime Disaster*. Gretna, LA: Pelican Publishing Co., 1992.

Ransom, John L. *Andersonville Diary, Escape, and List of the Dead*. 1881 (self-published). Reprint, Digital Scanning and Publishing, 2003.

Salecker, Gene Eric. *Disaster on the Mississippi: The Sultana Explosion, April 27, 1865*. Annapolis, MD: Naval Institute Press, 1996.

Speer, Lonnie R. *Portals to Hell: Military Prisons of the Civil War*. Mechanicsburg, PA: Stackpole Books, 1997. Reprint, Lincoln, NE: University of Nebraska Press, 2005.

Watkins, Sam. *Company Aytch: Or, a Side Show of the Big Show*. New York: Plume/Penguin Putnam, 1999.

DIARIES AND PERIODICALS

8th Indiana Cavalry. Reunion Booklet. Anne Woodbury collection.

Aldrich, Hosea. "Cahaba Prison: A Glimpse of Life in a Rebel Prison."

Elliott, Joseph T. "The Sultana Disaster." 1913. Genealogical Trails History Group.

Ely, John Clark. Journals. Jerry Potter; Memphis-Shelby County Library.

Hawes, Jesse. "Cahaba, A Story of the Captive Boys in Blue." Burr Printing House, 1888. University of California Library, Los Angeles.

Hoblizel, John. Civil War Diary. Madison Historical Society.

Indiana Magazine of History, June 1932; June 1943; December 1953; June 1955; March 1956; June 1956; June 1997; September 1998

McBride, Laura Harrison. "Civil War Horses." (www.us-civil-war. suite101.com).

National *Sultana* Survivors Association,. 31st Annual Reunion Proceedings Report. April 29, 1914. Gene Eric Salecker collection.

National Tribune. Nov. 30, 1887

Newton, Thomas, Pvt., Co. I, 6th Wisconsin. Memoirs. Theresa Peterson collection.

The Madison Courier (Weekly Courier) (dates cited in text).

Zettler, B.M. "War Stories & School-Day Incidents for the Children." Neale Publishing Co.

WEB SITES

www.sultana.org

www.roundaboutmadison.com

www.sultanadisaster.com

www.myindianahome.com

www.civilwardata.com

www.nps.gov/andersonville

www.itd.nps.gov/cwss

OTHER SOURCES

Official Records of the Rebellion

U.S. Census records

Civil War pension and military records, National Archives, and Records Administration

Various records, Madison (Ind.) library

INDEX